ABOUT THE BOOK

Replacing the Rainmaker is a practical guide to business development for accountants. It offers an array of tools, techniques and strategies to help accountants win more work. It gives you everything you need to launch a successful firm-wide business development effort. Each topic in the book culminates with three key takeaways and many topics include step-by-step processes to help put the ideas into action. The book is supplemented by additional resources, including online workshops, templates, spreadsheets and any other materials needed to jump-start your business development efforts. The book is written for any CPA, whether you're a sole practitioner, staff accountant or partner at a large firm. If you have an open mind and a desire to grow your business through calculated business development strategies, this book is for you.

REPLACING

– THE –

RAINMAKER

Business development tools, techniques and strategies for accountants

Ian Tonks

ISBN: 978-1-4834-2515-3 (sc)
ISBN: 978-1-4834-2516-0 (hc)
ISBN: 978-1-4834-2514-6 (e)

Library of Congress Control Number: 2015900988

Because of the dynamic nature of the Internet, any web addresses or links contained in this book may have changed since publication and may no longer be valid. The views expressed in this work are solely those of the author and do not necessarily reflect the views of the publisher, and the publisher hereby disclaims any responsibility for them.

Cover image courtesy of Shutterstock.

Rev. date: 3/16/2015

ACKNOWLEDGEMENTS

I'd like to take this opportunity to thank the following people for their help and support in bringing this project to fruition:

- Mom, Dad and Sis – For being three of the greatest influences a middle-age boy from "Blighty" could ever wish for. Love you always.
- Januaria and Sophie – For sacrificing countless nights and weekends to see this book into print. Vocês são lindas.
- Dr. Gary F. Russell – For seeing things in me at a young age when I and others did not. Thanks, GR.
- Bob Daoro, CPA, and the talented folks at Bay Area accounting and advisory firm DZH Phillips LLP – For their support, guidance and counsel.
- William (Bill) Burke, Elliott Bastien Morin, Molly Niffenegger, Paul Read and Ryan Svoboda – For their individual topic contributions. Thanks for adding your creativity and insights.
- Dr. John Caple – A friend first, and mentor second. Thanks for the perfect balance of support and suggestion. With deep appreciation, John.
- Dr. Christophe Morin of Sales Brain, Duane Sparks of The Sales Board, Tony Rutigliano and Gallup, Inc. – For contributing the building blocks of my business development philosophy.
- Last but by no means least, Stephanie Garlow – For her help in translating ideas into words. I cannot overstate her many magnificent contributions.

CONTENTS

PREFACE

This book has a simple premise: Accounting firms need to re-evaluate their approach to business development. Firms can no longer afford to depend on one or two rainmakers to bring in the majority of new business. To compete and thrive in a more globalized, more specialized, more technology-driven world, accounting firms must reframe business development as a firm-wide priority. The age of the rainmaker is dead; business development is now everyone's responsibility.

Why write this book

I decided to write this book to help accounting firms tackle this new world of business development. In running a consulting business, I've realized that most professional service firms don't have systems or processes in place to ensure their long-term success. Instead, as storied business developers retire, firms are left scrambling to replace their knowledge, intellectual capital and book of business.

Many of my insights come from the fact that I wasn't schooled in the existing accounting paradigm. Instead, I draw on what I learned from my two decades in the for-profit and non-profit sectors, bringing what worked there into the arena of accounting. In contrast, much of the available literature on business development for accountants is written by accountants themselves. As a result, most of their advice involves tinkering at the margins, rather than reimagining the future of business development at accounting firms. I have substantial experience providing sales and marketing expertise to small and large regional accounting firms, including serving in an outside sales capacity. I'm sharing tried and tested ideas that produce results.

What it's about

Much of this book tries to change preconceived notions about selling. Many accountants are unwilling to undertake important business development tasks because they don't consider themselves "salespeople." But one of my goals throughout the book is to challenge you to reconsider how you think about selling, overcome your resistance and instead embrace it as a way to help your clients seize opportunities and minimize liabilities.

This book defines business development as an amalgam of sales and marketing and focuses on how to improve your performance in both areas — from how to hone your elevator pitch to how to convert more prospects into clients. It's written for any CPA, whether you're a sole practitioner, staff accountant or partner at a large firm. If you have an open mind and a desire to grow your business through calculated business development strategies, this book is for you.

How it's written

The book is divided into 14 chapters, housing 96 short topics, typically two to four pages in length. Each topic culminates with three key takeaways and many topics include step-by-step processes to help you put the ideas into action. We've also developed a website that serves as an additional resource and a repository of templates, spreadsheets and forms. Throughout the text, you'll notice numbered www references — this signifies that the website contains additional information relating to the given topic.

For additional information

Please visit www.ReplacingTheRainmaker.com to learn more. Our website includes:

- **Book:** Purchase additional copies of the book in paperback, hardcover or ebook format.
- **Resources:** Follow the numbered (www) references in the book to access forms, templates and spreadsheets.
- **Workshops:** Many of the topics described in the book are available in workshop format. Each workshop runs for one hour and includes a workbook complete with activities, a continuing education assignment and a quiz.
- **Consulting:** Ian is available on a per diem or retainer basis to consult with firms either in person or remotely.
- **Marketing support:** Access our team of researchers, writers, graphic designers, web developers, social media specialists and videographers.
- **Alliances:** "Replacing the Rainmaker" has built alliances with several trusted service providers, including financial services professionals, software service providers and others.
- **Speaking:** Ian is available to speak on a variety of business development topics.
- **Academy:** A semi-annual three-day boot camp to give program participants an opportunity to interact with other accounting professionals and learn about business development best practices. Offered in San Francisco and other to-be-determined locations.

FOREWORD

An oft-used metaphor has it that there is a "road to success." But in working with more than one hundred sales forces and thousands of sales people, I've come to think that it's much more like an intersection. Success happens where talent, opportunity, knowledge, and technique converge.

With his rich understanding of sales and accounting, Ian Tonks gives you in this excellent book an encyclopedia of tools and techniques to help you build your business. Moreover, Ian understands and conveys that business development is not as much about "rainmakers" acting individually, as it is about building a culture and processes that ensure the growth of current clients and the acquisition of new ones. These cultures are those intersections where success is just more likely to happen.

You see, sales is everyone's business. Creating a climate in which customer service is a core value and where client expectations are consistently exceeded should be part of the job description of every professional and staff person in your firm. Such organizations rarely lose clients, and they consistently receive referrals for new business — the sort of marketing that you can't pay for.

When I think about building a culture that supports business development, Don, the CEO of a $3 billion construction firm, always comes to mind. When I asked Don to show me an organizational chart, he couldn't produce one, so he drew one out for me on the spot. On top was one word: "Customer." Below the customer were the various front-line service positions, then support staff, and finally, on the bottom of the page, Don wrote his own name. He told me that this highly successful, growing organization had to always place the customer's interests first and do all it could to support the people who tend to those interests.

What does the organization chart look like at your firm? Can you honestly put your customer on top? How much does customer engagement figure into your policies, practices, pay, and recognition? In your management committee meetings, how much time do you talk about the excellent service you're providing your customers and how you can do more for them?

Certainly, if you've bought this book, a part of your firm's strategy is top-line growth. But that part of your strategy is doomed to fail unless you create a climate in which service is a way of life. As one great business developer told me, "People don't care how much you know until they know how much you care." Plenty of firms can supply accounting expertise, but few of them can create powerful, mutually rewarding relationships with their clients.

This book has all the advice you will need to initiate and sustain such relationships. It is up to you and your team members to decide which lessons they can incorporate into their individual business-development repertoires. Sure, there's a wealth of how-to in the following pages. But, more importantly, this is a guide for helping you establish a climate in which each contributor can find a way to success that helps leverage the unique talents they bring to the wonderful game of sales.

Tony Rutigliano, best-selling co-author of "Discover Your Sales Strengths" and "Strengths Based Selling"

INTRODUCTION

Before I try to upend your notions about how to generate new business, let me convince you why your approach to business development needs to change in the first place. After all, plenty of firms have succeeded under the current model and it would be easy to dismiss the suggestions in this book as a lot of unnecessary work. But before you do that, I urge you to take stock of recent changes in the accounting industry. You've seen it all around you — firms are consolidating, specialization is increasing, partners who bring in the bulk of the firm's new business are retiring. Ask yourself: Are you well positioned to weather all these changes? Or is there more you could do to secure your firm's financial future?

First, consider the changing landscape of the accounting industry. According to the AICPA, globalization, technological change and generational shifts are just a few of the changes that threaten to disrupt the industry over the next decade. Accountants face increasing competition on all fronts, including from other professionals who want to marginalize the role that accountants play in advising their clients on financial matters. The falling price of compliance products only contributes to the commoditization of accounting work, further squeezing accountants. Finally, as experienced partners retire, they are leaving behind staff members who have little experience bringing in new business. Many firms will be left to stumble around in the dark, desperately trying to keep new business coming in the door.

Now the question is how to deal with these changes. You could ignore them, but you do so at your own peril. As consultant Peter Darling said, "If you hate change, you're hating the inexorable. It's like hating the sunrise. One way or another, it is going to happen, and if you are not out in the market responding to change, if you resist or deny it, you are at its mercy. And that is not a good place to be." Thankfully, it appears that most accountants aren't looking to bury their heads in the sand. According to a recent CPA Trendlines survey of more than 670 practitioners nationwide, 73% of tax and accounting firms plan to battle hard for new business this year, up from 65% last year. But how should you allocate your efforts? What will give you the most bang for your buck? Responding to RFPs hardly counts as a marketing strategy.

That's where this book comes in. It aims to provide a detailed roadmap for how to succeed in this brave new world. Its core argument is that business development success depends on establishing reliable and repeatable processes that guarantee you make the most out of every opportunity. It emphasizes that business development should be a firm-wide responsibility, with all staff members receiving business development training, starting with their first day on the job. It's the culmination of years of insight gained working at a variety of professional service firms, across a broad spectrum of industries, from law to engineering to accounting. It's jam-packed with tried and tested ideas that will work if you give them an opportunity.

The following 14 chapters will give you the tools you need to become a business development superstar. This is the answer you've been waiting for. Enjoy the journey.

Sources:

"CPA Horizons 2025 Report," AICPA, accessed June 8, 2014, http://www.aicpa.org/research/cpahorizons2025/pages/cpahorizonsreport.aspx.

"Trends for 2014 and Beyond," Public Accountant, accessed June 8, 2014, http://pubacct.org.au/trends-for-2014-and-beyond.

Peter Darling, "Why Business Development Matters," accessed June 8, 2014, http://peterdarling.typepad.com/business_development/why_business_development_matters.

Rick Telberg, "Why Now Is a Good Time To Be Shopping for a New Accountant," LinkedIn, accessed June 8, 2014, https://www.linkedin.com/today/post/article/20131228173857-458190-why-now-is-a-good-time-to-be-shopping-for-a-new-accountant.

CHAPTER 1
SOURCES OF NEW BUSINESS

Before you can start generating more new business, you need to know where to target your efforts. After all, no one wants to spend time chasing leads that go nowhere. In this chapter, we identify the six most common sources of new business and suggest a few best practices for generating new business from each of these sources. Our sources of new business include:

- **Clients:** Once you've delivered excellent work, you can sell more services to an existing client or ask for referrals to prospective new clients.
- **Colleagues:** Current colleagues with complementary areas of expertise can cross-refer business, while former colleagues can serve as valuable referral sources.
- **Wheels of influence:** These are the professional service people — including attorneys, wealth managers and consultants — who work with your existing clients. By collaborating with them, you can sell more services to existing clients and gain introductions to prospective clients.
- **Centers of influence:** These professional service people serve a similar clientele and can turn into some of your best referral sources.
- **Strategic alliances:** By teaming up with another type of professional service firm, you can meet more ideal clients and expand the services you offer to your existing clients.
- **Unsolicited lead generation:** In this case, you're not relying on people you already know. Instead, you're sending out mailers and making phone calls to solicit prospective clients to whom you have no personal connection.

CLIENTS

In most firms, clients are the single largest source of new business. The key to winning new business from existing clients is first to deliver excellent work, and then to take the opportunity to ask them for more business. You might be able to sell more services to existing clients, or they might be able to offer you introductions to prospective new clients. Both are invaluable sources of new business.

Build on your success

Clients have seen you in action. They know what you do and what you're good at. They like, trust and respect you. So why aren't they a more prolific source of business in firms? Two reasons: First, they don't know the full extent of your services and therefore don't realize you can serve them in other ways; and second, they don't think you're looking for new work. To overcome these hurdles, you need to get in the habit of educating your clients about what you do and for whom you do it.

Don't be afraid to ask

Once you've demonstrated your value to a client, it's time to leverage that capital by asking for new business, either by selling them additional services or by soliciting referrals. Be on the lookout for a good time to broach the subject. Saving a client time or money, helping them seize a new opportunity, serving as a resource on financial matters or making an introduction — these are all examples of "good news opportunities" and the perfect time to ask for more business. Yet, in my experience, many accountants are unwilling to ask for more work. They assume that doing good work automatically leads to more opportunities and referrals. Not so! Clients often believe that you have enough work and aren't looking for more, or they think that introducing you to others will dilute the level of service you give to them. You have to be willing to ask outright. I find that it's helpful to have specific language to use if you're uncomfortable asking. My two favorite "asks" are: "We're always looking for more great clients like you. Do you know anybody who could benefit from our services?" and "Is there someone else I should be talking to?" Try them out. If you aren't mining your client base for more work, you're letting business slip away.

Do more for your clients

In the client service topic in the next chapter, we outline a process for soliciting more work from existing clients. By seeking to understand the client's overall situation, you can connect their needs to the services that the firm or its strategic alliance partners offer. The important thing to remember is that you have to do great work to ask for more work. If they're happy with your work and if you understand their priorities, you're in a great position to win more of their business. Here are a few strategies to generate more from existing clients:

- **Classify your clients.** Use an "A", "B" and "C" rating system to classify your clients (www[1]). To decide where to place each client, use factors such as annual fees, realization rate, average billing rate, payment history, probability of increasing fees, probability of generating business referrals, niche relevance, business success and intangibles, such as willingness to follow advice. At the end of the process each person will likely have approximately 20%-30% of their clients in the "A" category, 30%-40% in the "B" category and 30%-50% in the "C" category. Now that you can quantify the value of your clients, you can focus on cultivating relationships with "A" and "B" clients. Partners should be freed up from spending too much time on "C" clients. Remember to continually re-evaluate client classifications.

- **Explore creative strategies.** Consider these strategies to uncover additional opportunities with "A" and "B" clients:

  - *Client spotlight:* A partner highlights a client who has significant potential upside. The partners brainstorm ways to grow the client's business and commit to an action plan to move forward.

  - *Client matrix* (www[2]): Each partner puts together a client matrix listing their top 10 clients. The matrix lists the client name across the top and all the firm's services down the side. The partner fills in the annual fees for each service provided to the client and leaves the other boxes blank. The matrix is then submitted to the group for ideas on how to cross-sell to that client.

  - *Data mining software* (see clients chapter): Utilize data mining software to identify prospective clients by business category. Document indicators that suggest that a current client is a good candidate for another firm service. For example, a tax client who has complained about tax liability or hasn't accumulated substantial assets despite having a high salary might be a good prospect for wealth management.

- **Conduct client service meetings** (see clients chapter): Conduct the client service process in person with all "A"-level clients and either in person or over the phone with all "B"-level clients. Have more junior staff conduct the client service process over the phone and via email with "C"-level clients.

Keep these other tips in mind to generate new business from existing clients:

- **Educate and inform.** Share new ideas and services with clients on a recurring basis. Send them communiqués and invite them to events. Constantly push the boundaries of what you do and how you can help them. The excuse should never be: "I didn't know you did that."

- **Track new business.** Additional revenue from existing clients has a habit of getting lost in new business reporting. Make sure you quantify and report all new opportunities with current clients as "new business." This will help ensure that sufficient energy is put toward this initiative.

- **Provide case studies.** When you succeed in up-selling or cross-selling a current client, turn the example into a case study for use internally or with other clients. Walk through the issue, solution and benefit to demonstrate how the new opportunity was born.
- **Maintain the matrix.** Maintain the client matrix for your top 10 clients. Revisit this regularly to identify new opportunities to better serve them.

Key takeaways

To generate new business from existing clients:

- Provide great service. It's all for naught if you don't do great work! Once you've done a good job, use the opportunity to ask for more work or referrals.
- Classify your clients. Focus on those who have historically brought you more business and referrals.
- Explore other creative strategies to identify opportunities. Follow your defined client service process.

COLLEAGUES

Both current and former colleagues are great sources of business for accountants. Current colleagues with complementary areas of expertise can cross-refer clients, thus keeping the client's business within the firm. Former colleagues can also be valuable referral sources, especially if they frequently interact with your ideal client. Much like clients, colleagues and former colleagues have witnessed your skill, expertise and dependability firsthand. Not only can they honestly vouch for you to their clients, but they also understand better than most who your ideal client is.

Current colleagues

In generating new business from colleagues, the biggest challenge is maintaining the other party's understanding of what you do, for whom you do it and what makes you different. In the case of current colleagues, your firm should offer multiple vehicles to help you uncover opportunities to collaborate, including business development meetings, staff meetings, lunch n' learn sessions and mentoring. Follow these tips when collaborating with current colleagues:

- **Educate and inform.** Be sure that colleagues understand one another's areas of specialty. You want to spend your time pursuing opportunities with clients who want what you have to offer. It's not useful if your colleagues are sending you dead-end referrals.
- **Deepen the relationship.** Build a level of like, trust and respect with your colleagues. Establish common interests, values and standards.
- **Model behavior.** Set an example by introducing colleagues to your clients. Model the type of introduction you want them to make for you.
- **Demonstrate value.** Find low-cost opportunities to demonstrate value, such as providing insight or sharing expertise. Chip away at the natural resistance to sharing client relationships.
- **Give it a try.** Start out small. Make sure this is a person you trust with your clients. If the initial collaborative engagement or referral goes well, more opportunities will follow.
- **Reciprocate.** Referrals are a two-way street. Help others by making connections with your clients and referral sources.

If all goes well, not only will you have a steady source of new business, but you also will have demonstrated your firm's value to the client by meeting all their needs in-house. This is especially relevant for firms that offer a wide range of services. The firm becomes a "one-stop shop" for the client, providing everything from bookkeeping and family office services, to employee benefits and insurance, to financial planning and asset management. Your clients won't be as tempted to look elsewhere if you're already taking care of all their needs.

Former colleagues

Similarly, former colleagues are a great source of new business if they like, trust and respect you and if they regularly encounter your ideal clients in their new position. In some cases, former colleagues will have remained in the accounting profession and now serve a different ideal client. Those who have moved on to smaller firms can refer up more complex or niche-specific matters; those who have left for larger firms can refer down work that's not sophisticated or profitable enough; and those who work at similar firms can refer work when they're conflicted out due to independence issues. In other cases, former accountants will have left the profession to take on other finance-related roles in business, such as CFO or controller. These people tend to associate with other financial professionals and can be prolific sources of new business, especially in industries such as technology where job migration is common. Follow these tips when cultivating relationships with former colleagues:

- **Stay in touch.** It seems like an obvious thing to do but so few of us do it. Connect with them via LinkedIn, keep them on your holiday card list, add them to the firm's communications list and invite them to special events. In short, create a recurring calendar appointment to stay "top of mind."
- **Paint the picture.** Be sure both parties know what an ideal client referral looks like. "C"-level referrals are relationship-killers. Avoid the urge to perpetuate the referral cycle by making introductions to professional contacts who are unlikely to become a referral source. Focus on referring one another to prospective clients.
- **Be a resource.** Sometimes a little thing opens the door to a new business opportunity. Offer a free piece of advice or make a connection to an expert in your network. Be a resource and referral business will follow.

Maintaining relationships with former colleagues isn't a huge time commitment and you don't need to do it with a lot of people. But if you do it well with the right people, a handful of former colleagues will become a big source of new business for you.

Best practices

Whether you're dealing with current or former colleagues, keep these tips in mind to generate as much new business as possible.

- **Deliver great work.** The formula for business development equals "do great work and ask for more." Only ask for more work, however, if you deliver great work on all fronts (high quality, on time, under budget, to specs, etc).
- **Steward the referral.** Keep the other party informed about your progress. Copy them on correspondence and invite them to participate in

the conversation whenever it adds value, such as by making the initial introduction in person versus via phone or email.

- **Say thanks.** In our recognition and reward topic (see management chapter), we talk about the importance of individual recognition and group reward. Acknowledge the individual's efforts with a handwritten note. Even if the referral doesn't ultimately lead to new work, thank them for thinking of you. Send them a personal gift that you know they'll enjoy. Even better, treat them to an experience, such as lunch or a sporting event.

Key takeaways

To generate new business from colleagues:

- Cultivate relationships with colleagues who have complementary expertise and whom you like, trust and respect.
- Look for opportunities to introduce colleagues to your clients. Model the behavior by making suitable introductions to your clients first.
- Maintain ties with former colleagues, whether they stay in public accounting or leave for a career in finance or business.

WHEELS OF INFLUENCE

Wheels of influence are professional service people who work with your existing clients. Think of a wheel with your client at the center, surrounded by their attorneys, bankers, wealth managers and so on. If you don't already know these people, you should because they can help you better serve your clients and they likely have other ideal clients whom you would like to meet.

Know your client's family

The wheel of influence is the most undervalued aspect of a professional network. Few accountants can name the professional family that supports each of their clients, and if they can, few have established a strategy to convert those resources into referral traffic. Yet these individuals have the potential to be among your best referral sources because they've seen the value you provide to a common client. Additionally, by taking the lead in organizing the client's professional service team, you can position yourself as the team's leader and win the role as the client's most trusted advisor. Remember that the wheel isn't necessarily made up of just one attorney, one banker and one wealth manager. Clients with complex needs may have a long list of professional service people who support them, including:

- Attorneys: tax, real estate, litigation support, family, immigration, estate, IP, business
- Bankers: investment, private, commercial
- Wealth managers: private equity, VC, hedge fund, charitable giving
- Insurance brokers: life, health, disability, property and casualty
- Consultants: M&A, HR, organizational development, strategic planning, life planning
- Accountants: client accounting services including bookkeeping, family office, etc

Build a bridge

Follow these steps to cultivate relationships with wheels of influence:

- **Create a map.** Log your wheel of influence contacts by client in a database (www[3]) or map (www[4]). Include name, contact details and a description of each contact. You can't cultivate them if you don't know who they are.
- **Introduce yourself.** If you don't know them, ask the client to connect you via phone or email. If that's not an option, reach out to them and reference your common client. Create a compelling case for building a relationship. There are at least two obvious reasons to get together: to explore ways to better serve your common client and to explore opportunities to cross-refer. They're unlikely to decline your invitation, but if they do, that tells you all you need to know. Move on.
- **Do your homework.** We talk extensively in the sales process chapter about the importance of doing research on key prospects. A wheel of influence is a key prospect. They might not be a prospect in the same way that a prospective client is, but they're an "A"-level referral source in the making. Do your homework. Find out about their ideal client, competitive advantage, claims and service capabilities. Ensure they know the same about you.
- **Deepen the relationship.** Like all relationships, you get out what you put in. Schedule recurring appointments to chat and get together for coffee or lunch. Generate like, trust and credibility.
- **Make connections.** As with any referral source, help them to build and enhance their network by making introductions to key contacts. Invite them to B2B and B2C events. Put them on the guest list for your "best of referral sources" mixer.
- **Keep track.** Keep a running tally of the number and dollar value of referrals in and out. Not all wheel of influence contacts will be referral sources. Some will just be resources to offer to clients when they need specialized expertise. Regardless of their role or value, track and allocate time and resources appropriately.
- **Play quarterback.** Take on the role of coordinating the client's professional service team. It doesn't take a herculean effort. Simply suggest to the client that you'd like to organize a meeting with the whole team, at no charge to the client. The goal of the meeting is to better understand the needs and wants of the client and, in doing so, to better serve them. Regardless of whether you come out of the meeting with more work, it conveys a level of commitment, deepens the client relationship and helps you earn the role of most trusted advisor.

Key takeaways

To generate new business from wheels of influence:

- Get to know your clients' professional service contacts, particularly those who share your ideal client profile.
- Play a quarterbacking role with the client. Position yourself as the trusted advisor and go-to person for questions and connections.
- Treat wheels of influence contacts like "A"-level referral sources until they prove otherwise. Help them to connect and encourage them to reciprocate.

CENTERS OF INFLUENCE

A center of influence is someone who regularly comes into contact with your ideal client as part of their job. For accountants, centers of influence will most often be attorneys, bankers, insurance brokers, consultants and other professional service people. You should share the same ideal client profile as your center of influence contacts, but you won't have any common clients (if you did, they would be a "wheel of influence"). These people have the potential to be among your best referral sources. The challenge is meeting the right people, who can be depended upon to deliver above expectation every time.

Mutual support

Centers of influence usually fall into one of three categories:

- **Resources:** Resources are simply people to whom you refer work or from whom you receive work without any expectation of reciprocity. The referring party is confident that their client will receive outstanding service, which is enough of a reward. Often, the timing of each other's service is such that one is not a good referral source for the other (see collaborators below). Don't undervalue resources just because they don't refer work to you; they're still an excellent contact to maintain if they provide excellent client service.
- **Referral sources:** Referral sources trade referrals and generally serve the same ideal client. Both parties deliver great work to strengthen client relationships and facilitate introductions to each other's clients and prospective clients.
- **Collaborators:** Collaborators serve as resources, are prolific sources of new business for one another and work together in such a way that the client sees them as part of the same team. They are the individual

equivalent of a strategic alliance. Their services are complementary and often take place in sequence or simultaneously (for example, a financial planner and a wealth manager or an auditor and a fraud assessment provider). Sometimes, the relationship is born out of independence issues.

Be selective

Not every attorney or banker you meet will be a good match for you. Here are some of the factors that make valuable centers of influence:

- **Trustworthy and credible:** You are entrusting your clients to your centers of influence, and they're entrusting you with theirs. It's critical to foster a sense of mutual trust so everyone knows their clients are in good hands.
- **Committed:** To get the most out of these relationships, you need to find people with a desire to grow their business and a commitment to the referral process. Professional service people who can't identify their ideal client or who aren't interested in learning more about your business are not going to be promising leads.
- **Business commonalities:** There needs to be some kind of overlap between your businesses. Maybe you serve the same clients, or you offer complementary services. You aren't competing against each other, but you aren't operating in totally separate spheres either.
- **Aligned sales cycles:** You may find someone who meets the above criteria, but if their sales cycle doesn't line up with yours, they probably won't be a good referral source or collaborator, though they could still serve as a resource. Your most productive centers of influence will be those whose work occurs soon before or after yours (for example, an attorney and an accountant who both work on estate planning issues).

There are plenty of networking opportunities for cultivating centers of influence. We talk about several in this book, including:

- **LinkedIn** (see social media topic in the marketing chapter): LinkedIn is one of the most valuable social media networks for connecting with people you know and would like to know.
- **Boards** (see networking chapter): Joining a board is a great way to meet potential "A"-level clients and hone your business development skills, while also serving the common good.
- **B2B groups** (see networking chapter): These groups offer a recurring opportunity to cultivate relationships with other professionals, who often turn into valuable referral sources.
- **Associations** (see networking chapter): Joining an industry or trade association helps you build your name and reputation, especially if you take on speaking positions or leadership roles.

Spend your time wisely

Once you decide to commit to finding centers of influence, you'll quickly realize that efficiency is the key to successful business development lead generation. Here a few suggestions for vetting potential centers of influence:

- **Think outside the box.** Professional service people aren't the only potential centers of influence. As Keith Ferrazzi writes in "Never Eat Alone," some professions are full of "super-connectors," individuals who maintain contact with hundreds and thousands of people. Examples include restaurateurs, executive recruiters and real estate agents. If these people routinely come into contact with your ideal client, it might be worth cultivating a relationship.

- **Refine your referral piece.** Your referral piece is a one- to two-page document that identifies who you want to be referred to, what you do and why you're different. The more targeted it is, the easier it will be to find suitable centers of influence. And if your potential center of influence doesn't have one, they might not be that serious about generating business through referrals. (See referrals chapter for more on referral pieces.)

- **Look for signs.** If they don't respond to email, if they're late for meetings, if they fail to follow up on commitments, you know all you need to know. They'll treat your clients the same way they treat you. If you're not willing to introduce these people to your clients, don't invest the time.

- **Give it a try.** Start with a simple request. Ask them to be a resource for an existing client or ask for advice that you ultimately deliver to your client. Don't give them instant access to your clients. Vet their interest and ability without risk. One of my personal favorite tactics is to see how they react with little time to prepare. You learn a lot about people by watching them respond under pressure.

- **Classify.** Figure out who the most and least promising candidates are. Here's a simplified way to do so for referral sources: "A"-level referral sources refer multiple ideal clients annually; "B"-level referral sources have referred an ideal client; and "C"-level referral sources have the capacity to refer an ideal client but have yet to do so. Allocate your time and resources accordingly.

- **Focus on quality versus quantity.** Only a small number of your centers of influence will consistently deliver quality work and referrals. Fewer still will become collaborators. That's okay. I know too many people who focus on the big number of how many people they know and not the number of people who are relevant from a business development perspective. To illustrate, I have 31 people I consider resources. Of those 31, only two are collaborators.

- **Reward and recognize.** Those 31 people are on my holiday card list, receive my family newsletter and make up the balance of my business development social calendar. These are people I like and trust. I try to thank them personally and reward them when appropriate. Whenever possible, I prefer experiences to tangible gifts as rewards.

- **Track your contacts.** Maintain a database (www[3]) that tracks all your sources of new business (clients, colleagues, wheels of influence, boards, B2B groups, associations, etc). Everyone in the firm should have access to that database to ensure contacts aren't being solicited by multiple firm members. In addition to recording contact information, classification and recent interactions, it's important to track the number and dollar value of referrals in and out.

Key takeaways

To generate new business from centers of influence:

- Build a network of contacts via B2B groups, boards, associations and other business networking resources.
- Don't be in a rush to add centers of influence to your inner circle. Create an audition process to demonstrate value.
- Look for ways to collaborate and invest the necessary time. Allocate your time and resources wisely.

STRATEGIC ALLIANCES

Strategic alliances are partnerships between accounting firms and other professional service firms. The two firms typically share an ideal client and team up for mutual benefit. Common strategic alliance partners for accounting firms include wealth management firms, insurance providers, employee benefit firms, outside CFO and outsourced HR firms.

A win-win

Strategic alliances are typically driven by the desire to meet more ideal clients or to provide more services to existing clients. Good strategic alliances are a win-win for all involved. Accountants benefit by expanding the array of services they offer to their clients, maintaining their role as a trusted advisor to their clients, deepening client relationships, garnering introductions to prospective ideal clients and earning additional money through fee-sharing arrangements. Clients benefit by gaining access to a broader range of services, meeting new trusted resources and implementing an integrated strategy with the guidance of their accountant.

Define your relationship

When looking for prospective alliance partners, look for people who work closely with your ideal client, provide a service your clients need and want, consistently deliver outstanding client service and are comfortable referring clients and sharing referral sources. In my experience, strategic alliances typically take three forms:

- **Resource-based:** One alliance partner serves as a resource by providing a valuable service without reciprocating new business referrals. In this case, the partnership's value comes from providing outstanding service for a client. That alone is sufficient value.
- **Reward-based:** One alliance partner is compensated for the relationship in the form of commission or fees. This is common for licensed CPA firms that form alliances with wealth management and insurance firms. While the accounting firm may not see an abundance of new client referrals from the alliance partner, they are compensated for the referrals they send to their partner.
- **Referral-based:** In the ideal scenario, the alliance partners cross-refer and are a considerable source of new business for one another. The accountant may receive commissions and fees, but this is a secondary driver in the relationship.

All of the above alliances can be beneficial to both parties, but it's important to know from the beginning what kind of relationship you'll have.

Form a team

Here are some keys to developing successful strategic alliances:

- **Select partners carefully.** Look for like-minded people who run their business along similar ethical lines. Seek out businesses that have established contacts in a particular industry or geographic region, but lack your expertise. An alliance must be a win-win to have a chance of success. Otherwise, one partner is likely to become frustrated and eventually resentful of constantly being underserved.
- **Do your homework.** Conduct a SWOT (strengths, weaknesses, opportunities, threats) analysis. Talk to references and testimonial sources and explore the opportunity by preparing questions and conducting a thorough needs assessment.
- **Be clear on desired outcomes.** Identify your expected revenue from the alliance, the number of hours you'll commit to the alliance, any concerns you have and the products and services you wish to promote and sell. Many business alliances fail because of poor communication so make sure you discuss all details to avoid misunderstandings and conflict.
- **Conduct a beta.** Strategic alliance partners often agree to something in principle, only to realize they can't honor their agreement. Establish a trial period to get an idea of the other firm's management style, attention to detail and investment in the project. Avoid the temptation to take the alliance beyond an initial trial until you have witnessed the other firm's commitment. Set measures for what has to be achieved to formalize the alliance.
- **Celebrate successes.** To maintain momentum in the partnership, it's important to record milestones, such as your first engagement letter or your first receipt in excess of $X. Celebrating shared achievements builds the relationship.
- **Review and improve.** As with anything, highlight positives and identify challenges. Always be on the lookout for how to strengthen the partnership.

Once you've moved forward with an alliance, follow these tips to get as much value as possible:

- **Promote from within.** Offer lunch n' learn sessions to educate staff about the partnership. Go door-to-door addressing any questions, issues and obstacles. Make sure your staff knows how to identify suitable candidates for the partner firm.
- **Integrate.** Create joint collateral to clearly articulate the alliance's value proposition and service set. Invite alliance partners to business development meetings and staff meetings and encourage communication between partner firms. Act as a team.

- **Communicate value.** Draft case studies when your alliance helps a client. Document the value in numeric and fiscal terms, including number of new accounts and dollar value of new business.
- **Reward and recognize.** Reinforce desired behavior, celebrate individual and team wins and share best practices.
- **Put in the time.** You get out what you put in. Left unattended, your alliances will flounder. Put in the necessary time, energy and resources to make the strategic alliance work.

Key takeaways

To generate new business from strategic alliances:

- Identify firms who serve the same ideal client. Do your homework to make a good match.
- Know your expectations of the partnership. Understand the value your alliance partner provides, whether as a resource or referral source.
- Invest the time. Make sure you're taking full advantage of valued partners.

UNSOLICITED LEAD GENERATION

Unsolicited lead generation is the process of identifying, cultivating and soliciting prospective clients to whom you have no specific connection; we also refer to this process as "warm calling." A warm-calling campaign involves a series of informational mailings, followed by a phone call. Warm-calling campaigns are most appropriate at firms that have the appropriate resources, such as an outside sales rep or business development coach, and that have exhausted other more productive aspects of business development.

Be persistent

Unsolicited lead generation won't make it into everyone's business development plan because it's usually the least fruitful of the possible sources of new business. That doesn't mean, however, that it can't deliver good leads, especially with a little bit of luck and good timing. Think about credit card applications. Everyone gets at least one per week, most of which are immediately discarded. But on that fateful day when the 101st credit card offer of the year arrives, it just happens to follow a conversation about earning points for an upcoming trip. The credit card company didn't necessarily do anything to separate itself from its competitors; its offer simply arrived on the right day. Unsolicited lead generation is similar. Of course, you need to deliver something relevant but just as importantly, you need to be persistent in hopes your offering will land on the right desk at the right time.

Sow your seeds

Unsolicited lead generation is most common in niche marketing efforts, when you've exhausted the usual universe of client and referral contacts. Additionally, non-profits can be a productive target for unsolicited lead generation if they're required to regularly undergo audits. When the goal is simply to be added to an RFP list, a warm-calling campaign can be particularly effective.

Each campaign consists of four stages: prep, mail, call, report. Typically, we recommend you send three mailings before making a call, unless the goal is simply to be added to an RFP list, in which case it's okay to send fewer than three. The purpose of the mailings is to build awareness, establish credibility and ultimately serve as a conversation starter. During the call, you want to qualify their interest and commit them to a next step, such as a phone call or meeting with an accountant at the firm. The following summarizes a schedule for a typical 12-week warm-calling campaign:

Prep stage	
Week 1	Develop an ideal client profile (www[5]). Interview the internal champion to perform a SWOT analysis (www[6]). Understand the strengths (clients, expertise, etc), weaknesses (lack of competitive differentiators, price sensitivity, etc), opportunities (associations, events, etc) and threats (competition, timing limitations, etc) associated with the campaign.
Week 2	Generate a one-page campaign strategy document (www[7]), including a campaign budget.
Week 3	Research and procure a list of prospective clients.
Week 4	Conduct data mining and list cleanup. Generate a call script (www[8]). Generate FAQs to address common objections (www[9]). Generate collateral piece #1.
Mailing stage	
Week 5	Mail collateral piece #1.
Week 6	Generate collateral piece #2.
Week 7	Mail collateral piece #2.
Week 8	Generate collateral piece #3.
Week 9	Mail collateral piece #3.
Call stage	
Week 10	Make first-round calls to confirm the prospect received your correspondence, to find out if the topic resonated with them, to ask if they're experiencing any issues with their current provider and to try to persuade them to take a call or meeting with the internal champion. Forward information about interested parties to the internal champion.
Week 11	Make second-round calls to prospects you didn't reach the first time.
Reporting stage	
Week 12	Produce a campaign report (www[10]). Include what you did well, what you would do differently next time, what you generated from the campaign and what follow-up you are planning to do.

Keep these tips in mind during the preparation and mailing stages:

- **Start with good data.** Acquire or purchase an up-to-date and targeted prospect list with accurate contact information. You'll waste a lot of time and money chasing ghosts if you don't.
- **Research.** Do a little research on the person and the firm before you get on the phone. You don't need a detailed profile but a little advance reconnaissance will help start the conversation.
- **Catch their eye.** Generate interesting and eye-catching mailing pieces by using unforgettable graphics. Send mailings by snail mail instead of email whenever possible because email is easier to ignore or delete.
- **Build your case.** Each mailing piece should stand as an independent piece while also building on one another. My favorite pieces are Top 5 lists because they're easy to read, topical, eye-catching and fit easily on one page. For example: "Top 5 Things To Look For In An Auditor" or "Top 5 Ways Your Auditor Provides Value Beyond the Audit."
- **Include a call to action.** At the end of each piece, tell them whom to contact or where to go to get more information. Let them know that you'll be contacting them within X days at the end of the third piece.

Once you actually have a prospective client on the phone, follow these tips:

- **Respect their time.** Think about how you feel when you receive a phone call from a solicitor. Be respectful of their time and acknowledge the lack of patience that typically accompanies a solicitation call. If you don't grab their interest in the first 60 seconds, thank them for their time and move on to the next call.
- **Nail your opening.** Begin with a statement to get their attention. Choose an opening that centers on the prospective client and that demonstrates you know something about them. For example, rather than opening with, "My name is X and I work at company Y," try, "I noticed that your company recently acquired company Z and wondered if you might benefit from learning more about how we've helped business like yours reduce resulting tax liabilities." Make it clear why you're calling.
- **Don't sell on the phone.** Your primary goal is to open a dialogue, not to describe all the features of your service. Focus on determining whether the prospective client is a good fit, but don't try to force them to buy. Prepare questions to help them understand whether they need your service. Anticipate their most likely questions and prepare answers.
- **Gain commitments.** You aren't trying to close a sale, but you do want to get them to the next step in the process, usually a phone call or meeting with a senior accountant. Even if they're not interested, try to get something out of every call, whether it's an agreement to stay on the mailing list or permission to call back next year to see if their situation has changed.

- **Don't get deterred by rejection.** Few prospective clients will buy immediately. Prepare a list of common objections beforehand and write down possible responses. For example, if a prospect says they can't afford your service, be prepared to explain how it will save them money.

Land a whale

If you really want to make unsolicited lead generation worth your while, don't just go after the small fish. Make a list of 10 organizations that would be game-changers for your firm. Build a campaign around soliciting those clients. Find out who is on their board, subscribe to their newsletter and sponsor their events. Do everything you can to win their business, because if you do, more business will follow. Think of it like this: If you want to be the go-to auditor for local private schools, and you can claim the most renowned private school as your client, all the other schools are going to trust that you can do the work they need. All the effort you put in to win that one client will pay off with the dozens of smaller clients that follow.

The easy way out

If this all sounds like it's too much effort for little return, consider a basic unsolicited lead generation campaign built around industry awards and announcements. When an individual is in the news or recognized with an award, send a congratulatory email or LinkedIn message. If they respond, follow up with a phone call. You would be surprised at how many people respond to fan mail. Sometimes it's all the opening you need to start a conversation. Even better, this type of unsolicited lead generation campaign is easy to do on your own, without much assistance from business development staff.

Key takeaways

To generate new business from unsolicited lead generation:

- Begin by sending informational mailing pieces to a targeted list of prospective clients.
- Follow up with a phone call to determine if the prospective client is interested and to commit them to a next step.
- Follow a 12-week campaign strategy to ensure your unsolicited lead generation efforts are short, measureable and manageable.

CHAPTER 2
CLIENTS

For many accountants, existing clients account for at least half of their new business each year, through up-selling, cross-selling and referrals. Invest in relationships with your clients, ask the tough questions and be a true trusted advisor on their financial journey and you will be rewarded in new business and referrals.

In this chapter, we discuss how to demonstrate your value to clients, how to earn more work from existing clients and how to dissuade clients from leaving. Individual topics include:

- **Client service:** Outstanding client service starts with an understanding of your firm's core client service values and a clear process for putting those principles into action.
- **Planning:** We discuss a range of planning vehicles that help you uncover new opportunities in the course of performing tax, assurance and advisory work for existing clients.
- **Data mining:** Perform analysis to identify prospective clients for specific products and services.
- **Evaluations:** Solicit feedback from clients about their relationship with the firm to identify ways to better serve them.
- **Change order process:** Document changes to the scope of work to ensure you're billing for the work you do.
- **Lost clients:** A three-part process to save clients who are considering leaving, to learn from their departure and to eventually win them back.

CLIENT SERVICE

Think about your best customer service experience. Whether it was a retail purchase at Nordstrom, a flight on Singapore Airlines or a stay at the Ritz-Carlton, all of these are companies that have built a commitment to great customer service into their DNA. Their dedication to delivering a five-star customer experience is embedded in everything they do, from the way they treat their employees to the way they interact with their customers. These companies aren't just claiming great customer service; they're demonstrating it day in and day out, which is the same approach your firm needs to take if you want to be known for your client service.

Outstanding client service starts with an understanding of your firm's core client service values. Those principles should then bleed into everything else you do, from your interactions with staff to communication with clients. Client service goes far beyond responding to emails quickly or delivering work on time as clients expect that everyone will do that.

The benefits of outstanding client service are obvious — it helps you retain existing clients and land new ones. So why don't firms do more of it? With all of the demands on accountants' time, something has to give. Though the things that "give" are small, it's the little things that make the difference between "satisfactory" and "outstanding" client service. Emails replace handwritten notes; generic thank-you tokens (the cured meats and salted gifts hamper at the holidays) replace personalized gifts (tickets to a favorite band).

Outstanding client service depends on understanding what clients want and providing it time and again. In this topic, we outline a two-step process for delivering outstanding client service:

- **Establish client service values:** Establish clear values that will guide your approach to client service. These values are your bedrock. They are the foundation of your competitive advantage and a key part of distinguishing your firm from the competition.
- **Institute a client service process:** This process helps you put your client service values into action. It guides your interactions with clients and ensures that you're always living by your values.

CLIENT SERVICE VALUES

The first part of establishing top-notch client service is deciding on your client service values. Think of retail companies with great customer service — some have a flexible return policy, others have deeply knowledgeable salespeople. Their priorities aren't identical; what's important is that each company is clear on its own priorities and deeply committed to them. The following outlines a six-step process for identifying your client service values:

1. **Reflect on your own experiences.** Gather the key decision-makers in your firm and ask each attendee to reflect on their best and worst customer service experiences. Discuss each person's responses and look for commonalities. Each person should answer the following based on personal experience:

    - Name a company with which you have had a five-star customer experience. What did they do to deserve a five-star rating? How did the five-star experience make you feel and what did it prompt you to do?
    - Name a company with which you have had a one-star customer experience. What did they do to provoke a one-star rating? How did the one-star experience make you feel and what did it prompt you to do?

2. **Know your target.** Try to answer the question, "Why is five-star service so important?" For example, my answers would be: Five-start patrons keep coming back, tell others unprompted about their experience and are loyal to your brand. One-star patrons start shopping elsewhere, publically complain about your business and force you to invest valuable time and money looking for new clients.

3. **Define good service.** List the characteristics of five-star customer service. Here are some examples of the types of responses you may get:

    - They identify and anticipate your needs.
    - They make you feel special, important and appreciated.
    - They're helpful, knowledgeable and courteous.
    - They routinely meet or exceed your expectations.
    - They resolve issues immediately and know how to apologize.
    - They remember your likes and preferences.
    - They ask for your opinion/feedback. They genuinely want to improve the customer experience.

4. **Decide on your priorities.** Selecting from the characteristics you've listed above, ask each person to individually score their top 10 client service characteristics, giving a 10 to the most important characteristic, and a 1 to the 10th most important characteristic. Add up the scores and create a top X list (usually with 5-10 characteristics).

5. **Figure out how to deliver.** For each client service characteristic in your list, state specific things your firm can and will do to earn a five-star

rating from your clients. Provide measures and metrics where applicable. For example:

Characteristic	Task	Measure
Responsiveness	Respond to all phone and email client inquiries within a specified timeframe. When unable to respond immediately, email the client thanking them for their inquiry and stating when you will be able to respond. Copy all pertinent staff members on all correspondence.	Initial response within two hours. Actual response by end of day.

6. **Live your values.** Once you have decided on your client service values, create visual reminders that employees and clients can see whenever they're walking the halls. You might hang posters or placards in cubicles, on notice boards and in conference rooms. This final step helps bring your values to life.

Know your true north

Having clearly defined client service values ensures there's consistency to your client service commitment; it's a way to make sure everyone is singing from the same hymnal. To your clients, it underscores that you have an enduring culture of client service versus a series of one-off events that make up client service. From an internal perspective, it provides you with "true north" principles that guide your decisions and ensures that new members of your firm are clear about what's expected of them. Finally, when every firm is claiming to have great client service, you'll have something meaningful to back up your claim. You'll be able to clearly communicate to clients and prospective clients what sets you apart from the competition and you'll be able to substantiate your claims by delivering real gains for your clients.

Key takeaways

To craft your firm's client service values:

- Know what makes a great customer service experience and what makes a horrible one. Learn from your personal experiences.
- Think about the benefits of great customer service. There's a lot of future business at stake in how you treat your clients.
- Decide what's important to you. You don't need to stand out at everything. Choose what you care about and how you're going to ensure you follow through.

CLIENT SERVICE PROCESS

The client service process is about demonstrating that you can deliver the kind of service that clients want. By following the steps outlined below, you'll showcase your interest in the client, your technical and industry savvy, your commitment to continuous improvement and your investment in helping clients succeed. All of these are traits that clients want from their CPA (you'll learn more about "what clients want" in the messaging chapter). Client service is an ongoing process, but as part of that, we suggest you conduct a one-hour unbilled meeting with clients to demonstrate your commitment to great client service.

1. **Interview the client (approximately 35 minutes).** Interview the client to better understand their needs, wants and issues. For example, you might ask the following questions:

   About them

   - How's business?
   - What are some of the goals your company is trying to accomplish this quarter/year?
   - Is there anything we can do to help you achieve these goals?
   - What have been your biggest challenges this quarter/year? How are you handling them?
   - What is the potential impact on your business if you don't address these challenges?
   - Is there anything we can do to help you address these challenges?

   About you

   - How are we doing as a firm? Can you provide any feedback in the following areas: staff, work, fees, marketing and communications?
   - What could we be doing better?
   - What should I focus on in the coming quarter/year?
   - How much do you know about our other service offerings? (List the other offerings your firm provides.)
   - Would you like more information about a particular product or service?

   End the interview with a thank you: "This has been great. I really value our relationship and appreciate your feedback."

2. **Share something of value (approximately 10 minutes).** Offer advice to help the client generate revenue, eliminate expenses or save time. Alternatively, you can use the opportunity to provide insights that demonstrate that you keep up to date in your field. You could draw on any of the following: new legislation, studies, reports, case analyses, relevant reading.

3. **Ask for referrals (approximately 10 minutes).** Asking for referrals is the Achilles heel of most accountants. They assume that if they do good work, referrals will follow. The dirty little secret, however, is that most of us need to be asked before proffering names of our contacts. The client service process presents a perfect opportunity to ask such a question. There are two approaches for asking for a referral — one is more direct, and the other avoids putting the client on the spot. If you take the StrengthsFinder assessment (as recommended in the management chapter), you'll understand which method is most appropriate given the client's personality.

- *The introvert approach:* Start out with, "I'm always looking for great clients like you." Tell the client that you would really appreciate it if they would pass your name along to anyone they know who would be interested in your service. Leave a few business cards and a copy of your referral piece (discussed in the referrals chapter).
- *The extrovert approach:* Ask the client, "I'm always looking for great clients like you and wondered if you know anyone else who could benefit from my services." Give the client a copy of your referral piece and say, "This one-page document highlights the type of individuals/organizations I'm looking to be referred to." Allow them to read it and pause in anticipation of their response. If they start naming names, write them down and ask if it's okay to contact the person directly or if they would prefer to pass the information along themselves.

4. **Close with commitments (approximately 5 minutes):** End the meeting with a commitment to follow up within a specified timeframe. For example, "Thanks for spending time with me today. I've been making note of the things I need to follow up on after this meeting, which are:

Action Item	Timeline
Ask X to call you about financial planning needs	By (insert date)
Ask Y to email you IRS interpretation of rule X guidelines	By (insert date)
Have Z add you to industry-niche email communications recipient list	By (insert date)

End by asking: "Did I miss anything?" Schedule any follow-up calls or meetings before you leave. This will demonstrate your commitment to the process.

5. **Summarize commitments via email.** Immediately following the meeting, send an email summarizing your "action items" (the items that you promised to follow up on). The email doesn't have to be overly

detailed but it should include the action items and timelines that you verbally committed to in the meeting.

6. **Execute commitments.** Complete the action items you listed in your commitments email. If an action item requires a colleague's involvement, check back to ensure they followed up as requested.

7. **Follow up on referrals.** Be sure to follow up on referrals. Your approach will vary depending on whether they offered any names when you first broached the subject.

   - *If they did not offer names:* Reconnect with the individual over the phone after a suitable period of time. Remind them of your interest and ask if they have identified any suitable referrals after your last meeting. If they do offer names, take them down and ask if it's okay to contact the person directly or if they would prefer to pass the information along themselves.

   - *If they offered names:* Reconnect with the individual over the phone to keep them apprised of any follow-up you've had with their referral contacts. Thank them for their help and ask them if they would like to be involved in the client solicitation process. You can also inquire about whether they've thought of any additional referrals since your last meeting.

An ongoing commitment

This seven-step process is merely a demonstration of your firm's commitment to outstanding service. That commitment should permeate all client interactions; it entails a lot more than a one-hour annual get-together. It has to be substantiated with other examples of your never-ceasing commitment to service. That effort might include recognizing special dates and achievements, offering ongoing client education initiatives and rewarding clients for referring new business opportunities.

Key takeaways

Having a clearly defined client service process gives you the opportunity to:

- Communicate your client service values in a real and meaningful way. Your commitment to client services goes above and beyond that of your competitors. This is a chance to show that off.
- Uncover ways to better serve your client. The first half of the interview is all about demonstrating your commitment to your client and your ability to help them succeed.
- Convert the outstanding client service experience into a networking opportunity to meet other ideal clients.

PLANNING

In this series of topics, we outline four planning vehicles designed to uncover new work from existing clients. We suggest using the process of preparing a tax return or performing an audit to open a broader conversation with clients about how to serve them. Though you already offer these services, you may not be taking full advantage of them from a business development standpoint. Don't think of a tax return as simply a compliance product. Instead, approach it as an opportunity to uncover new opportunities for the firm, its strategic alliance partners and its referral sources. You'll prove your value to your clients by helping them accentuate strengths and minimize weaknesses. You'll establish yourself as a trusted advisor and protect against poaching by other firms.

Our four planning vehicles include:

- **Tax planning:** Tax planning should take place regularly and in person. Offer it to all clients and focus on generating immediate benefits.
- **Tax planning observations and ideas:** Generate a series of observations and ideas for each line item in a tax return. Use these ideas and observations to open a broader conversation with the client about their needs.
- **Management letter comments:** Use the management letter comments section of an audit to suggest additional services that you can provide that will benefit the client.
- **Discovery planning:** Discovery planning focuses on understanding a client's hopes, goals, aspirations and fears with the ultimate goal of making recommendations to help the client prepare successfully for the future.

TAX PLANNING

Tax planning — in which accountants forecast client tax burdens for the up-coming year — is a core service offered by most accountants to their clients. It involves projecting taxable income, brainstorming how to reduce income and increase deductions, and forecasting actual tax liabilities. Nonetheless, many accountants are missing the chance to turn that process into a business development opportunity. A productive tax planning experience should almost always lead to better outcomes for the client, more opportunities for the firm and more referrals for the accountant.

Prove your value

Tax planning is a service that should be extended to all of a firm's clients, yet due to resource limitations often it is only offered to the firm's top clients or those who specifically request it. Additionally, many accountants don't open up the discussion enough, and miss the opportunity to probe other client needs. Follow these tips to generate more opportunities from your tax planning:

- **Make it a habit.** Tax planning should be part of the package extended to all clients. Sit down with your clients at least once annually to make predictions for the coming year and to assess if they should adjust their strategy. The process should entail reviewing their current situation, projecting what they will owe in taxes and brainstorming strategies for lowering their tax burden.
- **Look for immediate benefits.** Clients like tax planning because they often see immediate results. By suggesting, for example, that a client expecting a baby should open a 529 plan, you can help the client lower their future tax burden. The key is to ask enough questions to uncover ways for the client to seize opportunities or minimize liabilities. If you focus too much on just running the numbers, you won't uncover broader ways to serve the client.
- **Go back to the future.** A tax planning conversation provides a gate-way to a broader "discovery planning" conversation. If you want to be a trusted advisor to the client, you need to understand the totality of their needs, and tax planning is a great way to start that process. Think of it as the appetizer to discovery planning (see discovery planning topic later in this chapter).

Reel in the benefits

Tax planning is a great way for accountants to differentiate themselves from do-it-yourself software programs like TurboTax or "corner store tax accountants" like H&R Block. You can provide your clients with peace of mind by helping position them for the upcoming year. Even if you don't uncover any new ways to serve the client, you will have cemented your relationship by offering this value-added service. And if you are able to make recommendations or offer new services to the client, you'll clearly demonstrate your skills and create a loyal client in the process. As a result of this positive experience, you'll uncover new business opportunities and generate more referrals.

Key takeaways

The best tax planning conversations:

- Take place regularly and in person. You should focus on generating immediate benefits for the client.
- Demonstrate your value to the client. There's a value to hiring a real live accountant and tax planning is a great way to demonstrate that.
- Lead to a more strategic conversation about discovery planning. Clients probably don't know about all the ways you can help them. It's on you to start the conversation.

TAX PLANNING OBSERVATIONS AND IDEAS

This process, which we've named "Tax Planning Observations and Ideas," is a way to convert the exercise of preparing a tax return into a broader conversation with a client. The goal is to generate a series of observations and ideas for each line item in a tax return and to translate those into a letter that is mailed to the client. The letter should detail at least three suggestions for minimizing the client's tax burden. Ideally, that letter will spur an in-person meeting with the client, providing you with an opportunity to generate new business opportunities.

See the whole board

The observations and ideas process connects the conventional practice of tax planning with a more meaningful conversation about planning for the future at large. This formalized follow-up adds real value to the client relationship by turning a routine compliance process into an opportunity to lower the client's taxable income, increase deductions, identify new and underutilized credits and provide direction in areas including retirement planning, financial planning, will and estate planning and business exit and succession planning. It starts with a conversation about planning for the known and converts it into a conversation about preparing for the unknown.

Streamline the process

Use your tax return process as a springboard for a deeper investigation of the client's liabilities. Follow these steps:

1. **Draft a list of observations and ideas.** For each relevant line item in an individual or entity tax return, outline possible observations and corresponding ideas. For example:
   For "Wages," your observation and idea might be:

   > *Observation:* You're not making a contribution to a retirement plan on your W2.

   > *Idea:* If you're not in a qualified plan, you might consider setting up a deductible IRA, for between $5,000 and $6,000. Alternatively, if you are an employer, you might think about establishing a retirement plan, starting with a 401k plan, a 403b plan if you're a non-profit entity, or consider other types of retirement plans that are more expansive and that offer greater deductions.

   For "Itemized Deductions, Schedule A: Real Estate Tax," your observation and idea might be:

   > *Observation:* You are paying taxes on non-principal residence property/properties.

Idea: You might consider maximizing your deductions by reviewing the vacation home rules. Additionally, you might look into a QPRT (Qualified Personal Residence Trust), which allows you to gift your vacation home, retain your right to use the home and get that vacation home out of your estate.

For "Accounts Receivable/Bad Debt," your observation and idea might be:

Observation: You have accounts receivable but no bad debt expense.

Idea: You can write-off and take a deduction on bad debts so you might consider reviewing accounts receivable for uncollectible accounts to see if you can take a deduction now.

2. **Integrate an administrative process.** It should be easy for the individual preparing the return to note the relevant observations and ideas. You might create a single checklist so the preparer can check a box for each line item that deserves more attention. Make sure the partner reviews and signs off on the observations and then forward the completed observations sheet to an administrative assistant or business development coordinator.

3. **Merge the observations into a form letter.** The administrative assistant or business development coordinator should merge the appropriate observations and ideas into a form letter. The letter should explain the firm's proactive approach to tax planning, list the pertinent observations and ideas, and inform the client that a staff member will follow up within a given period of time (www[11]). The appropriate engagement partner or senior manager should sign the letter. You may have identified a multitude of observations, but don't include more than three here. Remember, the letter is just a means to start a broader conversation with the client about the future.

4. **Follow up with the client.** Someone — either a partner or administrative assistant, depending on the type of client — should call the client within a week of receipt of the letter to schedule a phone appointment with the appropriate senior manager or partner.

5. **Convert the phone conversation into a face-to-face meeting.** Discuss the observations and ideas contained in the letter in more detail. Use the Discovery Planning process outlined later in this chapter to explore other strengths, opportunities and fears.

6. **Keep track of all relevant follow-up steps.** An administrative assistant or business development coordinator should track all follow-ups. That includes date letter was mailed, date follow-up call was made, date follow-up meeting was scheduled, dollar value of opportunities

generated and dollar value of new business generated. You want to monetize the initiative by tracking the conversion of letters to calls to meetings to opportunities to new business won.

7. **Reward your team.** Multiple members of your team — from staff to supervisors to mangers and senior managers — play a role in this business development process. Recognize, reward and compensate them accordingly. The best way to motivate your staff to follow through on this initiative is to connect their efforts with career advancement or material rewards.

Know the pitfalls

It's important to make sure that firm members are comfortable having these conversations with clients. The person leading the conversation doesn't have to be an expert in estate planning and exit planning and so on. What's more important is that they're able to ask smart and insightful questions that get the client talking. They can then take what they've learned back to the office, discuss the client's needs with other specialists inside and outside the firm and return at a later time with solutions that address those specific needs. To feel more comfortable during the in-person conversations, they might bring others with them to address specific topics included in the presentation.

Key takeaways

The "Tax planning observations and ideas" process helps you:

- Demonstrate your commitment to better serving the client.
- Convert a compliance process into a vehicle for business development.
- Connect the more specific tax planning conversation with the broader topic of discovery planning.

MANAGEMENT LETTER COMMENTS

Management letter comments address concerns identified during the course of the audit. Many of the problems identified will relate to finance, and if unaddressed, they could result in inefficiency, ineffectiveness or even fraud. The process below outlines how auditors can capitalize on this opportunity to generate new business. For each audit, the auditor should draft a letter that suggests at least two specific services that benefit the client. The goal is to use the letter to open a conversation with the client about additional services that your firm or its strategic alliance partners can offer.

Don't hide behind independence

Making recommendations in the management letter comments section is a means to better serve your clients. It gives you the chance to suggest additional services that will benefit the client, and therefore helps you defend your client from competitors who will try to woo them by offering those services. Yet even though offering recommendations may be in the best interest of both the client and the firm, many auditors shy away from doing so, citing independence issues. While auditors are precluded from providing certain services such as valuation, there are several services they can offer. Auditors should be looking for more ways to serve their clients, and if they determine that an independence conflict does exist, they can always refer the work to another firm. It's a win-win. Either your firm generates new business or you refer work to another firm, which will likely reciprocate referrals down the road.

Offer advice

To generate new business from the audit process, we recommend requiring that each auditor submit a management observations letter at the end of each assurance compliance engagement. The letter should focus on specific services that the firm and its strategic alliance partners can deliver. Follow these steps to implement a management comments letter process:

1. **Draft a list of observations and ideas.** Create a list of observations that commonly arise during the audit process and ideas for how to address them. If you don't want to write the content yourself, there are plenty of textbooks that offer pre-written copy. For these observations to be business development-centric, it's important to connect them to services that your firm provides.
   For example, for "Convert to S Corporation," your observation and idea might be:

   Observation: The business is likely to be sold at some point in the future. The sale of a C corporation could result in double taxation, which could be avoided by the sale of an S corporation.

Idea: Company leaders should seriously consider converting to an S corporation because of the potential for substantial tax savings.

For "Review Insurance," your observation and idea might be:

Observation: The types and limits of insurance coverage are unclear.

Idea: Company should consider a thorough insurance review, with special attention paid to bonding coverage.

Include your firm's tax accountants in this process. Seek their suggestions and feedback about how to position your firm's services, as many of the observations and ideas that you come up with will be tax-centric.

2. **Compile observations and ideas.** You want it to be easy for the auditor to note the relevant observations and ideas. You might create a single checklist so the auditor can check a box for each observation and idea worth including. Auditors should be required to include at least two observations and ideas per audit.

3. **Merge observations and ideas into a form letter.** Draft a template to use for all audit management comment letters (www[12]). Have your administrative assistant or business development coordinator use the template to create a letter that includes the selected observations and ideas. Mail the letter to the client.

4. **Meet with the client.** Within seven days of the mailing, the administrative assistant or business development coordinator should contact the client to schedule a phone call with the appropriate manager or partner. Within 30 days, the manager or partner should meet with the client to discuss the recommendations in more detail.

5. **Keep track of all follow up.** The administrative assistant or business development coordinator should track all follow-ups. That includes date letter was mailed, date follow-up call was made, date follow-up meeting was scheduled, dollar value of opportunities generated and dollar value of new business generated.

Key takeaways

To generate new business from audits:

- Use the audit to identify ways to help improve a client's business.
- Identify key observations and ideas that you and your strategic alliance partners can deliver that ultimately benefit the client.
- Put a process in place to make management letter comments a critical step in the delivery of an assurance financial statement product.

DISCOVERY PLANNING

Discovery planning is designed to contrast a client's current reality with their envisioned future. It involves a one-hour conversation with a client that results in a roadmap outlining what they need to do to live the life they want. The ensuing recommendations often center on education and retirement savings, will and estate planning, asset protection and exit and succession strategies. Accountants should undertake this process with all new clients and every one to three years with existing clients. While other planning vehicles like tax planning offer a short-term tactical plan, discovery planning is a more strategic undertaking aimed at preparing for the more distant future. After completing discovery planning, clients should know their where they want to be, how much money they'll need and what tools to use to get there.

Peace of mind

Discovery planning provides clients with clarity, peace of mind and a set direction. It focuses on understanding the client's hopes, goals, aspirations and fears with the ultimate goal of making recommendations to help clients meet their long-term goals. Even if the client doesn't act on those recommendations immediately, you might succeed in educating them about something they will need down the road. An additional benefit of the process is that it gives clients perspective as to where they stand in relation to their peers; many people don't know how their own wealth stacks up compared to others.

Embracing the future

There are six steps to discovery planning. It is important to note that you should not bill the client for this time. Business opportunity will follow if you uncover new ways to serve the client; you shouldn't let money be an obstacle to getting the client through the door.

1. **Gather information.** Prior to an in-person meeting, provide the client with a brief survey to gain a basic understanding of their situation (www[13]). Information requested on that form might include contact information, personal assets, business assets, insurance coverage, liabilities, estate plan and advisors. Having this information allows you to prepare appropriate questions for your conversation. In many cases, clients won't take the time to fill out the form ahead of a conversation, in which case, it's fine to skip this step and move directly to an in-person conversation.

2. **Have a conversation.** The goal of this conversation is to probe the client's plan for the future. If you haven't done this type of long-range planning with a client before, you might need to explain why you're doing it now. For example: "We heading into (insert year here). This is a 'new normal.' We need to better understand where you're at and where you're heading to ensure we're minimizing your tax liability. I'd like to

assess where you are and where you would like to be in the following areas: tax planning, financial planning, retirement planning, estate planning and succession/exit planning." Proceed with your prepared list of questions to gather as much pertinent information as possible.

Tax
- Do you feel like something is getting missed?
- Do you feel like you're paying too much in taxes?
- Are you utilizing retirement planning instruments? (401K, SEP IRA, 401K with profit sharing, defined benefit plan, section 79 plan, etc)
- What's your risk tolerance?

Financial
- Do you have a household budget? If so, do you follow it?
- Do you have a financial plan? If so, when was the last time you reviewed it?
- What is the foundation of your financial structure?
- What do you own? What are your significant assets?
- Do you feel like you're saving enough for the future?
- What savings vehicles are you currently using (SEP, IRA, 401K, etc)?
- What are the holes in your current financial plan?

Retirement
- What does your retirement lifestyle look like?
- When do you want it to start?
- Do you know your number? Do you know what you'll need to retire?
- What are the unexpected, but possible, problems that could affect your long-term financial security?

Estate
- Do you have an estate plan? If so, when was the last time you reviewed it?
- Are you planning to do any gifting to family or charity?
- Are you thinking about trying to get something out of your estate?
- Do you have all the appropriate insurances?

- Do you have a living trust? If so, have you taken a look at it lately? Does it have the right benefactors in it?
- Do you have medical and financial powers of appointment?

Succession/Exit
- If there are multiple owners, do you have a buy-sell agreement? If so, do you have insurance to fund the buyout? Do you have a valuation formula to determine the value of the company? How do you buy out your partner at retirement? What happens if you sell the company?
- Do you have an exit/succession plan? If so, when was the last time you reviewed it?

- Do you understand your options (transfer to heirs, sale to employees, sale to employees via an ESOP, sale to a third party, etc) and the associated tax ramifications/liabilities?
- What do you think your business is worth? Have you had your business valued?

3. **Generate a report.** After the meeting, record the client's responses on a report form (www[14]). Detail any specifics mentioned by the client and take note of any services they may be interested in. You may choose to share this document with the client (a good way to avoid the common mistake of not following up on meetings). You can also send the client any appropriate articles or reference materials. Outline all the tasks to which you've committed and follow up in an appropriate time frame.

4. **Review your findings.** Review the report with others inside and outside of the firm to explore specific products or strategies that would benefit the client. A second meeting with the client may be required for other parties to fully understand the client's needs.

5. **Create a proposal.** Generate a proposal that specifies which products or services you recommend and how much they will cost. Forward the proposal to an administrative assistant or business development coordinator who should generate a personalized proposal from an existing proposal template.

6. **Give a presentation.** Meet with the client to review the proposal. Typical proposals include financial planning, investment allocation, insurance protection and tax minimization strategies to help the client meet their personal and business goals.

> As an alternative, you can take a more open-ended approach to the discovery planning conversation. With this approach, you ask a series of broad questions aimed at uncovering the client's strengths, opportunities and fears. This approach works best for accountants who are comfortable directing a more free-flowing dialogue. If you elect to go with this approach, see our website for a list of questions (www[15]) and the appropriate report form (www[16]).

Additionally, to successfully implement a Discovery Planning initiative, it might be helpful to host "lunch n' learn" sessions covering the key topics of tax planning, retirement planning, financial planning, estate planning and exit and succession planning. The more people know, the more comfortable they'll be leading the conversation in these areas. You can also create informational documents to better explain the product and service recommendations that are likely to result from these conversations. Here are typical topics that might arise in each category:

- Tax: Tax credits and incentives, inventory management, bad receivable write-offs
- Financial: 529 plan, financial plan creation, Sole K/IRA/SEP IRA

- Retirement: Retirement plan creation, life insurance, brokerage accounts
- Estate: Estate planning consultation, assorted trust vehicles, trust accounting
- Succession/exit: Section 79 plan, ESOP, sale to a competitor, sale to an employee, pass to family/heirs

Key takeaways

Discovery planning helps you:

- Understand your client's current financial situation.
- Picture where your client hopes to be in the future.
- Strategize how to make your client's goals a reality.

DATA MINING

Data mining involves performing an analysis on client data to figure out which clients have an unidentified need for services that you offer. Data mining identifies potential candidates for succession planning, wealth transfer, life insurance products, employee benefit analysis, retirement planning, sophisticated income tax planning and deferred compensation strategies. It is completed using data you have amassed from processing client tax returns and from qualitative information you've gathered from client conversations.

Uncover new opportunities

The upshot of data mining is that it helps you uncover specific opportunities for specific clients. In some cases, you'll gain a significant source of new business by identifying a need for a service that your firm provides (for example, R&D tax credits or hiring credits). In other cases, you'll add value to the client relationship by connecting the client with a strategic alliance partner (for example, insurance brokers or benefit plan administrators).

Slice and dice the data

Accountants generally use data mining in two ways: First, they run an adjusted gross income report to identify money that could be placed in tax-deferred vehicles; and second, they utilize screening software to identify candidates for specific products and services. The following steps detail how to utilize the second approach, which is more complex and less commonly used:

1. **Decide on the criteria.** For each product or service that your firm wants to promote, determine the search criteria that will help you identify candidates for that product or service. Many modern accounting software programs allow you to generate a report using multiple search queries (www[17]). The following list highlights search cues for products and services commonly offered by accounting firms:

Product/service	Search cues
SEP IRA	Schedule C earnings or Self Employment earnings greater than $50,000 and less than $200,000 with no line 28
Sole K	Schedule C earnings or Self Employment earnings greater than $50,000 and less than $200,000 with no line 28
Defined benefit plan	Schedule C earnings or Self Employment earnings greater than $200,000 with no line 28
Stock option planning	1040 Line 7 greater than $100,000

Product/service	Search cues
P&C insurance	Schedule A Line 10, 11 & 12 (any amount)
Employee benefits review	Schedule C Line 14; Form 1065 Line 19; Form 1120S Line 18; Form 1120 Line 24
Disability insurance	1040 Line 7 greater than $100,000; Lines 8a, 8b, 9a & 13 less than $1,000
Life insurance	1040 Line 6c; Line 7 greater than $100,000
Long-term care insurance	Schedule A Line 4 (any amount)
Charitable gifting	1040 Line 37 greater than $200,000; Schedule A line 16, 17 = zero
Debt refinancing	Schedule A lines 10, 11 and 12 greater than $80,000 in aggregate

2. **Run the report.** Choose a product or service that you want to focus on and crunch the numbers to identify clients in need of that product or service. You might analyze a different product each month, or organize your efforts seasonally (for example, toward the end of the year, you might focus on charitable giving). Distribute to each partner a list of their clients who might need that particular product or service.

3. **Pitch the client.** For each applicable client, game plan how to best present the information. You might have a conversation around a single opportunity or present multiple product options at once. Bring in other partners and senior managers with specific expertise, as well as outside strategic alliance partners. In many cases, you may have identified an opportunity in an area that falls outside of the engagement partner's area of expertise. The goal is to give the engagement partner enough information and support that they feel comfortable initiating the conversation.

4. **Track your progress.** Keep track of calls made, meetings completed, opportunities generated and new business won. You want to be able to monetize your efforts. As the great Stephen Covey famously said, "If you can't measure it, you can't manage it."

As an additional measure, it may be beneficial to hold "lunch n' learn" sessions that focus on each product or service. This will ensure that individuals have the level of comfort needed to broach the subject and the knowledge to understand if the client is a true candidate for that service. You might also consider converting key "lunch n' learn" content into one-page collateral documents that clearly explain the ideal candidate for each product or service, the features of the product or service and how clients will benefit.

Key takeaways

Data mining is an invaluable tool to help you:

- Uncover new opportunities. By mining the available data, you'll identify clients in need of a product or service that you can offer.
- Pitch specific products. You can focus your efforts around a specific product or service and then track your performance.
- Connect clients with strategic alliance partners. You may not perform employee benefit reviews, but if you know your client needs that, you can connect them with a firm that can help them.

EVALUATIONS

An evaluation is a chance to solicit feedback from clients about the services they receive and about their relationship with the firm. There are two main types: annual evaluations, which attempt to capture general information about the firm-client relationship; and service-specific evaluations, which focus on a product or service the client has recently used.

Forward-looking

The goal of administering evaluations is to identify ways to better serve clients and strengthen your relationship with them. The best evaluations are short, to the point and forward-looking. They don't fixate on events that have already happened, but instead focus on moving the relationship forward. In doing so, they to help identify potential business opportunities, generate new referrals and promote new products and services.

Annual evaluations

An annual evaluation is sent to all clients once a year (it should be done at the same time every year, either at the end of the year, or whenever makes the most sense for your firm). To ensure a high response rate, include an announcement explaining the purpose of the evaluation and what you intend to do with the information you gather. For clients whose feedback you particularly value, follow up with a phone call as emails and letters are too easy to ignore. Impress on them how important their feedback is and tell them what you plan to do with it.

Various online survey tools make it easy to create surveys and analyze the results. Sample survey questions (www[18]) are available on our website.

An annual evaluation involves four parts:

- **Introduction:** The introduction should clearly articulate why you value the client's feedback and what you intend to do with it. It should also make the case for why it's worthwhile for the client to complete the survey. For top-level clients, in addition to sending the survey electronically, you should call and offer to administer the survey over the phone or in person.
- **Satisfaction report card:** The first part of the evaluation uses a five-point scoring scale to evaluate client satisfaction with the firm. Clients are asked to rate the firm's staff, work, fees and marketing/communications on a scale of 1 (very dissatisfied) to 5 (very satisfied).
- **Additional comments:** The second part features open-ended questions that explore ways to generate new business opportunities by asking if the client has any goals or challenges with which they would like help. It also asks for referrals of friends, family members or other organizations.

- **Service offerings:** The third part includes a list of all services offered by your firm and asks clients to indicate whether they already use your firm for each offering, if they use another firm or if they would like more information about a particular service. The list should be grouped into major categories (for example, tax planning, wealth management services and business consulting services), and should break down the firm's offerings under each category.

It's crucial to follow up after sending the survey — no one likes to put work into something when it is ultimately overlooked. Whenever possible, perform an over-the-phone or in-person follow-up. Ask your clients to elaborate and get more detail about the areas where they expressed dissatisfaction. If they've requested more information about service offerings, inquire about what they're looking for and see if you can provide that service to them. Explore referral opportunities and establish next steps (for example, introduce them to another partner in the firm or connect with a strategic alliance partner for financial services expertise).

Once you've received the responses, summarize the findings in an aggregate report. Share findings with the entire staff as a way to highlight best practices and areas for improvement. And make sure individual evaluations don't get lost — the engagement partner and relevant personnel should receive copies of any evaluations that pertain to the work they've done. Distribute a version of the report to your clients so they know their input was valued (this version should be shorter and should be targeted toward strengths, weaknesses and recommendations for improvement). When you implement improvements based on these evaluations, communicate the change to your clients and detail how their feedback is helping to improve the firm's services.

Product-specific evaluations

These evaluations (www[19]) are much more limited in scope. They are sent to clients after they've received a specific service (for example, a tax evaluation is administered immediately following the filing of a tax return and an audit evaluation is administered immediately following the completion of an audit).

Include an email or letter with the evaluation that lays out the purpose of the evaluation. The letter should stress that the evaluation is aimed at strengthening client relationships, improving the specific service to which the evaluation applies and better understanding client priorities.

This evaluation is shorter and more targeted than the annual evaluation. It asks clients to rank their satisfaction with the service they just received. Importantly, it serves as a tool for business development by asking the simple question: "Would you refer us to a friend, family member or business associate?" As with the annual evaluation, you should follow up over the phone with top clients and explore any referral opportunities generated by the evaluation.

Beyond your grades

Most people think of evaluations as a tool for how to improve, but they're also a tool for identifying new business opportunities. They're a chance for clients to understand more about the firm and how it can help improve their financial situation. With that greater understanding, clients also have an opportunity to reflect on whether they know anyone who might also be interested in these services. Evaluations don't start and end with a survey — they're a way to begin a conversation, with the goal of converting that conversation into new revenue.

Key takeaways

The best evaluations:

- Are forward-looking. They don't focus only on past work, but also on offering tangible products to your clients.
- Make use of the information gathered. The information doesn't sit and gather dust. It's disseminated to staff, used to improve services and its value is communicated to clients.
- Promote other opportunities to work together, by soliciting referrals and offering products and services in which clients may be interested.

CHANGE ORDER PROCESS

Change orders allow firms to document changes that occur mid-project and to adjust the price and timetable accordingly. They offer a clear procedure to follow when billing disputes arise.

Control ballooning costs

It's a rare project that goes exactly as planned from start to finish. Goals change, unexpected problems arise and clients change their mind. When additional tasks are added mid-project, some accounting firms don't have a process in place to obtain formal approval for extra work, and end up losing significant amounts of money as a result. The key to handling these new demands is for accounting firms to formalize a change order process, which will in turn strengthen client relationships and generate new revenue.

Put a process in place

The first step in introducing a change order process is to create a change order form (www[20]). This form should include the reason for the change, a description of the work to be performed, an estimate for the cost and timetable of the additional work, and any terms and conditions (for example, how the additional work will be billed). It is important that the form requires both parties to indicate that they accept the changes. For change orders to be effective, it is imperative that the scope of work is clearly defined in the original engagement letter and that the process for approving change orders is documented in that letter. Next, staff need to be trained to identify and gain approval for change orders. Not all changes are significant enough to warrant a change order; each firm needs to create its own standard. In cases where a change order is required, a staff member should initiate a conversation with the client to talk through the change and obtain the client's approval. If at any point, the client contests the change, the staff member should bring the issue to the attention of the partner who negotiated the initial engagement letter with the client. Any changes that are approved should be documented in a change order form and signed off on by all parties. It is crucial that all change orders are submitted and approved before the work is done, not after.

A place of honor

If a firm doesn't emphasize the importance of change orders, they'll fall by the wayside, their potential benefits left unrealized. To counter this and to enshrine the importance of change orders, firms should adopt two key practices:

- **Count change orders as new business.** Change orders are often lumped in with old business in business development reports. Because of this, they aren't given a high profile and aren't recognized as a substantial revenue source. Tracking change orders as new business provides less-senior staff members with a means to contribute to the firm's well-being and underscores the importance of rigorously tracking change orders.

- **Reward staff for generating change orders.** This reward doesn't have to be monetary — it can take the form of recognition, gifts, goods or services, and can be awarded on either a team or individual level. These rewards raise the profile of the change order initiative.

A well-implemented change order process can be a great help in strengthening client relationships. Without such a process, the back-and-forth of negotiating additional costs can sour a client relationship and leave both the firm and the client dissatisfied. A change order process allows both sides to deal with potential problems as they arise and offers clarity for staff members and clients who will inevitably confront these issues.

Key takeaways

Creating a rigorous change order process will help to:

- Strengthen client relationships by eliminating unpleasant billing surprises.
- Reduce the amount of money currently lost on unbilled work.
- Create an additional avenue for measuring and tracking new business.

CLIENT ESCALATION PROCESS

Client escalation aims to repair a deteriorating client relationship. It involves a face-to-face conversation with disgruntled clients to hear their concerns and to develop a plan for improvement moving forward.

Turn that frown upside down

An unhappy client isn't necessarily a lost client. By confronting issues head-on, you can salvage relationships with these clients, turning them once again into successful partnerships. A well-defined client escalation process will allow you to understand the issues, address them and, in doing so, strengthen the client relationship. Not only do you save the client, but by demonstrating your commitment and responsiveness, you also have a chance to sell additional services to the client and to solicit valuable referrals. From adversity comes opportunity — if you fix the problem, you can emerge with a stronger client relationship than you had before because you've demonstrated your value and your commitment.

Talk it out

The client escalation process starts when a client expresses dissatisfaction with the service they've been receiving. They might submit a poor evaluation or verbalize concerns about missed deadlines or subpar work. Either way, as soon as a client makes their complaint clear, it's time to schedule an in-person meeting. At that meeting you should:

- **Involve senior personnel.** By including the engagement partner, the account managers and the firm's managing partner, you're signaling that you're serious about dealing with the issues.
- **Highlight the positives.** It's important to establish a positive framework for the discussion that follows. Don't rush past acknowledging all the productive parts of the relationship.
- **Listen to their issues.** Don't respond or react, and above all, don't get defensive. Acknowledge their complaints and accept blame for their frustrations. Ask good questions to better understand the root of the problem (for example, if they're unhappy about missed deadlines, try to understand why those deadlines were missed — was the scope poorly defined, was there a misunderstanding about the complexity of the work involved, etc).
- **Brainstorm solutions.** Allow the client to suggest solutions before offering your own. In some cases, you might want to offer special considerations in an attempt to salvage the relationship (for example, offer discounts or other firm benefits).
- **Make commitments.** Verbally summarize what you've agreed to do and then commit those agreements to writing. The agreement should include clear expectations, tasks, timelines and consequences. Give the document an air of formality — it should not be sent as text in an email.

The client escalation process doesn't end with one meeting. Check in with the client to see if the commitments have been honored. If you don't make good on your promises, you won't save the relationship.

If all of the issues have been resolved, you have a great business development opportunity. Use this chance to ask if they know anyone they could refer to your firm: "We're always looking for more great clients like you." Also ask if they have other work that they might want you to do for them. The door is open to learn more ways to better serve the client. Don't let the chance pass you by.

Key takeaways

A well-defined client escalation process will help you to:

- Avoid losing clients. Do it right and you'll keep the client and the money they bring in.
- Uncover new business opportunities. By opening a dialogue with the client, you may learn new ways to work together.
- Turn a negative situation into a showcase opportunity. You potentially gain a new referral source when you skillfully handle adversity and demonstrate your commitment to the client.

LOST CLIENTS POST-MORTEM INTERVIEW

A post-mortem interview is a conversation with clients who are taking their business elsewhere. It is a means to understand why they are leaving and to gather intelligence on your firm's strengths and weakness. A post-mortem interview isn't about persuading a client to stay; it's about learning from the client's decision to leave.

An investment for the future

By talking to departing clients about what they liked and what they didn't, firms learn valuable lessons about how to improve, rather than guessing at what they need to do. Post-mortem interviews can help a firm learn how to keep its existing clients happy and how to generate new opportunities. It's a proactive approach toward assuring a firm's long-term health.

Open, honest and non-confrontational

A post-mortem interview is a chance to turn a client's departure into a learning experience for the firm. It's important to see the interview as a learning opportunity and not to become defensive. The point is not to change the client's mind (see previous topic for how to save a damaged client relationship). Follow these key tips to ensure a fruitful post-mortem interview:

- **Do it soon (but not immediately).** Don't try to conduct a post-mortem interview at the same time the client ends the relationship. This will probably end poorly, with both sides upset. Instead, ask for a short appointment in the near future, no more than four weeks out.
- **Do it in person.** Online surveys are convenient, but they are unlikely to generate the kind of quality feedback you want. The best information will come from a conversation, ideally in person or over the phone.
- **Don't take it personally.** Don't get defensive and don't argue with the client's observations. Make sure the client knows you respect the decision to end the relationship. The point of the interview is to gather constructive feedback.
- **Really listen.** Practice active listening and ask follow-up questions that elicit more information ("Can you give me an example?" or "Do you mind elaborating?). This is a rare opportunity to hear an unvarnished opinion of your business.
- **Apply what you've learned.** All your hard work and time will be wasted if you don't make use of what you've heard. Reflect on what was said during the interview and consider how you can use it to improve your client relationships.

And remember, even though the client is leaving today, you may be able to work together again in the future. It's important to ask whether the client would consider your firm for special work or a consulting project (for example, would a lost tax or audit client be interested in consulting services?).

You may earn a new opportunity and you've left the door open to welcome them back. After all, the grass isn't always greener on the other side.

A list of questions you might ask to help guide the conversation:

- Before you decided to leave, how satisfied were you with our firm?
- Why did you decide to look elsewhere?
- Which firm did you choose to work with instead, and what do they offer that we don't?
- What could we have done better while you were our client?
- What should we take away from this experience to help us be better next time?
- Would you consider our firm for special work or consulting projects in the future? Do you have anything in mind now?
- Would you recommend our firm to others? Why or why not?

Learning how to do better

Post-mortem interviews allow you to glean valuable information from your lost clients about what went well during your relationship, what didn't and what ultimately led to their departure. You'll start to see common themes in the feedback that you can use to improve the services you offer. You should use that information to improve internal processes and to better train staff in areas of technical expertise or client service. If clients are willing to speak about what drew them to a different firm, you might even gain valuable insights about your competitors. All of this can inform how to craft your marketing materials to better highlight your firm's strengths. You might also learn to better identify clients who aren't a good fit. By listening to the issues, needs and wants of your lost clients, you'll understand how to better serve your existing and future clients.

Key takeaways

Post-mortem interviews with lost clients help you:

- Identify your firm's strengths and weaknesses.
- Put in place specific changes that will help you gain and retain clients.
- Win more work by offering services in line with what clients want.

LOST CLIENT CULTIVATION

Lost client cultivation focuses on re-establishing relationships with lost clients, with the goal of ultimately winning them back.

Never say never

Lost clients aren't lost forever. Maybe they left in search of cheaper fees or because it's organizational policy to change auditors every five years. No matter the reason, they may be open to returning down the line. But you'll never win them back if you don't try.

Back into the fold

For every lost client, follow these steps to make sure you stay on their radar:

- **Flag them as a lost client.** Update your database and mark them as a lost client. Be sure to enter information from your post-mortem interview in your account notes.
- **Assign a point of contact.** Assign them to a specific senior manager or partner, preferably someone who has built trust with them and maintained a positive relationship despite their departure. If they left on bad terms, consider assigning the account to someone new.
- **Keep in touch.** Keep them on your mailing list and stay on their mailing list.
- **Know how to reach out.** Identify the appropriate point of contact in the organization. Roles change and people move on. A new contact person doesn't necessarily have the same negative associations.
- **Stay in contact.** Check in periodically to see how their current CPA is doing. Use the opportunity to gather some competitive intelligence (for example, what is the other firm doing well).
- **Show your value.** Offer complimentary insights, expertise and assistance that can help them or their business.
- **Provide a referral.** Keep them in mind when opportunities arise that could help grow their business.
- **Open the door.** Make it easy for them to come back by providing them with a low-cost opportunity to re-engage with the firm (for example, a complimentary review of their prior year tax return).
- **Thank them.** Thank them profusely if they come back. Make them feel appreciated and welcomed. Be sure to address the issues that led them to leave in the first place.

And if you succeed, be comforted in knowing you've probably gained a loyal client. Clients who have left and had a negative experience elsewhere are likely to stay for the long haul once you've won them back. And the cost of winning that business back was probably considerably less than the cost of wooing a client you have yet to meet.

Key takeaways

Engaging with lost clients is a means to:

- Win back work that you've lost. After testing the waters elsewhere, clients might realize they were happy with the service you provided and bring their business back.
- Win new work. Even if a client wasn't a good fit for your tax services, they might be interested in your consulting work. You don't have to win back the exact work you lost.
- Efficiently allocate your business development resources. You already know these clients and what they want. By keeping in touch, you create an opportunity to win a valuable and loyal client.

CHAPTER 3
NEW CLIENTS

We've separated new clients from clients in this book because we look at new clients as an opportunity to start anew. While your existing clients may react negatively to change, your new clients have few expectations of how your relationship will go. Take advantage of the opportunity to test out new practices. Learn more about them and uncover more ways to serve them.

In this short chapter, we describe two practices for establishing your relationship with new clients:

- **Client welcome process:** This client onboarding process helps welcome clients to the firm. It's a chance to demonstrate that you deliver great client service. It's also a great way to introduce the client to all the services the firm offers.
- **Complimentary reviews:** Offer complimentary reviews to new clients to identify how well situated they are in a variety of areas, including estate planning, retirement readiness, insurance and employee benefits. See if there's an opportunity to better serve them right out of the gate.

CLIENT WELCOME PROCESS

Make a good first impression by welcoming your new clients to the firm with a client welcome process. You can do more than sending a generic information packet to new clients. Instead, utilize the new client welcome process to get to know the client and help them learn more about your firm. This process consists of a statement of your firm's standards, a call from the managing partner and an assessment of the client's financial situation. It should be extended to all new clients, whether individuals, for-profit businesses, non-profits or others.

Don't just talk the talk

Every accounting firm claims to have great client service, and yet one of the main reasons that clients leave a firm is because they don't think they're receiving enough attention. The client welcome process is a chance to demonstrate that your firm doesn't just talk about great client service, it actually practices it.

This 30-60 day client onboarding process establishes client service as a competitive advantage, introduces clients to the firm's areas of expertise and generates new business opportunities. It quickly demonstrates the value that your firm can bring to a client and sets the expectation that the client will receive top-notch service from your firm.

Demonstrate your commitment

Follow these six steps to welcome every new client:

1. **Mail a welcome packet.** Send the client a welcome packet that details the client welcome process. Include a document that lays out your firm's standards and its commitments to the client. This document could take the form of a Client Bill of Rights:

    > ### Client Bill of Rights
    >
    > As a valued client, you have the right to expect:
    >
    > - People who invest the time to understand and best serve your needs
    > - Efficient and prompt service from partners and staff who are easy to reach and responsive
    > - A comprehensive menu of services and staff with the skills and resources to perform the work
    > - Accurate and authoritative information
    > - Technology that serves you by providing fast and easy access to your account, as well as industry resources and reports
    > - Professionals who are active in their field and knowledgeable about changing regulations and standards
    > - Reasonable cost for services
    > - Specialized guidance to help you lower expenses, limit tax liability and maximize profitability now and in the future

2. **Connect over the phone.** The managing partner should call the new client to welcome them to the firm. During the call, the partner should highlight those commitments detailed in the Client Bill of Rights and should encourage the client to contact them directly if the firm ever fails to honor any of those promises. The partner should also mention the needs assessment form that is the next stage of the client welcome process.

3. **Conduct a needs assessment.** Ask the client to fill out a two-part needs assessment form (www[21]). The first part asks the client about their objectives and challenges. The second part lists the services the firm offers and asks whether the client is interested in any of these services. The assessment varies among individual, for-profit and non-profit clients. A needs assessment form for an individual might include sections on tax planning and wealth management, with questions such as "Do you participate in a stock option plan?" and "Do you want to transfer wealth to your children in the next X years?"

4. **Analyze the information.** The firm's business development liaison or an administrative team member should send the assessment to the relevant engagement partners and input the information into a database. In addition to using this information to better serve this particular client, you can use the aggregate data to identify areas you might want to target (for example, if multiple businesses suggest they need help evaluating employee benefit plans, you could update your marketing materials to advertise your expertise in this area).

5. **Get back in touch.** The engagement partner should call the client to review the needs assessment form (they can also arrange a face-to-face meeting if appropriate). After this conversation, the engagement partner should send the client a letter summarizing the firm's recommendations.

6. **Demonstrate value.** When appropriate, the engagement partner should introduce the client to other firm partners and service providers (for example, wealth management advisors or insurance brokers). This demonstrates to the client that you're part of a team that is here to help them. The partner should arrange the pertinent meetings and schedule the next interaction with the client.

The client welcome process can also be used as a courtship tool. Generate a Client Welcome Program flyer and share it with prospective clients to highlight your firm's commitment to service. It will demonstrate to prospective clients what makes your firm different from the others they're considering.

Build trust

Often the relationship between accountants and clients is purely transactional. The client welcome process breaks that mold. By understanding your client's needs from the outset of your relationship and by educating the client about the firm's capabilities, you'll find new ways to work together.

You'll build equity with your client and quickly become a trusted advisor, which will in turn result in more work and more referrals.

Key takeaways

There are many benefits to creating a client welcome process, including:

- Establishing your reputation for great client service. Others might tout their commitment to their clients, but you're demonstrating it from day one.
- Introducing the client to the firm's services. A client might come in for tax help, but you won't know what else they need unless you ask.
- Connecting the client with others who can help them. You'll add value to the client relationship by introducing your client to others inside and outside of the firm.

COMPLIMENTARY REVIEWS

A complimentary review is a free service extended to all new clients in which the firm offers to analyze financial documents such as a retirement plan or a buy-sell agreement. A review should take less than 60 days to complete and result in a report and presentation to the client. It can be offered as part of or instead of the client welcome process.

Invest in the relationship

Helping new clients better understand their financial situation is a great way to demonstrate your firm's value at the beginning of your relationship. A complimentary review requires only nominal time investment by both the client and the firm and it helps build trust and value with a new client. It can also result in new business, but is a worthwhile investment even it doesn't.

On the menu

Here are three easy steps for offering a complimentary review to your new clients:

1. **Extend the offer.** Send a print or electronic letter to the client listing the types of complimentary reviews you offer. This may include estate plan, retirement readiness and insurance reviews for individuals or shareholder agreement, employee benefits and fiduciary requirements reviews for businesses. For each type of review, summarize the requirements, expectations and timelines (for example, for an employee benefits review, the client would need to provide a census of full-time employees eligible for benefits, along with other relevant documents). Ask the client to check all applicable review categories and return the form. Here are some sample questions you might include for the different types of reviews, and the outcomes that might result from each one:

   ### Estate planning

   - Questions: Have your goals changed? Are there liquidity concerns if estate taxes are due nine months after death? Are there legacy or charitable goals you wish to achieve?
   - Outcomes: Minimize estate tax exposure, update will, trust, power of attorney and health care directives, achieve charitable objectives

   ### Retirement planning

   - Questions: Do you know how much capital you will need to live the way you want to live for the rest of your life adjusted for inflation? Have you reviewed your portfolio? Does your retirement planning take into consideration strategies to pay for post-retirement health care costs?
   - Outcomes: Provide the client with a clear estimate of how much money they will need to retire, identify any tax-favored strategies

to enhance capital accumulation, suggest small early adjustments that can make a big impact in the future

Property and casualty

- Questions: Do you serve on any boards of directors? Do you have adequate errors and omissions coverage? Are all your coverages coordinated under one umbrella and master billing? Have you explored all methods of asset protection?
- Outcomes: Comfort that coverage is in good order, suggestions of little tweaks that are beneficial, analysis of whether they're paying market rate for coverage

2. **Follow up.** Within 48 hours, the appropriate person would contact the client to initiate next steps. If the review work falls within your firm's area of expertise, someone in-house would conduct the review. For other areas, the work would be handed to one of the firm's trusted alliance partners (for example, with wealth management or employee benefit reviews). In this case, offering a complimentary review is a means of providing a valuable service to your client without significant investment on your part.

3. **Summarize results.** The person conducting the review completes the necessary due diligence in the allotted timeframe and compiles a report that summarizes opportunities, exposures and solutions. This should be an unobtrusive process that focuses on analyzing existing documents, contracts or policies. The engagement partner and the person who completed the review present the report to the client, who ultimately decides whether to adopt the recommendations.

Know the whole picture

The ultimate benefit of a complimentary review is that it puts you in a position to understand the client's financial situation. This positions you to better serve them as the relationship develops, and to grow beyond "the person who does their taxes" into a trusted financial advisor and advocate. The value of the complimentary review doesn't depend on whether you uncover any glaring problems. In many cases, telling a client they're well situated is just as valuable as making recommendations. It reassures them and helps build trust.

Key takeaways

Offer complimentary reviews to your new clients to:

- Establish your firm's value. If you save them money or improve their financial security, they'll appreciate it.
- Build trust. Just telling a client they're doing well financially is a great start to your relationship.
- Understand all their personal and professional financial needs. This can only help you to develop a strong relationship with the client.

```
┌─────────────────────────────────────────────────────────┐
│                                                           │
│   CHAPTER 4                                               │
│   MESSAGING                                               │
│                                                           │
└─────────────────────────────────────────────────────────┘
```

Messaging is your most powerful tool for separating yourself from your competition. In the words of Will Davis, CMO of Right Source Marketing: "The messaging guide … gives you the key points to talk about the company in a way that is unique, stands out, and resonates with your clients and prospective clients." Crafting your message starts with understanding what clients want from their accountants. If you can position your messaging to speak to those needs, you'll win more clients more of the time.

This chapter outlines a comprehensive process for how to develop effective messaging. Individual topics include:

- **What clients want:** Few firms fully comprehend what truly matters to clients. By utilizing industry research, your firm can learn how to better market itself.
- **Competitive analysis:** Study the competitive landscape to learn what others are doing. Understand the strengths and weaknesses of your competition.
- **Competitive advantage:** Use your knowledge of the competitive landscape to decide on your competitive advantage. Simply put, your competitive advantage is what you do better than the rest.
- **Elevator pitch:** Convert your competitive analysis into an elevator pitch. This short statement should explain what you do, what makes you different and why a client should choose you.
- **Issue-solution-benefit narrative:** Connect common issues with the solutions your firm can provide. For each issue, spell out your solution and explain how it will benefit your client.

WHAT CLIENTS WANT

Every firm has to make its case to prospective clients and persuade them to hop on board. Yet when trying to sell themselves, few firms fully understand what clients actually want. By utilizing industry research, firms can learn how to better market themselves. They can reserve their bragging rights for things that clients actually care about, and shelve the claims that won't help them make a sale.

Know the market

So what do clients want? According to industry surveys, clients want service that is:

- **Personal.** Accountants need to devote sufficient time to get to know their clients individually.
- **Responsive.** It's important that partners and staff are easy to reach and respond quickly to client concerns.
- **Comprehensive.** Firms should offer a full range of services performed by skilled staff.
- **Accurate.** Accountants should supply clients with accurate and authoritative information.
- **Simple.** Using the latest technology, firms should make it easy for clients to access their account and find industry resources and reports.
- **Knowledgeable.** The firm's staff should stay abreast of changing regulations and standards.
- **Affordable.** Services should be reasonably priced.
- **Specialized.** Firms should offer specialized services to help clients lower their expenses, limit their liabilities and seize opportunities.

Once you understand what your clients want, you can craft your message so it speaks to their priorities. Here is sample marketing copy that draws on the priorities listed above.

Our clients:

- See us as trusted financial advisors. We're more than just CPAs to our clients; we offer a full suite of financial services, including tax, estate and retirement planning advice.
- Trust us to address their financial concerns. They know our advice is authoritative.
- Know that they can reach us easily and that we'll respond quickly.
- Value that our staff members are well equipped to advise them on changing regulations that affect their business.
- Respect that we deliver accurate work on time.
- Realize that our technology is easy to use. We offer a multitude of services online, including document management systems, integrated tax and accounting suites and compliance solutions, knowledge management systems and client portals.
- Appreciate that we offer excellent services at a reasonable cost.

Craft your message

Try to read as much industry survey research as you can. We've outlined some of the main qualities that clients want, but it never hurts to know more. Use what you've learned when crafting language for your website, collateral materials, proposals and presentations (see the marketing chapter for more on developing your messaging in assorted marketing media). Be specific about what you offer. If you know that a client left their firm because they felt ignored, stress that responsiveness is a priority and detail the policies you have in place to anticipate their needs. Your messaging should explain to the client how you're going to fix their problems. Make sure they know how they'll benefit from your solutions — maybe they'll save time, or money, or be better informed when making decisions about their financial future. And don't forget: Practice what you preach. If you want a new client to stick with you, you have to deliver on your promises.

Key takeaways

Learn what your clients want and you will:

- Waste less time talking about things that don't matter to clients.
- Craft messaging that speaks directly to client priorities.
- Win more work in less time.

COMPETITIVE ANALYSIS

Competitive analysis helps you recognize the strengths and weaknesses of your competition. Understanding the competitive landscape will give you the necessary intelligence to determine your competitive advantage.

Know your competition

Many firms can't articulate their advantage when competing against a similarly sized or similarly focused firm. As a result, the client can't distinguish one firm from another and makes a decision based on price. Competitive analysis is a necessary first step in defining your firm's competitive advantage, and clearly articulating your competitive advantage will help you win more work.

Think it through

To figure out your own competitive advantage (what you do better than the rest), make a list of your competitors. For each competitor, supplement personal experience with information gathered from public records, including from their website. Analyze the services they advertise, their niche expertise, their marketing materials, their client testimonials and financial tools. Try to put yourself in your competitor's shoes: What would they tout as their strengths? What weaknesses would they try to downplay?

The following table is a competitive analysis of the types of firms that compete for tax clients. It lists the pros and cons of each type of firm. This is just a sample. To complete your own competitive analysis, you would want to make a similar table, but you would compare the advantages and disadvantages of your actual competitors.

Firm type	Competitive advantage	Competitive disadvantage
Self-preparers	Cheap, easy and can be done on your own timetable.	Requires more time and effort and involves a higher risk of error.
Individual tax preparers	Affordable and accessible. You deal with the owner, who is conveniently located.	The owner might have limited expertise and limited access to resources. There's no support team.
National tax preparer	Offer a systematic approach.	Staff members with limited expertise will push their own product. The more forms you complete, the more they get paid.

Firm type	Competitive advantage	Competitive disadvantage
Small local firms	You will receive plenty of attention. You have a whole account team and access to the firm's partner.	Less expertise than bigger firms on certain issues.
Large local firms	Offer specialized service and are able to handle more complex issues. They put a premium on service and are competitively priced. You have a whole account team and access to the firm's partner.	You're likely to see the partner less and deal with senior managers more.
Regional firms	Still nimble, but have the resources of a larger firm. Offer personalized service and expertise.	Work is pushed further down the chain of command and the firm's growth might result in quality control issues.
National firms	They do it all, and can grow with you. They're willing to take on initial engagements at a loss to make money later when your company grows.	More expensive and work is pushed further down the chain of command.

You should go through this exercise for each type of service your firm provides (for example, tax, audit, private client services, consulting, etc). Some advantages and disadvantages will be consistent across all service types, while others may vary by category. Armed with this information, you're in a better position to articulate your competitive advantage.

Over the course of performing this research, you'll come across certain claims that are nearly universal. For example, everyone claims "client service" as a key differentiator. Take note of what proof firms are offering for these common claims. When you go to craft your own claims, you'll need to demonstrate that you offer a level of service that goes beyond what your competitors are offering, otherwise you won't be able to substantiate your position.

As an unintended consequence of completing a competitive analysis, you may identify opportunities to specialize. If there's less competition for a certain service or in a certain niche, you have a great chance to gain market share quickly.

Key takeaways

Perform competitive analysis to:

- Better understand the strengths and weaknesses of your competition.
- Learn how to define your true competitive advantage. You'll avoid making hollow claims that sound like everyone else's.
- Know the bar. If you're making a common claim, you'll know what standards you have to meet to substantiate this claim (for example, if you're claiming outstanding client service, you'll know what you have to do to deliver on that competitive advantage).

COMPETITIVE ADVANTAGE

Simply put, your competitive advantage is what you do better than the rest. You have a competitive advantage in areas where you provide your clients with a greater value, even at a higher price, or the same value at a lower price.

Stand out from the crowd

Clients trying to choose an accounting firm often encounter a sea of uniformity — every firm claims to be "responsive" and "client-focused." Faced with the same claims everywhere, the lowest common denominator becomes price, unless you can tell clients what makes you unique — that's your competitive advantage. Not only should you stress what differentiates you from everyone else, but you should focus on the things clients care about. You may be the only firm with a waterfront view, but clients aren't paying for your view. Tell clients what you do best and you'll position yourself to win more work.

Define yourself

Before deciding on your competitive advantage you need to research what your clients want and what your competition does best. Once you've done that, gather the firm's key decision-makers and try to answer the question: "What can we claim to be the best at or, at the very least, better than our competitors at?"

Typical answers to that question fall into one of three categories: **people**, **process** and **performance** ("The Three P's"). With that in mind, consider the following questions:

- **How are our people better?** Are they more qualified, more seasoned, more invested in the community, more experienced in a particular niche?
- **How are our processes better?** Do we offer more checks and balances, better use of technology to minimize human error, more processes that focus on better serving the customer's needs?
- **How do we perform better?** Do we offer a faster turnaround time or money savings, or do we solve more problems or generate more ideas to help clients?

Pick measures and metrics that corroborate each claim. Be specific and avoid making claims that can't be substantiated. A weak claim: We're number one in client satisfaction. A better claim: Seventy percent of our CPAs have an MBA, CVA or CFP.

You may find a number of areas where you offer superior services, but you want to choose the most important three — this will make it easier for you to articulate your competitive advantage and for your audience to remember it. You might decide on three claims in a single category or your claims might be spread across the different categories; either is fine, and it varies from firm to firm. Create a summary document that lists the three claims that make up your competitive advantage. This document will help you craft your elevator pitch (see the next topic). The following table details a hypothetical firm's competitive advantage relating to its people:

Category	Claim	Validation
People	Our people are more responsive	We do more than just respond to your needs. We also work hard to anticipate your needs through a complete and thorough understanding of your personal and business affairs. If you contact us and we're not immediately available to answer your inquiry, we have a two-hour reply policy. Additionally, we assign multiple contacts to each client. If an individual partner or staff member is temporarily unresponsive (for example, they're off-site or on vacation), another member of our client service team will be available to answer your questions.
People	Our people are more experienced	For our partners, senior managers and managers, the average tenure with our firm is 13.2 years. In accounting, experience equates to vast technical knowledge, increased industry specialization and a thorough understanding of our clients' needs, wants and opportunities.
People	Our people are more industry specialized	Our firm was one of the first in the state to establish niche practices in technology and real estate. We are regarded as thought leaders by our peers, and are often called on to speak at industry events, write for industry publications and comment for local media outlets.

Don't be a wallflower

Crafting your competitive advantage allows you to stand out where others blend in. You'll attract more and better prospects if you clearly highlight your competitive advantage in your marketing materials. And when talking to prospective clients, you'll be able to focus the conversation on areas in which your firm excels. Connecting the needs of your client to the things that your firm does best is a recipe for business development success.

Key takeaways

Deciding on your competitive advantage will help you:

- Define what you do best. You talk all the time about what you offer clients. You might as well be talking about the traits that make you special.
- Stand out from the rest. Separate yourself by making uncommon claims that are substantiated with metrics.
- Focus on the areas where you excel. Match up what you offer with what clients want and you'll win more work.

ELEVATOR PITCH

An elevator pitch is a summary statement that quickly explains what you do, for whom you do it and why you're different. The name "elevator pitch" reflects the idea that it should be possible to deliver the summary in the time it takes to ride an elevator (about 10-45 seconds).

Less is more

You've invested a lot of time and effort in your messaging by analyzing your clients, your competition and your own strengths. Crafting an elevator pitch is about finally putting all that information to use. Now when someone asks you "so what do you do?" or "so why should I pick your firm," you'll have a simple, quick and eloquent answer that will set you apart from your competition.

Rehearse your lines

I advise my clients to draft two versions of their elevator pitch: a long version (30-45 seconds) for speaking introductions, prospect presentations, print and electronic collateral, etc; and a short version (10-15 seconds) for networking events, prospect introductions and such. The short elevator pitch will be your "go-to" version and the one you use most often. You'll be light-years ahead of your competition if you have that version nailed down.

To craft your pitch, gather the key decision-makers in your firm. Try to connect the three claims you identified in your competitive advantage summary document into a single flowing 30-45 second statement. Once you're comfortable with the longer version, edit it down to arrive at your short version. Your short version should be as concise as possible — it will be tough to let go of key words, but if you do, your message will stick with your intended audience.

Here are examples of long and short form elevator pitch statements for a fictional firm:

- **Long** (30-45 seconds): Our advantage revolves around our people. We're committed to serving our clients by anticipating their needs. We invest significant resources in ensuring that all our accountants remain on the cutting edge of the accounting industry. Everyone at [insert firm name] is an expert in their field. Because we invest in our people, they stay with us for the long haul. This depth of experience allows us to deliver a consistently high level of service.
- **Short** (10-15 seconds): Our advantage revolves around our people: our accountants have decades of experience and deep industry expertise. We're committed to serving our clients by anticipating their needs.

Practice your elevator pitch until it rolls off the tongue. The shorter version is the one you'll use most of the time, for example at networking events, during conversations with referral sources and future clients.

Key takeaways

Crafting a clear, concise elevator pitch will help you:

- Have a great answer to the inevitable questions: What do you do? Who do you do it for? Why are you the best at it?
- Convert networking event conversations into meaningful next steps.
- Close the deal quicker. Once you convince a prospective client that you're qualified, they'll be more open to hearing your ideas.

ISSUE-SOLUTION-BENEFIT NARRATIVE

The final step in developing your messaging is connecting the needs of your prospective clients with the areas in which you excel (your competitive advantage). We call this the issue-solution-benefit narrative (or ISBN for short, easily remembered because it is also the unique identification number assigned to every book). It's a way to identify the most common client issues, lay out your solutions and explain how they'll benefit your clients. You'll put this information to use later in the sales process chapter, but for now, you want to focus on gathering and rehearsing the narrative.

Don't narrow your sights too soon

In my sales training process, I put my clients through an exercise I call "Ian's life plan" (www[22]). I have created a visual representation of my life plan (what's important to me, where I'm going, where I need help, etc).

The accountant, who can't see the image, has 30 minutes to interview me and identify as many of my priorities as they can. Inevitably, they're drawn to one aspect of my life: my business. Within five minutes, they've identified something I don't know and they stop asking questions. They turn the spotlight on themselves and start telling me how to solve the issue, and though their recommendations may be correct, they're not getting to the heart of my needs. We end up spending 90 percent of the time talking about 10 percent of my plan. The issue-solution-benefit narrative is a way to avoid this concentration risk. It's about identifying as many of the client's needs as you can, so you can connect those needs to the things the firm does best.

ISBN

Developing an issue-solution-benefit narrative is about identifying your strengths and connecting those strengths to the needs of your prospective clients. We'll discuss in the sales process chapter how to actually use this information during a face-to-face meeting; this chapter is about preparing and rehearsing your claims.

The issue-solution-benefit narrative consists of three parts:

- **Issue:** Make a list of your prospective clients' top 10 issues. Typical issues include: lack of responsiveness, failure to meet deadlines, lack of personal attention, lack of technical expertise, staff turnover, excessive fees, etc.
- **Solution:** For each issue, come up with an explanation of how you or your firm solves that issue. Include measures or metrics to substantiate your claims (for example, instead of saying that your turnover rate is "lower" than your competitors' turnover rate, say that it is, "6%, half that of our competitors").
- **Benefit:** Explain how the solution benefits the client (for example, how they'll save money or sleep better at night). This is the most important part of the pitch — it tells your client what's in it for them.

Here are a few examples of how to craft the issue-solution-benefit narrative:

Issue: Staff turnover

Solution: Our annual turnover rate for staff, seniors, supervisors, managers and senior managers is 6%, half that of our competitors.

Benefit: You see the same people year after year. Our people will know your business inside and out and you won't have to continuously educate new staff about your operations. The time savings to you are considerable!

Issue: Lack of industry expertise

Solution: We offer expert advice from dedicated people in the following specialized areas: (insert here). That experience amounts to more than 100 years in relevant fields.

Benefit: You can be sure your work is completed by industry experts who possess the knowledge and expertise to do the work right. We also share industry best practices to help you improve and grow.

Issue: Lack of personal attention

Solution: We want each of our clients to have a five-star client service experience. To this end, we work hard to anticipate your needs by returning calls and correspondence within two hours, and determining deliverables and timelines ahead of time so there are no surprises.

Benefit: You'll feel "taken care of" and secure in the knowledge that the right people are taking your needs seriously.

Issue: Excessive fees

Solution: Our audit process goes beyond the expected advice to help improve your business, at fees that are typically 15-25% lower than at your current firm. Additionally, in addition to projecting fees ahead of the work, we adhere to a detailed change order process that requires your approval before additional expenses are incurred.

Benefit: You get more than you expected for less than you are accustomed to paying.

Key takeaways

Creating an issue-solution-benefit narrative will:

- Position you to eloquently verbalize your strengths and how they help your clients.
- Allow you to connect the things you say you do best to the needs of your prospective clients.
- Eliminate the unnecessary "fluff" that permeates most sales presentations. It keeps you focused on the issues that clients care about.

CHAPTER 5
MARKETING

Many accounting firms take exactly the wrong approach to marketing. They simply copy other firms when they create websites, collateral, social media and event marketing. It's as if they're going out of their way to look like everyone else. Frankly, it's boring. Firms should want to be different; they should aim to be special and exceptional. Marketing is a prime opportunity to do this. Take the opportunity to demonstrate who you are. Consider the words of famed business author Peter Drucker: "The aim of marketing is to know and understand the customer so well the product or service fits him and sells itself."

In this chapter, we'll highlight several important marketing strategies. Individual topics include:

- **Style guide:** Create standards for all design elements like font, colors, graphics and images. When a client opens a letter, it should be obvious it's from you because it carries your unique style.
- **Website:** Your website is your store window; it showcases what you have to offer. It should explain who you are, what you believe and how you're different.
- **Social media:** This topic focuses specifically on LinkedIn, because it's a powerful vehicle for communicating with your professional network.
- **Testimonials:** Instead of singing your own praises, find someone else to do it for you. The best testimonials feature interviews with real clients talking about what your firm does best.
- **eCommunications:** Don't clutter up everyone's inboxes. Instead, develop compelling content, package it nicely and send it to relevant contacts. It will ultimately serve as a conversation starter.
- **Collateral:** This is your chance to showcase your personality, culture and expertise. To make great collateral, you need to perfect both your copy and your design.

- **Proposals:** To get the best return on your investment when responding to RFPs, create a master proposal template. This will save you time and help you draft clear, concise, value-driven proposals.
- **Presentations:** Presenting is about more than what you say — it's about how you stand, where you look and how you modulate your voice. Develop your non-verbal skills and you'll become a more effective presenter.
- **Case studies:** Use case studies to illustrate your solutions to common client concerns.
- **Media:** Get your name out. You can keep a blog, post to social media, host webinars or speak at workshops. Position yourself as a thought leader in your field.
- **Advertising:** The best ads are targeted, creative and compelling. Choose a powerful visual and use as few words as possible.
- **Events:** Throwing events helps you increase brand awareness, foster new connections and boost morale. Common firm-sponsored events include business-to-business mixers, business-to-client mixers and virtual events such as webinars.

STYLE GUIDE

Creating and following a style guide ensures your firm's content is formatted consistently across all platforms. The style guide lays out your standards for design elements like fonts, colors, graphics and images. It will be clear that all of your materials, whether presentations, flyers or emails, are from you because they carry your unique style.

Define your brand

If you pay attention to the smallest detail in your promotional materials, down to the footer text in a flyer, it sends a message to your clients about the level of care they can expect from all your work. In contrast, firms that have very little brand uniformity come across as disorganized and careless. You might not notice these things, but clients do, and they matter.

Pick your style

The easiest way to ensure uniformity in your branding is to hire a marketing agency. For a more economical solution, creating your own style guide will help inhibit the use of rainbow fonts and clip art graphics. A style guide should include standards for the following elements at a minimum (www[23]):

Style elements

- **Logos:** You may have different logos for different parts of your business; include all logos and specify the specific cases in which they should be used.
- **Colors:** For your firm's primary colors, list the color codes in various formats including pantone, RGB (for online use) and CMYK (for print use). Also provide additional color shades and specify when they should be used (for example, a less saturated version of the main color in your logo might be used to fill Excel spreadsheet cells).
- **Fonts:** Specify your firm's primary and secondary fonts, the cases in which each should be used and where they can be found (include a download link when appropriate).
- **Bullets:** Decide whether your bullets will be round, square, triangular, etc.
- **Punctuation:** List any punctuation rules, such as whether you use the Oxford comma or whether you use a single or double space at the end of a sentence.
- **Images:** Include a list of approved images and their uses. For example, if you have small business clients, specify which images should be used for small business messaging. Your employees should only use these images; they should not pull unauthorized images from the web. Save all images to a central and easily accessible location.

Brand messaging

- **Opening and closing document paragraphs:** Consistency is about more than design. To achieve consistency in your messaging, include in your style guide opening and closing paragraphs that should be included in all client correspondence. These paragraphs should reiterate your brand's competitive advantage.
- **Email signature:** Everyone in the firm should follow the same format for their email signature (no fancy fonts). Include name, title, logo, contact information and relevant social media profiles (like LinkedIn).

Sample documents

Include sample templates for all document types including letters, flyers, newsletters, proposals and presentations. Specify any unique style elements for each type (for example, the font size for newsletters).

Once you've created your style guide, you have to ensure that it is enforced. A few suggestions to facilitate its adoption:

- Circulate the style guide to all staff and make it available on your network/intranet.
- Meet with staff to explain the importance of brand consistency.
- Have an individual oversee the implementation of certain features to make sure they're implemented within the stated timeline (for example, updating email signatures or resetting default email fonts).
- For a set period of time, have a staff member "police" the standards you've set (for example, by reviewing customer-facing documents).
- Make document templates easily accessible on your internal network.
- Delete old versions of each document template from your internal network, as well as from each individual's computer.
- Circulate the style guide to relevant third parties, such as strategic alliance partners. Police their use of your standards.

Key takeaways

Creating and enforcing a style guide for your firm will:

- Create consistency. All of your communications will sound and look like they come from you.
- Demonstrate your values. By policing every detail of your communications, you're sending a message about your commitment to stability, regularity and precision in all your work.
- Set you apart. Branding is an easy way to differentiate your firm from the competition.

WEBSITE

Your website is often a prospective client's first introduction to your brand. It's your equivalent of a store window. Thus it should adequately snapshot who you are, what you believe and how you're different. It should also be a resource for clients when they need to find relevant and timely information. There are two basic elements to crafting a good website: content development and web design.

What you see is what you get

I'm reminded of the first joke I ever heard: A man walks into a pet store and asks to buy a pet wasp. The store clerk replies, "Sorry sir, but we don't sell wasps here." "That's funny," the man retorts, "you've got one in the window." Apart from the fact that I've always wanted to tell the joke out loud, it reiterates the importance of your store window. Your website is often your first chance to make a good impression. A good website alone won't win you new clients, but a bad one will definitely drive them away.

It's not just for show

Any good website should achieve all of the following:

- Articulate your firm's competitive advantage and claims.
- Define your firm's areas of service and industry specialization.
- Serve as a place to go to get more information.
- Highlight your firm's culture and showcase your people.
- Demonstrate your firm's currency.
- Connect users to supporting forms of social media.

How to write content for your website

Follow these steps to generate content for your website:

1. **Create a navigation map.** Try to limit the number of navigation links in your menu bar. We suggest no more than six. For example, your navigation links might include firm, services, industries, contact, client login and social media. Each category can contain further subcategories. For example, your "services" navigation link might house tax, audit, wealth management and consulting. Your "firm" navigation link might house why us, team, client testimonials and communications.
2. **Craft your homepage.** Your homepage is unlike any other page on your site. Typically it will be more visual and less wordy. It will also serve as a secondary navigation point, connecting the user to other sections of your site (for example, clicking on one of the claims pictures might take the user to the "why us" page). Your homepage should achieve three things:

   - Articulate who you are and why you're different.
   - Spell out your claims.

- Allow the user to easily connect to important pages on your site. In the example below, the **bolded** links should be updated regularly to direct viewers to topical content.

Here's an example:

Your Firm Name Here		Firm Services Industries Contact Client Login Social Media	
Who you are/why you're different copy here			
Claim #1 Visual supported by a single sentence of text	Claim #2 Visual supported by a single sentence of text	Claim #3 Visual supported by a single sentence of text	**Links** **Nonprofit Newsletter** **Midyear Tax-Planning Guide** **Director of Audit Position** **Museum Hospitality Event** **RSVP** **Resource Center**
Site Map Privacy Policy Terms of Use			

Don't use your homepage as a dumping ground for content. Include only topical and worthwhile links, and remember to take them down before they get old. Having your midyear tax-planning guide on your homepage in December will have a damaging effect.

3. **Write copy for individual pages.** Create a consistent page format, with a consistent word count for your individual pages (tax, wealth management, team, etc). Use bullets to summarize specifics, such as to list the services you provide. This makes the copy easier to digest and makes the page less busy. To achieve consistency across all pages, have one person write or edit the copy or educate all contributors on your writing format ahead of time.

4. **Avoid the curse of brochure-ware.** You don't want your website to be static media that never changes. It's important to have a few sections of your site that are frequently updated. These include:

- *Communications:* Archive each of your electronic communications. Make sure you include a publication date so that your viewers know when the content was written.
- *Resource center:* Add readings, white papers and publications that are relevant for your clients. This can be content that you've produced or content from outside sources. Promote it as the "go-to resource" for information on a wide range of finance and accounting topics. Make it search-friendly by categorizing it by topic or by adding search functionality.

Finally, pay attention to search engine optimization (SEO) guidelines when customizing your design, functionality and content. Creating unique and accurate page titles, using the description meta tag, improving the structure of your URLs, optimizing your images, using heading tags appropriately, making the site easy to navigate and updating the content frequently will help improve your ranking in search engine results. Be sure to keep up-to-date on these guidelines, as they change frequently.

Here are a few additional tips for what to include on each page:

- **Why Us:** Focus on your competitive advantage and claims. This is your chance to differentiate yourself from the competition. Make it count.
- **Team:** Write interesting bios for your team. Tell your readers what makes your staff members unique and include personable, emotive images. If you've done your job, a prospective client should be able to identify their "ideal candidate CPA" from comparing the various bios. For each team member, include areas of expertise, talents, academic background, qualifications, affiliations and personal interests.
- **Clients:** Include your ideal client profile, testimonials from clients and case studies.
- **Communications:** Organize publications by type (for example, firm newsletter, non-profit newsletter, etc). Archive past editions to make them easily searchable.
- **Resource Center:** Archive white papers, legislative updates, tax planning guides and so on. Categorize content by topic and offer title or keyword search functionality. In short, make it easy for your clients and prospective clients to find stuff.
- **Events:** Provide short descriptions of events with links to invitation collateral and online registration. Again, make it easy for your clients and prospective clients to get more information and to RSVP.
- **Strategic Partners:** List your strategic alliance partners and link to their websites.
- **Services and Markets:** If you have a "go-to" person for a specific service or industry, include a link to their bio here. Don't make it hard for clients or prospective clients to locate relevant expertise.

How to design your website

Don't overlook the importance of your website aesthetic. It says a lot about who you are and what you stand for. For example, look at your competition's websites. You'll likely notice commonalities: dark colors, conservative images with professionals shaking hands over a conference room table, and words like reliable, trustworthy and dependable. If this is who you are, then be true to it. Own it. If you want to stand out from the crowd, however, look for ways to separate your firm from the rest.

Colors, fonts, images and words are the "big 4" tools at your disposal. For me, the most important of those are images. Pick images that get the reader to stop and pay attention. One of my personal favorites is the M&A image of the big fish chasing the little fish. With little translation, most everyone knows what that image means. As we'll talk about in the advertising topic, there are lots of royalty-free websites where you can buy great photos at an affordable price. In web design, this is the best money you can spend. Regardless of how good your copy is, bad images will kill your site.

Before you hire someone to design your website, take the time to figure out what you want. Look at the competition's websites to find design concepts that inspire you and repetitive elements that you want to avoid. More importantly, look at the websites of non-professional service firms. I personally prefer to look at the websites of graphic designers and web developers because they're usually on the cutting edge of style and design. Create a "design ideation" document to keep track of the ideas you like. Clearly articulate your competitive advantage and claims to your designer, as they'll be able to draw design concepts from your words, concepts and themes.

When hiring a designer, be sure to interview and audition them. Their portfolio is important, but also ask them to sketch out how they would design your website around your competitive advantage, claims and content. Don't put too much stock in industry-specific experience. Try to get outside of the professional services paradigm by considering people who bring a different perspective to the process.

Key takeaways

To create a website for your firm:

- Focus on your homepage. It's your store window. Make it attractive and compelling and build it around your competitive advantage and claims.
- Write consistently across all pages. It shouldn't feel as if a different person wrote each page.
- Make your website a relevant resource by updating it with recent communications and relevant documents. You don't want a static site.

SOCIAL MEDIA

Unlike most of the enduring principles highlighted in this book, social media is a relatively recent phenomenon whose face is changing daily. There are many ways to reach out to clients, prospective clients, referral sources and others via social media. The question is not whether social media is relevant, but where and how to invest your efforts.

From Facebook to Google+ to Twitter and YouTube, a seemingly endless succession of products has popped up to help us communicate, interact and connect. Three years ago, Facebook was all the rage — Super Bowl commercials were littered with invitations to visit company Facebook pages and little blue icons began to appear on the homepages of even the stodgiest of professional service firms. Firms struggled to know what to do with Facebook. Many duplicated the content on their websites; others used it to communicate with the college crowd and younger prospective employees. The fad, at least in accounting circles, appeared to be short-lived. Yet while many social media pages sit idle, LinkedIn continues to offer an invaluable resource to accountants. While not ignoring other forms of social media, this chapter will focus on LinkedIn as a vehicle to communicate with and expand your network of professional contacts.

Make the most of your connections

Once you've joined LinkedIn, here's a game plan for how to use it more effectively:

- **Connect with people you know.** You only need to spend a minute or so each day to connect with the people listed under "People You May Know." Broadening your network is crucial to getting the most out of LinkedIn, but remember that you should only connect with people you actually know. If you would like to connect with someone you don't know, ask one of your contacts for an introduction via LinkedIn. Make sure you follow the company pages of your current clients and top prospective clients.
- **Look for leads.** LinkedIn allows you to see the connections of your connections. Spend a few minutes each day going through the list and making note of whom you would like to meet. You should also join LinkedIn groups, where you can share insights with others. LinkedIn lets you connect with people who are in groups with you, giving you another way to build out your network of prospective clients.
- **Be an active participant.** Post a quick "update" each day by sharing an article or video that is relevant to your clients and prospective clients. The goal is to add value and share expertise, not to sell your services through these updates. You can also use updates to celebrate the accomplishments of others. When you see a post that shares good news

about a client, prospective client or key contact, share the news as a status update and recognize the individual with an "@" reply.

- **Write recommendations for others.** Instead of waiting for others to recommend you, take the initiative and post recommendations for your clients and key contacts. Your recommendation will show up on their profile page, reinforcing your relationship with the contact and serving as a promotional piece for you and your firm. It also increases the chance that your contact will want to return the favor, either with a referral or recommendation.
- **Share your video testimonials.** If you have client testimonials, be sure to include them in your profile. As discussed in the testimonials chapter, third-party testimonials are a great way to showcase your strengths from the perspective of a happy client (see the next topic in this chapter).
- **Make it a habit.** To make the most of LinkedIn, invest 10 minutes daily or one hour weekly in the activities listed above. Spending six hours a day for a week straight followed by months of inactivity won't help you.

Sell yourself

LinkedIn is an extremely powerful tool that when used correctly can greatly amplify your marketing and networking efforts. It's an easy way to build your own brand and promote your firm because it automatically communicates your updates to all your contacts. By compiling recommendations, video testimonials and your own expert advice in one place, your LinkedIn profile becomes a great way to sell yourself. You'll grow your professional network and learn more about your clients, prospective clients, referral sources and competitors.

Key takeaways

The keys to a great LinkedIn presence are:

- Connection. Add others to your LinkedIn network to grow your professional network.
- Communication. Send daily updates to keep in touch with your connections. It doesn't help you to be a silent presence.
- Dedication. You need to consistently devote time to LinkedIn to harness its power.

TESTIMONIALS

A testimonial is a written or verbal statement by a third party that praises a particular person, product or service. The most effective testimonials in the accounting world are those that speak about common client concerns, the solutions that your firm offers and how those solutions benefit your clients. The best testimonials also praise specific individuals by name and single out their contributions. This helps establish the firm's personality and builds the reputation of those individuals.

Hear it from someone else

A third-party testimonial is one of the most effective ways to win over prospective clients. Instead of touting your own talents, someone else with "no dog in the fight" does it for you. That person has no vested interest in recommending your services; they're simply doing it because they believe in you and want to help you grow. When you talk about yourself, most prospective clients will assume you're exaggerating, but when someone else talks you up, and has no material motivation to do so, the prospective client will assign more weight to their comments.

Lights, camera, action

Gone are the days of written testimonials; today you want to flatter yourself on camera. The best testimonials feature interviews with real clients talking about what your firm does best. Seeing a person on film (their voice, their passion, their conviction) will bring the words to life. Video testimonials are also surprisingly affordable, but short of having a professional do it, you can always use a handheld video or cell phone camera (www[24]).

Follow this quick "how to" guide for shooting great video testimonials:

- **Craft your claims.** If you followed the advice laid out in the messaging chapter in this book, you will have clearly articulated your competitive claims. You want your video to focus on those claims because they are your most important talking points.
- **Select great subjects.** You want subjects who are raving fans of your work. They should also be charismatic, engaging and interesting on camera.
- **Prepare subjects prior to the shoot.** It is essential that your interview subjects are as relaxed as possible. Send the subject a list of questions three days before the interview (do not overwhelm your subject with more than 9-12 questions). Tell them the interview will take place in a conversational tone and that no significant preparation is necessary on their behalf. The goal is to limit anxiety and avoid scripted responses.
- **Help your subjects feel comfortable on camera.** As the interviewer, you must ooze positivity. Sitting in front of a camera and lights can be nerve-wracking for your subject; you want to smile, stay positive and help them relax. Begin the interview by asking the subject easy

questions about who they are, what they like, etc. You probably won't use most of this footage — you just want the subject to relax before you start with the important questions.

- **Coach subjects live in the room.** Sit straight because your subjects will mirror your posture. Maintain eye contact and stay engaged. Subjects will lose focus and confidence if you do not make it clear they have your undivided attention.
- **Aim for 10-15 second sound bites.** Your final cut will be made up of 10-15 second sound bites. Use the rhetoric that you want the subject to use and imply the responses you are looking for with the phrasing of your questions. After you ask the question the first time and the subject has gathered their ideas, rephrase the question or ask them to clarify one point. The goal is to encourage them to restate their answer in a more concise, more eloquent form. Shorter sentences carry more power so aim for questions that encourage short summarizing statements.

Once you've captured your footage, you can compile it in any of the following formats:

- **The individual video.** One person speaks to each of the firm's claims. This is most relevant if you have a particularly enthusiastic and engaging subject.
- **The claim video.** Multiple subjects speak to one of the firm's claims (for example, three different clients speak about how responsive you are). This is the most widely used format.
- **The documentary.** Multiple subjects speak to each of the firm's claims interspersed with additional "B roll" footage (shots of the building, the people, etc). This requires more work but is a great tool to have in your arsenal.

Once you've created your video, find as many ways as you can to maximize its distribution. Embed videos in electronic newsletters and post on the firm's homepage and social media sites. Consider creating a firm YouTube channel.

Finally, convert the material you've gathered into a written format. Not everyone will have the time or capability to watch the video, so it's still important to disseminate quotes that simply and eloquently capture your claims.

In a rare situation, you might have a client who is willing to deliver an in-person testimonial, most likely when you are wooing a prospective client referred by that client. An in-person testimonial is your trump card, followed by a video testimonial, then a written testimonial. Don't forget: Any testimonial is better than no testimonial.

Key takeaways

Testimonials are a great way to:

- Showcase your strengths. Testimonials help you hammer home your message.
- Take the pressure off yourself. Someone else will do the selling for you.
- Bring weight to your claims. Everyone saying the same thing consistently adds credibility to your claims.

eCOMMUNICATIONS

Accountants now have an arsenal of options for communicating with their firm's clients, prospective clients, strategic alliance partners, referral sources and employees. When used correctly, electronic communication is a great method for conveying your expertise to an array of constituencies. Yet the simplicity and affordability of email has resulted in an abundance of ill-targeted newsletters clogging up everyone's inboxes. This chapter highlights some best practices to help your emails stand out from the crowd.

Master the mass email

Your overarching goal is send the right content to the right people. Here's how to do that:

- **Identify your targets.** The first step is to create a database of contacts that can be sorted by type (clients, prospects, vendors, etc) and then subtype (industry, niche, etc). The more categories you include, the more targeted and effective your communication. This is especially important when writing for niches (for example, you might only want to send an email to those people who work in health care non-profits, as opposed to everyone on your non-profit list). Ideally, this database will connect easily with your client accounting software so that you don't have to maintain two separate communications databases. If that's not possible, review and update your email contact list regularly to ensure it includes a current list of contacts.

- **Decide on your messaging.** There are several types of eCommunication that accounting firms typically use to communicate with their target constituencies:

  - *Firm news:* Articles that spotlight the gamut of services the firm offers (tax, assurance, private client service, client accounting services, consulting, etc)
  - *Client news:* Articles that highlight the accomplishments of firm clients (awards, recognition, publicity, etc)
  - *Niche news:* Articles that discuss hot topics specific to one of the firm's areas of niche expertise
  - *Tax news:* Articles that spotlight proposed solutions to legislative changes
  - *Employee news:* Articles that share new team member announcements, merger and acquisition announcements, etc

  Don't feel pressure to generate all this content yourself. You can buy pre-edited articles from recognized sources for $50-$100 apiece so you don't have to break the bank to produce good copy.

- **Make it easy to read.** Keep your articles short. The best articles are 400 words or less. If you have to write more, always try to say it in less. Adhere to the "rule of three" — not more than three topics per category (for example, three articles about tax, three articles about assurance) and not more than three key takeaways per article. It often helps to spotlight one important article per email. The teaser for that article might include a summary and image that takes up a significant chunk of the available real estate. Your other two articles would be shorter and take up less room. As with any messaging communiqué, connect the content to your competitive advantage and claims.

- **Dress it up.** Make the publication "visually attractive." Include compelling images, adhere to the standards laid out in your style guide and use reusable templates to facilitate uniformity (see earlier in this chapter for more on how to create a firm style guide). Try to come up with attention-grabbing headlines; you don't have to sensationalize, but try to do more than simply tell the reader what the article is about. For each article, include a headline and summary paragraph so readers can choose what they want to read. Every article should be hosted on your website and the email should link to each article. This makes for easily digestible emails and also supplies you with a steady stream of content for your website.

- **Create the chance for conversation.** Think of each article like an infomercial — every infomercial ends with a screen telling you how to order. You too want to make the next steps clear by telling the reader where to go to get more information. Make sure someone is in charge of replying to any inquiries. Make it easy for readers to share or forward the content and integrate social media links. Solicit feedback and encourage readers to suggest topics for future consideration; you want audience interest to drive your subject matter. Remember, one of the main goals of eCommunication is to insert yourself into the client's consciousness, reminding them of your relationship and creating an opportunity for further conversation.

Key takeaways

eCommunication is a great way to:

- Communicate with your entire network or targeted subsets of that network.
- Stay "top of mind" with your key constituencies.
- Start a conversation, and hopefully generate new business development opportunities.

COLLATERAL

Your flyers, brochures and other pieces of collateral are your chance to showcase your personality, culture and expertise. Your collateral shouts to the world who you are and what you do best. To make great collateral, you need to perfect both your copy and your design.

Great collateral copy:

- **Hits the important points.** Your collateral should explain how you're different than the competition. We know by now that we must be sounding like a broken record but like any sales piece, collateral is focused on two things: who you are and what you do best. Stick to this formula and it's hard to go wrong!
- **Focuses on solutions and benefits.** Instead of dwelling on the features of your service, explain how your clients benefit from your service.
- **Is easy to read.** Use language that your target audience understands.
- **Creates a call to action.** Always encourage your audience to get in touch. Tell them how to reach you and where to go to get more information.

Great collateral design:

- **Relies on great visuals.** Choose interesting and appropriate images that speak to your personality. Balance your use of words and images. Incorporate non-photographic visuals like charts when appropriate.
- **Follows a consistent style.** Style elements like colors, font and layout should be consistent across all pieces of collateral.
- **Reflects your personality.** Your choice of card stock, colors, fonts and design all speak to who you are. Dark colors scream consistency, reliability and tradition; light colors suggest creativity, flexibility and fun. Conventional fonts like Times New Roman imply you're traditional. Straight lines, perpendicular and parallel accents, conventional column spacing and pictures of buildings and bridges all speak to conformity; abstract use of space, a unique way a document folds and use of abstract images all speak to imagination and invention.

Types of collateral

We've simplified the many types of business development collateral into four forms:

1. **Firm brochure:** Typically 4-12 pages in length with a large emphasis on images. It should follow a similar navigation format as your website, organized by firm, services, industries, contact, etc.
2. **Firm sheet:** Typically two pages in length. A condensed version of your firm brochure that focuses on your competitive advantage and claims. It provides a list summary of services and industries.

3. **Industry or niche brochure:** Typically 4-8 pages in length with a large emphasis on images. It addresses your firm's services in a particular industry or niche, including client needs and wants, expertise, experience and solutions.
4. **Individual service sheets:** These offer a more detailed description of individual services the firm provides. They are typically inserted into a promotional folder with any of the three documents listed above.

Each of these documents should be designed in a similar size and format, making it easy to customize an informational folder for a prospective client based on their areas of interest.

Control your image

Follow these steps to create your collateral:

1. **Go from big to small.** Start by writing copy for the web. Your website will include a wealth of information about everything you do. Edit down from what's on the web to produce your collateral copy.
2. **Have a design strategy.** Follow your style guide to ensure consistency from piece to piece (see earlier in this chapter for how to create a style guide). Keep all your documents the same size to make folder customization easy.
3. **Write consistently.** If you don't have your own writing process, consider a version of our writing formula (see the media topic later in this chapter):

   - **Who:** Your ideal client.
   - **What:** A description of your products or services. Focus on the benefits versus the features.
   - **How:** An explanation of your methodology or process. This is particularly important if process is one of your claims.
   - **Why:** An argument for choosing your firm. Detail your competitive advantage and claims.

   As a famous British comedic pianist once commented, "These may be all the right notes but not necessarily in the right order." Experiment with the order of delivery until it reads sequentially, from concept to action.
4. **Design with intent.** Your design communicates as much as your words. The way something looks and feels says a lot about your personality. "Conservative" isn't necessarily better or worse than "progressive"; each will appeal to a particular type of client. Pick a personality that's consistent with who you are. What's most important is that there's congruency between what you look like on paper and how you act in person.
5. **Choose your designer.** Create a "design ideation" document that includes samples of design concepts you culled from elsewhere. If you hate excessive text in sidebars, note that; if you really like bold colors, note that. Look at a designer's portfolio and ask them to sketch some ideas

based on your design ideations. It may take longer and cost a little more money but a good designer, much like a good web developer, is worth a lot. Don't place too much emphasis on whether a designer has done work for similar firms.

6. **Package for presentation.** Create an attractive collateral folder to house assorted materials. Make all print documents accessible in an "assembly room." Create a request form so it's easy for support staff to assemble an informational folder for you.

7. **Go paperless.** Going paperless will save you a lot of money. If you're worried about going paperless, think about why you're hesitating. If it's because firm members are uneasy about the change, it might be worth getting over the fear. If your clients actually value receiving paper documents, it probably makes sense to stick with paper. You can always ask prospective clients if they would like to receive documents electronically or in print. As you go paperless, promote the move as an illustration of your firm's commitment to doing right by the client (by saving money) and right by the planet (by saving trees).

Key takeaways

To create great collateral:

- Remember that less is more. Get to the point. If people want more information, tell them where to go to get it.
- Write persuasive copy. Focus on your competitive advantage and claims and how your clients benefit from your services.
- Make it visually appealing. Balance words and images and adopt a consistent style.

PROPOSALS

While accounting firms submit many types of proposals, including engage-ment letters for tax clients, this topic focuses on audit proposals generated in response to RFPs (requests for proposal). In the process outlined below, we recommend that you generate a proposal master template, and then convert that content into a proposal template for each industry (for example, real estate), and ultimately sub-industry (construction firms, developers, pri-vate owners, etc). While time-consuming up front, this process is a lifesaver in the long haul.

Avoid the RFP black hole

RFPs are a huge time drain. Without the benefit of a needs assessment meeting, you have no guarantee that you're hitting the right notes in your proposal. You're spending a lot of time and effort on a proposal that could be way off the mark. This process aims to solve that problem in two ways. First, by creating a master template, it aims to reduce the work involved in responding to an RFP. And second, it helps you craft a clear, concise, value-driven proposal that will stand out from the rest. Remember, the goal of a proposal is to get you past the first round and into a room with key decision-makers.

Don't be boring

We'll lay out a detailed process for creating a master template below, but first, consider these overarching principles for crafting an audit proposal:

- **Focus on your competitive advantage and claims.** Don't waste too much time talking about your process, such as approach, plan or time-table. Those factors won't vary significantly from firm to firm. Instead, try to get to the root of the prospective client's issues and explain how they'll benefit from your solutions. You would be amazed at how many audit proposals fail to identify the mark and hit it.
- **Be brief.** Most proposals are too long and are padded with too much fluff. One suggestion: Once you've created your proposal template, cut it down to a four-page executive version. The executive version should focus on what makes you different and highlight the need-to-know information. If you make it to the presentation round, you can use this version to snapshot your most important points, rather than recycling the longer version that you've already submitted.
- **Focus on the benefits.** Audit clients want to know how you're going to make their life better. Speak to how you'll help them. If their previous audit experience was "painful," describe how yours is "pleasurable." If they felt like their prior auditor was "out to get them," tell them how "you're on the same side."
- **Be emotive.** Audits can be intrusive, drawn-out and time-consuming for clients. Any such situation is made easier by working with people

whom you like and respect. Add personal touches to your proposal to connect with your readers.

Master your proposal

You'll save yourself a lot of time by generating a master proposal template that you customize for each RFP. Follow these steps to create a master template:

1. **Create chapter headings.** These will be the "chapters" in your proposal template. In the example below, the **bold** headings are for the copy that needs to be customized for each individual proposal. The rest is generic copy that doesn't change from proposal to proposal. Here are sample headings:

Chapter	Description (what it is)
Cover	Graphic cover including name of firm, prospect, date, etc
Cover letter	Introduces competitive advantage, claims, relevant experience, etc
Why your firm?	Details competitive advantage, claims, relevant experience, etc
Needs	Presents an understanding of their needs and wants
Solutions	Provides specific solutions to their needs and wants
Team	Introduces the key people who will likely work on their account
Approach	Provides a high-level overview of your process
Plan	Breaks down your process into steps
Timeline	Breaks down each step into an overall project timeline
Fees	Details fees and expenses
Testimonials	Provides suitable client contacts for reference checks
Other services	Summarizes other services the firm can provide (both audit services like internal controls and non-audit services like tax)
FAQs	Gives you a place to add unique content
Summary	Highlights your competitive advantage and claims again

2. **Write generic copy.** There are three types of copy in a proposal:

Generic copy	Pre-written; same in every proposal	Team, approach, plan, etc	60% of total copy
Industry-specific copy	Pre-written; same in every industry-specific proposal	Cover letter, references, etc	10% of total copy
RFP-specific copy	Can't be pre-written; customized for each client	Needs, solutions, dates, fees, etc	30% of total copy

The first step is to draft the generic copy that will be the same across every proposal. This will cover most of the content in the headings above. You'll want to draft a cover letter that includes an introduction to your firm, a description of your competitive advantage and claims, and information about your staff and audit process. You should note places in the text that require industry-specific customization. For example, in the sample below, the bold text corresponds with content that would be customized per industry:

> "Our firm provides a passionate team with deep expertise in the areas of **(insert industry knowledge here)**. We have years of experience working with **(insert clients here)**."

3. **Write industry-specific copy.** Write industry-specific copy that can be dropped into the generic template. For example, if you specialize in real estate and retirement communities, you would generate copy for each of those industries:

   - *Real estate knowledge areas:* cost segregation, property-tax reassessment, entity restructuring and leveraging real estate for gift and estate planning
   - *Real estate past clients:* construction firms, developers, private owners, property managers and affordable-housing advocates
   - *Retirement communities knowledge areas:* proper trust-fund recording and relationships with subsidiaries
   - *Retirement communities past clients:* single- and multi-entity communities, related entities and residence and life-care communities

4. **Create industry-specific proposal templates.** Now it's time to turn your master template into industry-specific proposal templates. Use the industry-specific copy you generated above and add industry-specific imagery. For example, you would take the paragraph above and insert your real-estate specific copy:

"Our firm provides a passionate team with deep expertise in the areas of **cost segregation, property-tax reassessment, entity restructuring and leveraging real estate for gift and estate planning**. We have years of experience working with **construction firms, developers, private owners, property managers, and affordable-housing advocates**."

5. **Add unique requests to the FAQ section.** Your FAQ section is a list of questions and answers to tell your prospective client more about you. Every time you receive an RFP with a unique question, add the question and your response to the FAQ section. A sample question you might include: "Provide information on the last three audit clients you lost. Why did you lose them?" The more insightful information you provide, the more transparent you look.

6. **Generate your proposal.** Even though 70% of the proposal template is pre-written, you can't do everything in advance. Have a clear plan for completing proposals on time. Working backwards from the proposed submission date, assign tasks by timeline. Ensure your administrative support team has sufficient time to pull your customized contributions together. Always have a member of the accounting team proof the final document for content and grammar.

7. **Create sub-industry templates.** The more specialized you become, the more versions of your industry-specific template you'll create. A template that used to work for technology will split into multiple templates for types of technology clients (for example, SaaS, green, biotech, etc). Customize with appropriate images and references.

8. **Archive content.** One of the biggest timesavers in proposal writing is knowing where to go to find relevant content. Create an archiving system that allows you to easily locate old proposals.

9. **Share best practices.** Share best practices across industry groups, and update industry-specific templates accordingly.

If you would like to streamline this process even further, you can hire a software engineer to create a program that will allow you to generate proposals by checking boxes and adding content to pre-formatted fields. There's a high up-front cost, but it may be worth the time savings in the end.

Key takeaways

To get the most return on investment with audit proposals:

- Write proposals that are detailed but brief. Cover a lot of ground in as few words as possible.
- Focus on your competitive advantage and claims. Connect your strengths with the prospective client's needs.
- Minimize the time required to turn around proposals by generating master templates that you can customize accordingly.

PRESENTATIONS

There are two parts to giving a great presentation: generating your content and delivering that content effectively. Because we've talked extensively in other parts of the book about how to craft your messaging around your competitive advantage and claims, we'll focus primarily in this chapter on the techniques and non-verbal skills that make you a better presenter.

No need to jump in the casket

Knowing how to give a good presentation is essential for any accountant, whether you're pitching a prospective audit client or speaking at a convention. Presentation skills will serve you even in informal settings, where you need to gain support for your ideas among colleagues, prospects and clients. Yet many people dread giving presentations. Consider this Jerry Seinfeld quote, "According to most studies, people's number one fear is public speaking. Number two is death. Death is number two. Does that sound right? This means to the average person, if you go to a funeral, you're better off in the casket than doing the eulogy." It's worth getting past the fear.

Writing content effectively

Let's say that you have to give a presentation and you've come up with all the content you need, but you're not sure what to include and what to omit. We suggest you think about it this way: Only include what you need to deliver a tightly crafted presentation with a clear message. You want content that is:

- **Persuasive.** Use stories, anecdotes and real-life examples to bring your content to life. You want your audience to listen attentively and take action once the talk is over.
- **Well-reasoned.** Highlight the evidence behind your claims. Follow up every argument with proof.
- **Focused.** Stay on course. Adhere to a single theme throughout the presentation.
- **Concise.** Less is always better. When was the last time you heard someone say, "I just wished that presentation were longer!" Time is people's most precious commodity.
- **Clear.** State what you want to talk about, then talk about it and then tell your audience what you told them. Think about it like this: Would your mother-in-law walk out understanding the key points of your presentation if she were in the audience?

A few other delivery recommendations:

- Customize your presentation to your audience. Include shared history or interests.

- Help the audience relate to your message. Use stories or analogies that will resonate with them.
- Ask questions. Get the audience involved.
- Focus on what's most relevant to the audience in front of you. Often presenters spend a lot of time hammering home their talking points, without considering what their audience wants to hear.

Finally, consider how to format any accompanying materials. If you're using a slide presentation, we urge you to use striking visuals and as few words as possible. The best presentations include no written words at all. When you do use words, abide by the "rule of six": not more than six bullets per slide and not more than six words per bullet. To help you organize your presentation, consider creating a "presentation skeleton" that includes the slide number, slide title and slide talking points (www[25]). You can use the information contained in this skeleton to create bullets and choose relevant images. Here are a few sample slides from a "presentation skeleton":

Slide number	Slide title	Slide talking points
1	Step 1: Discovery process	We begin by identifying the dangers, opportunities and strengths that will inform your exit plan. We'll ask questions such as: What do you want to do? Who are the up-and-coming leaders in the business? How much money do you need to retire? What do you think your company is worth? Do you have charitable interests you want to pursue?
2	Step 2: Feasibility evaluation	Feasibility involves evaluating potential and benefits, such as: Is there a market for this business? What are the potential outcomes and how will they affect cash flow? This step allows us to analyze potential courses of action and anticipate their end results.
3	Step 3: Value computation	We'll perform a complete assessment of the value of your company and its overall marketability. Additionally, because your business is likely the largest asset in your portfolio, we will assess your personal financial plan. Monetizing your business must work in concert with your overall financial picture.

Delivering content effectively

Now that you've written your presentation, you need to deliver it with gusto. We'll focus on presence, visual aids and live Q&A as three essential skills for delivering your content effectively.

Assert your presence

To establish your presence in front of a group, you need to master the following presentation skills: eye contact, stance, volume and tone, speed and pitch, and gestures. Of these, eye contact is by far the most important.

Maintaining eye contact with your audience helps keep the tone conversational, which will make your talk more engaging. Audience members will also feel that you have genuinely connected with them. Follow these tips to establish better eye contact:

- **Shrink the room.** Imagine that the person you're looking at is the only person in the room. For those few seconds you're having a one-on-one conversation with just that person.
- **Move to another person at an appropriate time.** At the end of a sentence or paragraph, switch your focus to someone else.
- **Look for a reaction.** After an important point, look for a reaction to what you've just said.
- **Keep your eyes up.** Discipline yourself to keep your eyes up until you've finished your sentence, then look down. Look at your notes in silence. When you're ready to continue, look up, find someone to talk to and then start talking.
- **Don't be a lighthouse or a tennis umpire.** A lighthouse presenter goes systematically around the room; a tennis umpire presenter looks first to the left, then to the right.
- **Respect people who are uncomfortable.** Some people in your audience may show that they're uncomfortable with eye connection by looking away. Respect that by making less direct eye contact with them.

When delivering a presentation while standing, you want to adopt a neutral stance with your shoulders back, chest out, stomach in, knees relaxed, feet slightly apart, hands open and relaxed by your side, head tilted slightly upward. It's fine to move around occasionally and purposefully, but avoid aimless weight shifting or pacing as it conveys nervousness and a lack of confidence. At a seated presentation, make sure you sit confidently, with your back straight and shoulders back. Demonstrate your confidence by taking up your space at the table instead of slouching or shrinking and don't let your nerves show by fidgeting or tapping your foot.

Your voice is a powerful tool when presenting and you need to be aware of your volume, tone, speed and pitch. Remember that we all sound louder to ourselves than we do to an audience so try to speak to the audience members who are farthest away from you. Use your voice to show confidence in your abilities and your material — speak firmly, enunciate each word and don't mumble or slur your words. Slow down when making important points to give the audience time to understand and absorb your message.

Finally, pay attention to the power of gestures. Gestures are particularly appropriate when addressing an emotional subject or driving home a point. The bigger the audience, the bigger the gesture needs to be. If gesturing seems unnatural to you, start by adding gestures to words like large, tall, small, all, etc.

These are all skills that you can practice on your own before you get up in front of an audience. You can even practice giving presentations that have nothing to do with accounting. For example, I ask my clients to write an introductory speech about someone influential in their life. Record yourself and ask others for feedback to help you improve.

A picture's worth a thousand words

You have a variety of visual media options depending on the formality of your presentation, prep time, audience size, room size and the type of presentation. A few of the most common options include PowerPoint, Prezi, flip charts and handouts. These visuals aids can bolster your presentation, but don't let them prevent you from focusing on the audience.

When presenting, first look at your own visual to refresh your memory and then turn to the audience, maintain eye contact with one person and deliver the information from the visual. You can continue to expand on that piece of information, or you can return to the visual to pick up more information, but be sure you are talking to the audience, not to your visual aid. If you choose to use handouts, we recommend you distribute them afterwards to ensure that the audience stays focused on your presentation. If you want to use your handouts interactively (for example, to allow the audience to make notes), distribute them at the beginning and be sure to specify when the audience should refer to them.

The ABCs of live Q&A

The Q&A session is one of the most critical moments during a presentation. Because the Q&A section is unscripted, your audience has the opportunity to surprise you. If you can't answer well, your credibility will suffer. The following steps are designed to help navigate a live Q&A. They should be used with an audience of 5+ people up to very large groups.

1. **Raise your hand.** This is your way of signaling that you're ready to take questions. It also sets the process for the Q&A session, as questioners who raise their hands will be selected. This helps to reduce the chance of questions being called out, which can be confusing in a large audience setting.
2. **Select.** Select the next questioner by indicating with an open palm. Don't point, it can appear rude.
3. **Listen to the question.** The first impulse most presenters have when an audience member asks a question is to try to think of the answer. That's

the wrong impulse because it can cause you to miss a key part of the question and therefore give an off-target answer. Maintain eye contact with the questioner and listen to the entire question before starting to think of your answer.

4. **Break visually.** Once you have listened to the questioner, before speaking, move to another audience member. This will begin the process of including the rest of the audience in your answer.

5. **Rephrase the question.** While maintaining eye contact with an audience member, rephrase the question by putting it into your own words. This ensures that everyone heard the question, confirms that you have understood the question and buys you valuable thinking time.

6. **Answer the question.** As a courtesy to the questioner, begin your answer with him/her. Then, using eye contact, continue your answer to different audience members.

7. **Choose where to end.** If you end on the questioner, he/she may ask you another question. If the questioner is a key decision-maker, it might be a good idea to elicit another question. In a large audience, it is better not to end your answer on the questioner but on another audience member. This prevents a one-on-one dialogue that excludes the rest of the audience.

8. **Raise your hand.** This signals that you have completed your answer and are ready for another question.

Go off script

Keep in mind that some of the best presentations are not tightly scripted. You don't have to start with a slide deck and end with questions to give a great presentation. Instead, allow the audience to drive the direction of your presentation. This helps you to focus on what your audience wants to hear. Consider the following opening to achieve a more free-flowing presentation: "I'm prepared to tell you who we are, what we do and why we're different. But in order to make the best use of your time today, I'd like to focus on what you would most like to learn." This suggests that while you've done your homework and are prepared to deliver a more conventional presentation, you're also willing to diverge from your script to provide the audience with the best possible value. This is a particularly useful strategy when you know your content well, as you're able to jump between slides and talking points to align your presentation to your audience's interests.

Key takeaways

To give a great presentation:

- Write great content. You want clear, compelling, concise content.
- Deliver your presentation skillfully. This involves mastering three skills: delivering with presence, presenting with visuals and handling live Q&A.
- Practice makes perfect. Record yourself and practice with colleagues to get feedback to help you improve.

CASE STUDIES

A case study is a written document that illustrates how you approached a particular client issue, how you solved it and how the client ultimately benefitted. It allows you to promote your competitive advantage from a client's perspective, as with a testimonial. But in this case, you get to write the script and control the message.

Show the real world applications

Case studies showcase practical applications of theoretical concepts. Readers relate to them because they highlight real world issues, solutions and benefits. They're another tool in your arsenal for telling client success stories. They're also a powerful vehicle for selling ideas internally to partners and staff. If you're trying to persuade other accountants to accept a new idea, one of the most effective approaches is to demonstrate to them how it will benefit their clients. Rather than getting lost in the theory behind a new idea, you can use case studies to illustrate its practical advantages.

Know your audience

In crafting case studies, consider both your ideal client and your competitive advantages and claims. You want your case studies to resonate with your ideal clients; after all, they are the people whose business you covet. For a case study to be relevant, the reader must be able to connect it to their own situation. You also want case studies that highlight your competitive advantage and support your claims. In the messaging chapter, we talked about the three P's: people, process and performance. Take your claims for each category and convert them into case studies. For example:

- **People:** If you claim to have more bench strength in a particular service line or industry, illustrate how that depth of expertise and insight benefited a particular client.
- **Process:** If you claim to deliver outstanding client service, provide examples of how your client service values or client service process helped a client to prosper and grow.
- **Performance:** If you claim to be quicker, more efficient and more affordable than the competition, provide a case study where a client contrasts their prior experience (slower, inefficient, more expensive) with their experience working with you.

Craft your narrative

Follow the steps below to create your case studies:

1. **Introduce the issue.** This can be as simple as stating the challenge facing the client. It is sometimes helpful to list the factors that originally contributed to the issue and list some of the client's questions and concerns.

2. **Break down the solution.** Explain to the reader how your firm walked the client through the options and detail the steps ultimately involved in solving the issue.
3. **Show how the client benefitted.** Whenever possible, substantiate the narrative with measures and metrics that validate your claims. Remember, readers remember numbers long after they forget words, especially if the numbers are profound. And be specific. If the number is 11.2%, say 11.2%; don't round to 11% or say "about 11%."

Case studies should be short. Get your point across and don't overcomplicate the story. If you've generated an issue-solution-benefit narrative, you can draw on those points in your case studies (see the messaging chapter for more on the issue-solution-benefit narrative). Once you've written your case studies, employ them in as many vehicles as possible, including on your website, as one-page inserts in your promotional collateral, in newsletters and other prospect and client communications and in business development meetings as a way to introduce new services and illustrate best practices.

The following is an example of a case study describing whether to ESOP or not:

Client issue

A single business owner was considering leaving his company. He wanted to know if he should sell the company — which had generated fairly consistent earnings — to an ESOP. He had a number of questions, including company valuation, classification as an S-corporation or C-corporation at the sale date and timeline for completing the sale.

Solution

The firm conducted a feasibility study. The study offered a basic calculation of the company's value, identified the value drivers of the business, provided useful benchmarking data and projected the impact of several ESOP transactions on both the P&L and the Balance Sheet. The study also addressed succession issues and discussed ESOP governance at length.

Benefit

Within a month, the client had a strong grasp of an ESOP and had a game plan for executing the ESOP transaction.

Key takeaways

Case studies are a useful tool to:

- Showcase how your firm ultimately helps its clients.
- Give clients the chance to talk about what you do best, but in a forum where you control the message.
- Tout your competitive advantages and claims to your ideal client.

MEDIA

Use various forms of media to get your name out there. Publish articles, record podcasts, give speeches, organize webinars and so on. The objective is to establish yourself as a thought leader. Clients are willing to pay for genuine expertise, and if you're the go-to expert in your field, you'll stand out from your competitors. A media strategy is especially important if you're building a niche because you need to be able to demonstrate a mastery of your subject matter.

Commit to it

There's no way around it — establishing a media presence requires a lot of time and effort. The key is to repurpose your ideas in as many formats as possible. Thus a white paper becomes a series of articles, a speech, a webinar and a workshop. It will still take time, but the return on investment is significant. This list summarizes the types of media most useful to accountants:

- **Press releases:** A press release is a short statement about a recent piece of news. Press releases should always be timely and news-driven. For example, a practice combination announcement might warrant a press release.
- **Media source:** Be the person whom the press interviews when they need to talk with an expert about a particular topic. To get on the radar of local media outlets, send them your contact information and a summary of your topic expertise.
- **Articles:** Contribute articles to outside publications to build your professional reputation. When pitching an article, aim for ideas that are innovative, insightful and interesting. If a publication has already written five stories about a new SEC rule, don't propose a sixth.
- **Blog posts:** You can start your own blog or contribute to an existing blog. Either way, for blogging to be an effective strategy, you need to write regularly. It also helps to stick to a common theme, rather than bouncing around too much. You want to give readers a reason to keep coming back to your blog.
- **Social media:** Facebook, Twitter, LinkedIn, Google+, etc. For more on social media, see earlier in this chapter.
- **Podcasts:** Podcasts might cover much of the same material as blog posts, but a podcast will be an audio or video file, not a written post. People can listen to podcasts on their phones, music players or computers. Stick to a single topic in each podcast and keep it simple. Again, you'll want to create a regular series to build your brand.
- **Webinars:** Webinars are online seminars that can be attended by a large number of virtual participants. They're a great way to establish your expertise and can drive sales more effectively than more passive forms of communication. For example, you might create a webinar

planning series where you address a different planning topic at each seminar.

- **Speaking and presenting:** Putting yourself at the front of the room is a surefire way to build credibility. Choose an interesting topic, but keep it simple. For more on public speaking, see presentations earlier in this chapter. You can also lead workshops or roundtable discussions.
- **White papers:** A white paper is a comprehensive report that helps readers understand a topic. Because white papers are time-intensive, choose your white paper topics wisely. Today people often prefer content in a shorter and more digestible form.

Put it on paper

Your ultimate goal is to reach as many people as you can. If, like me, you're not the greatest writer, here's a simple process to help convert your ideas into polished prose. It basically follows the format that we followed in writing this book:

1. **Create a template.** You're writing for someone who is less knowledgeable on the topic than you are. To simplify the topic, create a simple content generation template like this:

Topic	Your subject matter
Preamble	Relevant background that adds perspective
What	A basic description of the subject matter
Who	A description of who you're writing for
Why	An explanation detailing why the topic is important and why the topic is particularly relevant now
How	The steps, the process, the things you want them to do
Key takeaways	The three things you want them to remember from the content

2. **Get it down on paper.** Don't waste time trying to wordsmith your thoughts. Just start writing. Group your thoughts under the appropriate headers in the template and don't worry about repeating yourself. The key is to get your source content into a format that can be edited.
3. **Pick an initial format.** My recommendation is to start with a 1-2 page piece that can be easily communicated in multiple formats (newsletter, blog post, podcast, etc). Resist the temptation to write an opus. While having more content gives you greater flexibility from a repurposing standpoint, the sheer time commitment is an unnecessary barrier. Also, people are less inclined to read lengthy narratives these days.
4. **Work with a writer.** If you were not blessed with natural writing ability, consider working with a writer to convert your thoughts into finished content. If you don't have someone on staff to fill that role, hire a freelance writer. In auditioning writers, be sure to give them a

demonstration test that mirrors the type of written assignment you'll be giving them in the future. Have them interview you to get you to elaborate on areas that require more detail.

5. **Consider your repurposing options.** Armed with your finished 1-2 page piece, think about ways to repurpose the content. Include it in your company enewsletter, send it to relevant publications, convert it into a video and post to your firm's YouTube channel, or break the article into 140-character chunks and communicate it daily via social media. You've already invested the time and money to create the content; now try to make sure that it reaches as many people as possible.

6. **Make an ongoing commitment.** Becoming a thought leader requires persistence and repetition. With every innovative, insightful, interesting impression, your reputation will grow as a go-to resource on the topic in question. Do this well over a sustained period of time and you will no longer need to create your own media, the media will come to you.

Key takeaways

To devise a media strategy:

- Focus on innovative, insightful and interesting content.
- Repurpose your ideas in as many formats as possible.
- Position yourself as a thought leader in your field.

ADVERTISING

Advertising helps you build awareness, gain credibility and target your message to a specific audience. Most local or regional accounting firms aren't going to create an ongoing ad campaign, but you might consider spending on advertising if you are building a niche or if your firm is undergoing significant change, such as combining with another practice. For most firms, that will mean placing targeted ads in regional print and electronic media.

Hit a home run

What makes a great ad? Think about your personal favorites, and you'll realize there are a few unifying principles. Great ads are:

- **Targeted.** They speak to a specific ideal client. When your ideal client reads your ad, they should relate to the storyline, subject matter and characters. You want an ad that resonates with its target audience.
- **Creative.** The best ads use intelligence or humor to communicate their message.
- **Compelling.** Ads don't just educate and inform; they cause you to act. That's why every infomercial ends with the immortal words: "Here's how to order."

Aim for picture perfect

In creating low-budget print and electronic ads, adhere to this basic formula:

1. **Decide on your message.** Draw on your issue-solution-benefit narrative to craft an ad that speaks to your firm's competitive advantage and claims. Start by identifying an issue that is common among your prospective clients, discuss how you'll solve the problem and explain how your clients will benefit. Infomercials do a great job of establishing this "case" in 60 seconds or less. In scene 1, an item breaks and disastrous consequences ensue; in scene 2, the advertised product is tested, often in a situation that exceeds normal use; in scene 3, a happy customer enjoys a better experience as a result. For example, your ad might target prospective clients who are unhappy about the rate of staff turnover at their current firm.

Issue	Staff turnover
Solution	Our annual turnover rate for staff, seniors, supervisors, managers and senior managers is 6%, half that of our competitors.
Benefit	You see the same people year after year. Our people will know your business inside and out and you won't have to continuously educate new staff about your operations. The time savings to you are considerable!

2. **Pick a visual.** Choose an eye-catching visual that will dominate the page. In most cases, you'll want an image with a person as the focal point. When viewers glance at the image, they should immediately understand the problem you're promising to solve. If you want, you can supplement the image with no more than 10 words to set the scene, often by asking a question ("Sick of never seeing the same accountant twice?"). It's important to know that there are plenty of royalty-free image sites that offer suitable stock photos for less than $10 per image.

3. **Choose your words wisely.** State your solution to the issue in 10 words or less. Explain how the client will benefit in 10 words or less. Tell the viewer where to go to get more information. Here's an example of what an ad might look like:

Struggling to Save More Money?

Let us help you create an easy-to-follow plan that'll give you the knowledge and tools you need to prosper.

Call us at (insert number) or visit us at (insert website) to learn more.

Another option: membership listings

In addition to placing graphic ads, you might consider listing your firm in membership directories. This could be offered for free as part of an association membership or you may have to pay an additional fee. These listings aren't graphic ads, so you have a little more text to work with. When writing copy for these listings, it's important to articulate three things: your areas of service, your ideal client profile and your competitive advantage and claims. Many firms spend too much space talking about what they do, and not enough explaining what makes them different from the competition.

Key takeaways

Create ads that:

- Are targeted, creative and compelling.
- Support your competitive advantage and claims.
- Are visually engaging. Supplement the image with words that help to tell the story and compel the reader to act.

EVENTS

Events are a way to get your name out there and to bring people together, and as such should play an important role in your overarching marketing strategy. Firm-sponsored events most often include business-to-business mixers, business-to-client mixers and virtual events such as webinars. Because we've discussed the individual event types elsewhere in the book, this chapter focuses on how to get the most out of your events.

Party like it's 1999

There are a myriad of benefits to throwing events, from increasing brand awareness, to fostering new connections and boosting morale. Events are a great opportunity to connect people from across your network, including employees, clients, prospective clients, vendors, strategic alliance partners and referral sources. Good things can happen when you get people together. Events also build your public image. They're a way to celebrate your successes and increase your exposure. They'll get people talking about you and may even generate press coverage.

Get up and boogie

Follow these suggestions to get the most out of your events:

- **Partner up.** If you struggle to get people to attend your events, partner with another organization such as a strategic alliance partner to double your potential audience.
- **Offer compelling events.** If the idea is interesting, topical or unique, people will come.
- **State the benefits outright.** Make sure the value proposition of your event is clear. If one of the benefits of attendance is the chance to network with fellow professionals, make that clear in your collateral.
- **Top X lists are always good.** Spell out the reasons to come quickly and clearly. At this event, you'll learn 1), 2) and 3).
- **Promote like crazy.** You don't want to annoy people, but one email invitation won't get the job done. Use multiple types of media to remind people repeatedly leading up to the event. Persistence pays off. And make your invitation compelling. Invitees are more likely to take notice of a well-written, well-designed invitation, versus one that was thrown together with little creative consideration.
- **Utilize social media.** Don't just send out an email invite. Promote your event on Facebook, Twitter, LinkedIn and so on to raise awareness.
- **Make registration seamless.** Use technology to make it easy to sign up and add guests.
- **Run great events.** There's no better way to get people to future events than by throwing a great event. Put on a stellar show and people will not only come back but they'll also tell others.

- **Record the event.** Especially for informational events, record the proceedings so you can repurpose the content into a podcast, video clip or blog post.
- **Follow up.** This is the most important part. To get the most out of your event, you have to follow up with attendees. Give them a call to thank them for coming and to restart the conversation.

Key takeaways

Throwing events is a way to:

- Promote your firm's personality. This is especially important if your competitive advantage and claims highlight your people or culture.
- Add depth and substance to your pitch. Other marketing elements like your website and collateral are important, but they're one-dimensional. Events help define who you are.
- Cross-pollinate multiple constituencies and instill a sense of pride in both employees and clients.

CHAPTER 6
REFERRALS

There's no better way to think about referrals than these words by entrepreneur Bo Bennett: "In sales, a referral is the key to the door of resistance." Without referrals, everyone starts from the same place. With a referral, you're off the mark and 50 yards down the track before the starting gun goes off. Earning these valuable referrals depends on reciprocity — you send business to a contact, they send business to you and everyone wins. As more successful referrals are exchanged, the relationship grows and you become collaborators, part of an extended team of trusted professionals.

In this chapter, we emphasize the importance of reciprocation, rewards and recognition and offer tips for how to cultivate referral sources. Individual topics include:

- **Referral piece:** A referral piece is a one- to two-page document that describes who your ideal client is and explains why you and your firm are a good fit for your ideal client.
- **Referral meeting process:** The referral meeting process provides a roadmap to follow when meeting with referral sources. By following a defined process, you can leave each meeting with specific commitments.
- **Referral email:** Introducing others is an important part of solidifying your value to your contacts. Take care when writing an introductory email and make sure to steward the introduction to ensure a successful connection.
- **Referral agreement:** A referral agreement is a formal agreement to compensate an individual for referring new business to your firm.
- **Referral program:** A referral program rewards and recognizes individuals who are important sources of new business for you. By thanking others for their help and reciprocating with referrals, you build an enduring relationship and a steady stream of new business.

- **Referral letter:** A referral letter is a letter sent by more junior staff to friends and family to ask for their help in finding new business.
- **Referral tracking:** Keep track of all business generated from referrals. Allocate your time to helping your best referral sources.

REFERRAL PIECE

A referral piece is a document that can be distributed to referral sources and that addresses three critical pieces of information: who your ideal client is, why you are a good fit for your ideal client and why your firm is a good fit for your ideal client.

A source of clarity

If referral sources don't know what kind of clients you want, they won't be able to consistently provide you with high-quality referrals. A referral piece is designed to solve that disconnect. It encourages firms to clarify their competitive advantage and to form a clear picture of their ideal client. By communicating that vision to referral sources, firms ensure that they aren't wasting their time chasing prospective clients who aren't a good fit.

Know yourself

A referral piece should be a one- to two-page document that can be distributed in print or sent electronically to a referral source. To see a sample, visit our website to read my referral piece (www[26]). Follow these steps to develop a well-written and well-thought-out referral piece:

- **Define your ideal client.** Your ideal client profile should include both quantitative and qualitative measures (www[5]). Quantitative measures include income, net worth, business revenue and number of employees. Qualitative measures include issues the client is trying to solve, specific product needs they have and intangibles like "pays their bills on time." The ideal client profile should not be so specific that it's nearly impossible to find matching prospects. If you serve multiple constituencies, you should provide an ideal client description for each (for example, you might create an ideal client profile for both brokers and hedge funds).
- **Highlight your talents.** Focus on your skills and how you use those skills to help your clients. Don't regurgitate your resume by listing where you went to school and what organizations you belong to; talk about what makes you a valuable asset for your clients. Use the information you learned from the Gallup StrengthsFinder profile to connect your talents to the skills that clients want (see the know your strengths topic in the management chapter for information on the Gallup StrengthsFinder profile).
- **Emphasize the firm's competitive advantage.** Connect your firm with the skills and expertise that the client is seeking. Talk about the specific services you would provide to your ideal client, as well as the firm's ability to serve the client's broader needs. The pitch should be customized to the specific situation (for example, if your ideal client is a green technology company, talk about the firm's competitive advantage in the green technology space, versus the broader technology arena).

- **Use it well.** Your end product should be a polished document that adheres to your firm's graphic standards and includes contact information and your photo. The content should be organized into three areas: about your ideal client, about you and about your firm. Create a low-resolution version for electronic use and a high-resolution version to print. Usually the information included in a referral piece is conveyed verbally to referral sources during a face-to-face meeting (at the same time, ask the referral sources about their ideal client and competitive advantage so you can send referrals to them as well). After the meeting, send an electronic copy of your referral piece. It will provide the referral source with a tangible reminder of your conversation.

Get rid of the guesswork

By defining who your ideal client is and conveying that vision to others, you'll take the guesswork out of referrals. You'll provide clarity to your referral sources about who is the best fit for you. When a "C"-level referral comes along, you won't waste time chasing them. And when an ideal client comes knocking, you'll be able to explain clearly why you and your firm are the best fit. Plus, by applying the same strategy in directing referrals to others, you'll make valuable connections for other people, who in turn will send high-quality referrals to you.

Key takeaways

To get the most out of a referral piece:

- Know your client. You need to clearly define your ideal client so that you know and others know whom you're looking for.
- Sell yourself. It's not just about your firm. Potential clients want to know you and trust that you're the right person to address their needs.
- Sell your firm. A client may come in for one thing and need another down the line. You want to convey what your firm does best.

REFERRAL MEETING PROCESS

The referral meeting process outlines how to spend your time cultivating referral sources. The process is designed to ensure that both parties cover the relevant information and leave with specific commitments to move the relationship forward.

Avoid endless chitchat

Consider how most referral meetings go. Two people meet for lunch and chitchat for a few minutes, neglecting to look at the menu by the time the waiter returns. Eventually they get down to business and after some discussion, one person looks at their watch and realizes 55 minutes have passed, yet little progress has made been. The parties hurriedly try to save the meeting by generating tangible next steps. Most often, however, this involves scheduling another meeting to do what they should have done the first time. The referral meeting process aims to weed out this inefficiency, so that you accomplish your business development objectives at each and every referral meeting. Adhering to the referral meeting process allows you to make the best use of the time available, to weed out suspects from prospects and to avoid an endless string of fruitless meetings.

Guide the conversation

To get more out of referral source meetings, you have to prepare beforehand, skillfully guide the conversation and follow up afterward. Before each meeting, know what you want to achieve from the meeting to move the sales process forward. Send the referral source an email summarizing your goals. For example, "I'm looking forward to learning more about you, your business and your business development efforts so we can explore ways to help each other grow our respective businesses."

During the meeting, focus on the other person for half the time — their current situation, their wants, their needs and their objectives. Then turn the attention to yourself. It's not enough for one person to come out of the meeting with a long list of prospective clients; you want to navigate the meeting agenda so it's productive for both parties. Here's how to guide the conversation:

1. **Relationship (10% of total time):** Start with general open-ended conversation starters to get to know the individual or to catch up on what's new. You might discuss family, life, shared interests or work-related topics. The goal is to establish a conversational tone to the meeting. You want both people to feel at ease.

2. **Current situation (15% of total time):** Ask broad business-related questions such as, "How's business been for you lately?" or "What have you been doing to generate new business in this economy?" Ask specific follow-up questions when relevant. For example, if they share ways they've been trying to generate new business, you may follow

up with, "How successful has that been?" or "In what ways has that helped you?"

3. **Value proposition (25% of total time):** Ask them how you can help grow their business. Usually this conversation will focus on referring prospective clients and referral sources or providing a specific expertise or service to clients. Most often, client referrals will dominate the conversation. Before proffering names, ask them to answer the following questions to help you better match them to a prospective client:

   - Who is your ideal client?
   - Why are you a good fit for your ideal client?
   - Why is your firm a good fit for your ideal client?

4. **Plan (5% of total time):** Tell them how you plan to help them. Identify prospective clients and suitable referral sources if appropriate.

5. **Next steps (5% of total time):** Tell them what you plan to do after the meeting to follow up on the conversation. For example, you can offer to contact prospective clients and referral sources to gauge their interest in speaking with the individual.

6. **Switch the spotlight (40% of total time):** Up to this point in the conversation, the focus has been entirely on them; now it's time to shift the conversation to your wants, needs and objectives. If they don't instinctively segue to asking about your current situation, take the lead yourself. You might say: "If you don't mind, let me take a few minutes to talk about me, my business and how you can help me." Tell them if you would like them to refer prospective clients or referral sources or to provide a specific expertise or service. Share your referral piece to help them understand your ideal client, your personal value proposition and your firm's competitive advantage (see previous topic). Then it's time to ask the critical question, "Can you think of anyone?" Depending on the referral source's personality, it's up to you to decide how direct you want to be. Introverts don't like being put on the spot, in which case, ask them to consider your request and tell them you'll call in a week to see if they've thought of anyone. Extroverts (like me) won't mind a more direct approach, in which case, you should pause once you've asked the question and wait for their response. If they offer names, write them down and ask if you can contact the people directly or if they would prefer to pass your information along.

After the meeting, send them an email that day summarizing what both of you committed to do. Be sure to follow up within a reasonable timeframe if you haven't heard back from them or established a next step. It's okay to be persistent.

Key takeaways

When meeting with referral sources:

- Establish clear objectives going into the meeting.
- Follow a defined meeting process to ensure objectives and goals are met for both parties.
- Summarize commitments at the end of the meeting and send a follow-up email that day.

REFERRAL EMAIL

There are two types of referral emails: one in which you introduce two people to each other and one in which a third party introduces you to someone else. Both types of emails should be well crafted, substantial and informative to ensure that a successful connection ensues. Don't think of an introductory referral as a throwaway email — it's a chance to spark a valuable connection, and that deserves thought and effort.

Introducing others

Introducing two people in your network isn't a task to be taken lightly. You are helping your contacts and solidifying your value in the process. An introductory email deserves time and effort, yet too often an email is fired off without a second thought.

A well-written introductory email should be:

- **Substantial:** Tell each person something substantial about the other person. It should include a link to each person's bio and website.
- **Detailed:** Establish common ground between the two people. Try to include three details about each person.
- **Personal:** Include a personal testimonial for each person.
- **Forward-looking:** Attempt to steward the conversation beyond the email.

Here is an example of a poorly written introduction:

> "James, meet Julia. Julia is a writer and just moved to Denver. Feel free to talk among yourselves."

Here is an example of a well-written introduction:

> "James, meet Julia. Julia, meet James.
>
> James is a senior manager at [insert firm name]. He's developed several successful niche practices at the firm, most recently with education-focused non-profits. You can learn more about James at [insert website here] and about his firm at [insert website here]. James spends most of his free time volunteering in his neighborhood or climbing mountains and is the owner of the most adorable golden retriever you'll ever meet. James and I are both board members at a local charity, and he's a real visionary when it comes to growing an organization. James' firm is growing rapidly — they've recently acquired two other firms — and James is looking for someone to help rebrand the firm and revamp their marketing materials.
>
> Julia is a wonderfully talented writer who just moved to Denver with her husband, two sons and their black lab. Her work has been published in the Wall Street Journal, Forbes and just

about every other business publication you can name. You can learn more about her at [insert website here] and read some of her recent work at [insert website here]. Julia covered the 2008 financial meltdown in New York, before moving to Brussels to write about the euro crisis. She's a wine and cheese expert, a motorcycle enthusiast and reads more books than anyone else I know. She is new to the area and looking to start her own writing and marketing business.

I think it would be advantageous for the two of you to connect. Feel free to copy me on correspondence and let me know if there's anything else I can do to facilitate this introduction."

Being introduced

The same principles apply when you ask someone to introduce you to someone else. You want that person to draft a thoughtful email that helps spark a connection. To facilitate this, provide the other person with a copy of what you would like them to include about you. They can always tweak it as necessary, but it's helpful to give them a nudge.

An email introduction should include three parts:

- **Connection:** The first part should explain how you and the referral source know each other. It might explain how you've helped the referral source directly, or how the referral source has witnessed how you've helped others.
- **Summary:** The second part should explain what you do, who you do it for and why you're different. Include both personal and professional information.
- **Testimonial:** The third part should include an endorsement of you. The referral source should explain why they think the other person should value the introduction.

In the example above, if James were asking for an introduction, he would send the following text to the person making the introduction:

"James is a senior manager at [insert firm name]. He has successfully developed several niche practices at the firm, most recently with education-focused non-profits. He's made a name for himself in the accounting world and regularly presents at conferences on how to develop a niche. You can learn more about his work at [insert website here]. Outside of work, he volunteers at a foundation that raises money for local schools."

The person making the introduction would then add personalized content, including an explanation of their connection to James, a testimonial to the quality of his work and a call to action that explains why it would be advantageous for the two individuals to meet.

To see another example of how to write a referral email, visit our website to read my own referral email (www[27]).

Key takeaways

Writing well-crafted introductory emails will:

- Represent you well in dealings with your professional contacts.
- Successfully steward connections among your contacts.
- Lead to others helping you make valuable connections in the future.

REFERRAL AGREEMENT

A referral agreement compensates an individual for introducing the firm to prospective clients. Most of these individuals do not work in accounting or related fields, but instead are people who network for a living; they make valuable connections among people they know and get paid for it.

Outsource the handshaking

It takes a lot of time to convert professional contacts into reliable referral sources. A referral agreement is a way to pay someone else to do that legwork, so the firm receives a steady flow of new business without committing significant resources to finding prospective clients.

The right fit

To reap the benefits from a referral agreement you need to find the right person and provide a clear idea of your ideal client. You also need to make sure the terms of the agreement are clear. Follow these steps when entering into a referral agreement:

- **Identify a suitable candidate.** Find an individual with the appropriate contacts and knowledge who wishes to be paid for connecting you with ideal clients.
- **Agree on the referral process.** To get the most value out of a referral agreement, you need to provide a clear description of your ideal client, including quantitative considerations such as income and net worth and qualitative considerations such as niche relevance and business growth. The referral source is usually tasked with initiating an introduction between the prospective client and the firm. Once that introduction is made, the referral source steps back and plays no role in selling the firm's services. Be sure that you are clear about what happens if the referral isn't a good fit.
- **Decide on compensation.** There are a number of options for compensating referral sources. Fixed, percentage and commission fees should only be paid upon receipt of payment from the client; you do not want to be advancing payment on unpaid fees. Often a mix of the following is appropriate:
  - *Introductory fee:* A nominal fee paid to the referral source for initiating an introduction with a promising prospect.
  - *Fixed fee:* A flat fee paid to the referral source once the prospect becomes a client.
  - *Percentage fee:* A variable fee paid to the referral source based on the value of the initial client transaction.
  - *Commission fee:* An ongoing commission fee based on the value of transactions between the firm and the client over a specified period. Be sure to factor in profitability in deciding on commissions (for example, tax versus audit, or recurring versus nonrecurring).

- **Generate and sign a referral agreement.** Most referral agreements detail the services to be provided, the amount of time for which the agreement is valid, the compensation terms, the conditions for terminating the contract and any confidentiality restrictions. You should download and customize your referral agreement from a reputable source and consult your attorney to ensure it contains all necessary provisions.
- **Track referrals.** Provide the referral source with ongoing reports about the status of the business they referred. You should tell the referral source where you are with each prospect in the sales process, what type of work you expect to perform for the client and how much you expect to bill. By providing this information, you'll ensure the referral source continues to provide "A"-level introductions. It's especially important to track referrals when you've agreed to pay an ongoing commission fee.

Key takeaways

Formalizing a referral agreement will:

- Save you time and effort. You can pay someone to find your ideal clients for you; all you have to do is close the deal.
- Help you meet the right kind of clients. These referral sources are connecting every day with the kind of clients you want to serve.
- Provide a steady pipeline of introductions. It's in everyone's best interest when the referral source introduces you to someone who turns into a client.

REFERRAL PROGRAM

The goal of a referral program is to provide a systematic approach to generating and recognizing referrals in any form, whether from employees, clients, business contacts, friends or others. The process can be formal or informal, and should be based around the Three R's: recognize, reward and reciprocate. You want to **recognize** people who are driving new business to you, **reward** them for their efforts and **reciprocate** by sending referrals to them as well.

Let others help you

A referral program is an inexpensive way to gain new clients because it draws on the experiences of others who know you and your product. One-time referral sources often turn into repeat referral sources, giving you a pipeline of new opportunities without the wasted effort of more traditional techniques like warm-calling. And remember to do good work or the referrals will dry up quickly.

Set up a structure

Referrals are key to gaining new business, and the referral program is designed to ensure that you have a steady flow of referrals coming into your firm. The reward program doesn't have to be based on a strict dollar-for-dollar formula, but it should recognize individuals who are helping grow your business. Follow these key steps to make sure your referral sources don't go unnoticed:

1. **Get out the word.** If your business relies on word-of-mouth referrals, let people know. They'll mention you when it's appropriate and be glad to contribute to your success.
2. **Recognize the referral source.** As soon as you learn that someone has sent a prospective client your way, call and thank them for the referral. Let them know you'll be in touch and follow up to tell them how it turned out. You can also invite them to participate in the client solicitation process — most won't accept but they'll appreciate the invitation. And if they are interested, they can provide an invaluable testimonial about you to the prospective client.
3. **Send a note.** Within 48 hours, you should send a genuine and personal thank-you note. If it's the first time they've referred someone to you, include a small personalized gift (for example, a sleeve of golf balls for a golfer or an iTunes gift card for a music lover).
4. **Keep them updated.** Let them know once you've connected with the prospective client. Update them on how the meeting went and thank them again.
5. **Reward them.** Send the referral source a more substantial gift if their introduction produces a new client for you (for example, tickets to a game for a sports fan). Include a handwritten note to thank them for

the referral and briefly summarize the work you'll be doing, without disclosing confidential details.

6. **Reciprocate the referral.** The best way to drive referrals to your firm is to keep a steady flow of referrals going out. If you've referred work to someone, they're more likely to refer work to you. Invite the referral source to lunch to learn about what they're looking for in an ideal client. Use that information to introduce them to potential clients or others who might help them. Remember, reciprocity isn't always a one-to-one exchange. Some referral sources just want to know their clients are being well served.

7. **Welcome them to the family.** Keep the referral source apprised of developments in your firm and add them to your communications database if they would like. Invite them to firm events and consider asking them to a business development meeting to share their experience as a referral source.

8. **Track your referrals.** Create a database to track the number and dollar value of referrals in and out. Calculate your referral conversion (percentage of referrals that become actual clients) and use that information to improve your approach to referrals. Report on your referral successes in business development meetings. Identify commonalities among your best referral sources and use that to improve your cultivation of other referral sources.

Key takeaways

To create an effective referral program:

- Recognize individuals who send business to you. This can be as simple as a heartfelt note, but don't let their efforts go unnoticed.
- Reward others for helping you. If a referral turns into real business, do something nice for the referral source. You don't need strict rules that correlate specific gifts with dollar amounts, but send something they'll appreciate.
- Reciprocate referrals. The best way to keep referrals coming your way is to send referrals to others.

REFERRAL LETTER

A referral letter is a letter sent by staff accountants (more junior staff) to friends and family to ask for their help in finding new business. It's a great way to kick-start a staff accountant's business development effort, as contacting people they know is often easier than joining an organization or walking into a room full of strangers.

A place to start

Staff accountants usually haven't had the chance to establish a network of professional contacts. They may be young, or new to the firm, or they may not have taken the CPA exam yet. Business development prowess is a great way for them to get noticed at their firm and start climbing the career ladder, but without many professional contacts, they often don't know where to start. We suggest that staff accountants begin by mining their personal lives for potential contacts. By considering who they know from each chapter of their life — childhood, college, first job, etc — they'll likely realize they already know a significant number of people who can help them bring in business.

Make your case

Follow these steps to craft a referral letter:

1. **Identify contacts.** A business development coach or mentor should interview the staff accountant to document the chapters in their life and identify potential referral contacts in each chapter. These are individuals who would be willing to open and read the letter and talk over the phone or in person to discuss any opportunities. Potential referral contacts include college classmates, family friends and former colleagues, among many others.
2. **Craft a letter.** Write a letter that makes the case for why they should help (www[28]). It's often helpful to frame the request as asking for support: "I have been very grateful for your friendship and support in the past, and I could again use your help as I work to demonstrate my business development skills. I hope you might be willing to help me find new clients or to refer me to individuals who could connect me with potential clients. It would go a long way in helping me take the next step in my career."
3. **Set meetings.** Mail the letter to all the contacts you have identified. Make appropriate follow-up contact and, for qualified candidates, try to set up calls or meetings with a senior person in your firm. Let that person do the heavy lifting. The staff accountant is merely the booking agent.
4. **Coach for success.** Coach the individual regularly around what's working, what's not and how to do it better. When they succeed, make a big deal about it. Make an announcement at the business development meeting, publicize their success in your firm business development

report, give them "lead generator" credit in your sales database and send them a thank-you note and a gift voucher. In short, reward the behavior you want to instill.

Key takeaways

Consider these tips to help staff accountants start to generate business:

- A staff accountant doesn't need to have a deep rolodex to generate a list of referral source contacts. If they build their case around helping them advance in their career, family and friends will only be too happy to help.
- The letter is merely the conversation starter. It's nothing more than "junk mail" unless follow-up contact is made in a timely manner.
- Jump up and down when they succeed. You only have one chance to make a first impression so make it a great one. Shine the spotlight brightly.

REFERRAL TRACKING

Referral sources can be clients, colleagues, wheels of influence, centers of influence, strategic alliance partners or association contacts, among others. Whoever they are, it's important to track the business referred to and received from each referral source. Most importantly, you want to record the number and dollar value of referral opportunities.

Keep a ledger

Referrals are built on reciprocity. If your database says that a referral source has brought more business to you than you have to them, or vice versa, it may be time to get the equation back in balance. And once you start tracking referrals in and out, it will be easy to grasp who your best referral sources are. You want to allocate your time and resources to helping the people who are helping you.

Money in, money out

Most sales databases allow you to easily record the business you give to and receive from referral sources. If you don't have a sales database, consider using a spreadsheet to keep track of referrals (www[3]). Follow these tips for tracking your referral sources:

- **Draft a master list.** Create a list of all your referral sources. Categorize each referral source by type (client, colleague, strategic alliance partner, etc) and industry (accountant, attorney, banker, etc). When possible, include further industry categorization (for attorneys: business attorney, litigation attorney, immigration attorney, etc). Classify each referral source as "A"-level, "B"-level or "C"-level so you know where to prioritize your efforts.
- **Track referrals in and out.** Record the number and dollar values of referrals given and received from each referral source. Track whether a source's referrals actually resulted in new business. This will help identify which referral sources produce high-quality leads.
- **Follow up.** If you've given a referral, follow up to ask if the referral source was able to convert the opportunity and what the referral equated to in dollar terms.
- **Stay in balance.** Keep a running total of net number and dollar value of referrals (given minus received). Try to balance that number as much as possible. Note: Some referral sources simply want to make sure their clients are well cared for; in these cases, you don't need to be concerned about evening the score.

Make sure you keep the information up-to-date and keep an eye out for imbalances. Update it after every business development meeting referral discussion and produce a monthly report that ranks your referral sources by the number and dollar value of referrals given. Use the information to talk about best practices: What are you or others doing to cultivate your best referral sources? What behaviors can you replicate?

One of the biggest benefits of this system is that you will have a created a comprehensive list of professional contacts. Your database should be the go-to resource for members of your firm to consult when asked by a client to refer a professional contact (for example, "Do you know any immigration attorneys?"). Everyone needs to know how to access the information in the database.

Remember to recognize and reward your best referral sources accordingly, whether in the form of a thank-you card, a personalized gift or ongoing invitations to special informational and hospitality events (see earlier in this chapter for more on how to recognize your referral sources).

Key takeaways

Tracking referrals:

- Tells you where to invest your time and resources when generating referrals for others.
- Provides a best practice roadmap to help the firm generate more referral traffic as a whole.
- Helps you to build a list of endorsed professional contacts the entire firm can access when a client requests a professional referral.

CHAPTER 7
NETWORKING

Networking: it's the oatmeal of business development. You know it's good for you, but more often than not, you end up choosing something else. Yet networking is a crucial part of business development; it's not just something you do if you have time. Who you know is just as important as what you know. My natural instinct used to be to stand in the corner and keep to myself, but I've taught myself how to network effectively. I know what it feels like to stand uncomfortably in a room of strangers, but I also know how to overcome that fear and end up walking away from a conversation with a tangible gain. After all, if we have to endure another evening of cheap wine and rubber chicken, why not have a little fun doing it!

In this chapter, we discuss types of networking events, a process for organizing your networking efforts and offer suggestions for how to work the room. Individual topics include:

- **Networking calendar:** Track all your firm's networking commitments in one place.
- **B2B mixers:** These events are a great opportunity to showcase your firm's expertise and to establish connections with other individuals and firms.
- **B2C mixers:** Get to know your clients in a new setting. Offer informational events to better educate clients about important topics. Throw hospitality events like holiday parties so everyone can mix and mingle in a relaxed setting.
- **B2B groups:** Join these groups to meet valuable referral sources. Be discerning about finding a good group, and focus on forging worthwhile relationships that will result in new business for both parties.
- **Industry and trade associations:** Interact with your peers, prospective clients and industry experts in a friendly environment. You'll build brand recognition while learning about your competition.

- **Boards:** Joining the board of a non-profit can be a great way to meet potential "A"-level clients. And you get to do some good in the process.
- **Networking tools and techniques:** A series of suggestions for how to get the most out of networking events.

NETWORKING CALENDAR

A networking calendar tracks all of the firm's networking activities in a single place. Commitments that belong on the calendar include business-to-business mixers, business-to-client informational and hospitality events, business-to-business groups, industry and trade association events and board meetings. Managing the calendar should be the responsibility of a sole individual, either the firm's office manager, business development coordinator or administrative assistant.

Get your money's worth

Firms spend untold dollars investing in memberships and events; a networking calendar helps make the most of that money. Many firms incorrectly assume that individuals are making the most of their networking opportunities, yet in reality other priorities often take precedence and networking events get lost in the shuffle. With a networking calendar, all your networking events will be catalogued in one place and there will be a designated person to make sure that events are suitably attended, attendees are well prepared and appropriate follow-up takes place.

Keep all your ducks in a row

First, decide who will coordinate the calendar. Whoever you select, they will need access to everyone's calendar. Managing the calendar involves three main tasks:

- **Identify the opportunities.** Anyone with business development responsibilities will already have made networking commitments. It's the administrator's job to record everyone's commitments and add them to the calendar. This includes networking groups, board meetings, firm-sponsored events and so on. Next, the administrator needs to determine if the firm is using its resources well and assign attendance accordingly (for example, the administrator should step in if 10 people are attending a business-to-client mixer, while everyone is skipping the trade association meeting on the same night).
- **Make the most of it.** Succeeding at a networking event is about more than showing up. The administrator should make sure that attendees are well prepared for these events by providing advance materials like attendance lists. Attendees should arrive with an ample supply of business cards and should have a list of people they want to meet (for more networking tips, see later in this chapter). Afterward, the administrator can help facilitate the appropriate follow-up.
- **Monetize the investment.** Firms spend huge amounts of money on networking opportunities, but they're not all equally valuable. The administrator should keep track of the outcomes of all networking events by recording contacts made, leads initiated, opportunities generated, etc. The goal is to come up with a dollar figure for the value you

received from a specific membership or event. Use this information each year to determine which networking resources are most effective.

Key takeaways

Having a central networking calendar helps you:

- Keep track of your commitments. There's little point in paying to be a member of a group if you skip every meeting. A networking calendar tracks all your commitments in one place and helps ensure events are appropriately attended.
- Maximize your investments. The staff member in charge of the calendar should make sure that attendees are well prepared and that they follow up after events.
- Spend your money better. Tracking the value of each networking commitment ensures that future networking spending reflects your return-on-investment.

B2B MIXERS

A business-to-business mixer is a great vehicle for establishing the foundation of a strategic alliance with another organization. B2B mixers provide an opportunity to showcase the depth and breadth of your firm's experience while facilitating introductions among relevant individuals. By spending an hour or two talking to members of another firm, you'll gain a sense of whether a formal or informal alliance would benefit both parties. The acronym "T.E.A.M.," or "Together Everyone Achieves More," has never been more true than in this capacity.

Erase your bad experiences

Everyone has endured a horrible B2B mixer — the longwinded introductions where every speaker drones on about where they went to school; the managing partner talking ad nauseam about how the firm got to where it is today; and the interminable amount of time spent listening to presentations. The goal here is to outline how to do away with the painful B2B mixers of your past and replace them with an event that doesn't eat away your precious time. Here is a list of before, during and after event strategies to maximize your events:

Before the event:

- **Choose participants wisely.** There should be four to 12 attendees from each firm and one firm shouldn't have significantly more attendees than the other firm. The best B2B mixers have a cross-section of "titles" and "areas of expertise" in the room. B2B mixers are a great opportunity to incorporate managers and senior managers into the business development fray as they can sharpen their networking skills in a relatively low-pressure environment.
- **Decide on a location.** The two organizations should collaborate to pick a date and location. Some groups prefer to meet over breakfast in the morning; others prefer after work during the "cocktail hour." There's no single best way. Typically one group will host the event at their office or at a client location (for example, if your client owns a restaurant or art gallery). An administrative assistant or business development coordinator should handle food and beverage needs and should set up the room to facilitate open dialogue (open space, no tables, no chairs, etc).
- **Prepare a brief presentation.** Each group should prepare a short presentation summarizing the following:
  - Who we are (elevator pitch)
  - What we do (services)
  - Who we serve (ideal client, markets, niches, etc)
  - Why we're different (competitive advantage, claims, etc)
  - How we can help you (referrals, expertise, etc)
  - How you can help us (referrals, expertise, etc)

- **Study the attendees.** The administrative assistant or business development coordinator should circulate an attendance list that includes names, titles and other biographical information. This will allow each person to target the individuals with whom they want to talk. The sponsoring firm should encourage the other party to do the same; after all, strategic alliances only work if they are mutually beneficial.

During the event:

- **1-on-1 networking:** The first 30 minutes of the event should be devoted to 1-on-1 networking. At least one individual from the host firm should be assigned to greet guests. That person should welcome each individual, give them their nametag and direct them to an appropriate person at the host firm (ideally someone who has identified them as a "person of interest"). See later in this chapter for more on getting the most out of networking events.
- **Formal presentations:** The presentation section should not exceed 30 minutes and will typically start with the host managing partner welcoming the other firm. Any introductions should be brief and should avoid name-dropping. The managing partner will then give a presentation for not more than 10 minutes (this can just be a verbal presentation or it can be accompanied by visual aids). The other firm's managing partner should repeat the process, and at the end, the host managing partner should set the stage for networking to occur by encouraging individuals to mix, socialize and enjoy the refreshments.
- **More 1-on-1 networking:** The final hour should be spent networking with more individuals from the other firm. A good B2B mixer should not last for more than two hours and individuals will typically leave at their convenience.

After the event:

- **Circulate contact information.** The administrative assistant or business development coordinator should send to the other firm a single document that lists the contact information for all the firm's attendees.
- **Send a note.** The managing partner should pen a brief note to the other firm's leader thanking them for their attendance and outlining the next steps (for example, a meeting to discuss the particulars of a formal strategic alliance or an exchange of materials or resources). This follow-up is essential. All too often, valuable conversations take place at a mixer but nothing ever comes of the investment. Converting a great conversation into a meaningful business development opportunity is the difference between a good mixer and a great mixer.

Key takeaways

B2B mixers are a great way to:

- Facilitate introductions. Key individuals from your firm can meet key individuals from another firm.
- Form an alliance. You'll learn whether there's a good fit to merit a formal or informal partnership.
- Sharpen networking skills. B2B mixers offer a relaxed small-group setting where managers and senior managers can gain experience networking.

B2C MIXERS

There are typically two types of business-to-client mixers: informational events that center on a topic of interest and hospitality events that feature a firm announcement or celebration. A talk about retirement planning is an example of an informational event while a party celebrating the end of tax season would be a great hospitality event. Both types of events give relevant constituencies — including clients, prospective clients, partners, staff, strategic alliance partners and vendors — a chance to mix and mingle.

Show off your best self

Business-to-client mixers are good news opportunities that offer a chance to convert positive feelings into business development gains. Informational events showcase your firm's intellectual knowledge and hospitality events are a way to recognize, reward and thank key contributors. In both cases, there's a tremendous value from cross-pollinating clients and prospective clients. As discussed in the testimonials topic in the marketing chapter, a recommendation from a third party can help build trust with a prospective client.

Run events like a pro

Here are a few keys to running successful informational or hospitality events:

Informational:

- **Pick topics that have broad appeal.** Time is a precious resource. Many of the people whom you invite won't come and as a result, you need to pick a topic that appeals to a broad audience. One idea is to create a "planning series" that rotates through different planning topics, including tax planning, financial planning, retirement planning and estate planning. If you have a consulting practice, consider introducing business-centric planning topics like strategic planning and exit and succession planning.
- **Draw a headliner.** The more recognizable, the more revered, the more respected the speaker, the more likely it is that your invitation will grab the reader's attention.
- **Make the event short.** Most of these events drag on far too long. An hour is about right, or an hour and a half tops. Most events include a welcome, introductions, the keynote, questions and refreshments.
- **Pick an appropriate time.** Most people want to go home at the end of the workday, and yet that's when most events take place. Consider hosting your events at unconventional times and try building the event into the conventional workday (for example, a breakfast presentation from 7:30 a.m.-9:00 a.m. or a lunch gathering from 11:30 a.m.-1:00 p.m.). You can experiment to determine what resonates with your audience.
- **Repurpose content.** If you have a keynote speaker, record the audio, synch to slides and post the presentation online to make the content

available "on demand." You can also record segments of the presentation and post to your firm-sponsored YouTube channel.

Hospitality:

- **Make it family friendly.** If you're going to throw a holiday party, add elements that appeal to the whole family. Provide activities for the kids and encourage all three generations to attend. After all, if you want to understand the totality of your clients' needs, creating an environment where you can meet their extended family can only be a good thing.
- **Build the event around other activities.** The best hospitality events I've run took place early in the evening. Attendees were able to go from there to dinner or the theater. Thus our event was the pre-party.
- **Don't mix too much business with pleasure.** The worst hospitality events are thinly veiled advertisements for the firm or one of its strategic alliance partners. It's fine to thank parties for sponsoring the event, but don't allow the sponsor to pop up a tent and start pitching. The valuable business development opportunities at these events come from 1-on-1 networking.
- **Make the event about recognition, reward and thanks.** If you're going to say a few words, make the focus about the audience — their contribution or their importance.
- **Find the host with the most.** If you have hospitality-oriented clients like restaurants or art galleries, consider hosting the event off-site. Attendees will enjoy the event more and you may help the host to drum up a little interest for their establishment. That's a win-win!

Both:

- **Create an eye-catching invitation.** Spend a few dollars creating an invitation that grabs the eye, whether in print or electronic format. One of my personal favorites was a parchment paper scroll inside a plastic bottle. It certainly stood out when it arrived in the mail. Even people who didn't come to the event remarked on how much they appreciated the invitation.
- **Remind, remind, remind!** If it takes six impressions to make a sale, think of the initial invite as impression one. Follow up repeatedly with mixed media reminders (electronic invite, print postcard, follow-up phone call, personalized email, etc). Don't be an annoyance but be persistent.
- **Publish dates in advance.** The best-attended events are promoted far in advance.
- **Follow standard networking guidelines.** Provide staff with a list of attendee bios ahead of time so they can selectively network, place hosts at all entry points to ensure guests are welcomed and directed to appropriate attendees when they arrive, and remember not to get

locked into a single conversation (see later in this chapter for more on how to network effectively).

- **Send something tangible to each attendee after the event.** For an informational event, it may be an article or a copy of the speaker's book. For a hospitality event, it may be an online photo album of the event. Use the follow-up as a way to re-engage and suggest a next step.

Key takeaways

The best business-to-client mixers are:

- Well promoted and well thought-out. You want to attract as many attendees as possible.
- Informative or fun. Attendees should feel the event is a good use of their time.
- A jumping-off point. The goal is to convert a nice conversation into a meaningful business development opportunity.

B2B GROUPS

Business-to-business groups are made up of professionals interested in growing their network and expanding their business development outreach. These groups offer a recurring opportunity to cultivate relationships with people you know, like and trust, which is crucial for subsequently generating referrals.

How to choose

As someone who has attended events sponsored by everyone from the local chamber of commerce to the local community foundation, I'm not promoting a spirit of "just do it." You want to be discerning about how you invest your time and resources. Find a group that has a limited membership of 30-100 people. It needs to be small enough to be intimate but large and broad enough to pack a networking punch. Some groups are non-industry specific (for example, a collection of accountants, bankers and consultants), while others are industry specific (for example, the Fair Value Forum or the Fair Value Exchange for valuation specialists). Most important is that they promote a sense of team; you want a group where members are asking, "How can I help you?" Look for a group that offers the following characteristics:

- They have a regular/recurring meeting schedule (anywhere from weekly to monthly).
- They limit the number of participants by professional specialty (for example, they cap the number of accountants, attorneys, engineers, etc).
- They provide opportunities for participants to "showcase or spotlight" their expertise or business.
- They provide networking opportunities that promote like, trust and credibility among members.
- They encourage additional "small-group" networking to take place outside of regularly scheduled meetings.
- Membership is driven by the membership through recommendations and referrals.
- They may or may not "keep score" of how much business is referred or generated, but they do recognize and acknowledge those in the room who are helping others.

For a sense of the kinds of groups that you might consider, check out the following groups. You don't need to join these specific groups; these are listed to provide you with a flavor for the kind of group you want.

- **BNI:** This group allows one person per specialty in each group and carefully tracks how many leads you give and receive. It exists worldwide and is relatively affordable.
- **ProVisors:** This is a smaller and more expensive option for professional service people. Each group aims for diversity among specialties, but the restrictions are less strict than at BNI.

- **The Association for Corporate Growth:** This association focuses on helping middle market companies expand their business. Business development is included, but is not the group's exclusive focus.

Senior staff might consider joining a leadership group like Vistage instead. These groups are typically smaller and focus more broadly on business issues. They still provide a sense of kinship and introduce you to people with similar interests and issues, but the focus on business development is less pronounced.

Once you've narrowed down your focus to a specific group, follow these tips to determine if it's a good fit:

- **Speak to existing members.** Ask them about their experience and inquire how helpful the group has been for networking and winning new business.
- **Guest.** Some groups allow you to guest multiple times and with multiple groups. Use those "free passes" to audition the organization and the specific group.
- **Attend the small group events.** Outside of the regularly scheduled meetings, attend a small group "breakout" meeting to see how much business development takes place in more intimate 1-on-1 and 1-on-2 settings.
- **Ask yourself the ultimate referral question.** Would you refer someone in your network to the group? Are you willing to attach your name and reputation by referring a trusted confidante to the group?

Once you've joined

Now that you've joined, you want to make the most of the opportunity:

- **You have to show up.** It's meaningless to join a great group only to attend meetings and breakout sessions sporadically. You get out what you put in.
- **Take on positions of responsibility.** You don't have to go from bus boy to president overnight but look into committee positions or volunteer to organize an event. As with association marketing, work to the front of the room!
- **Turn on the spotlight.** You only get one chance to make a first impression so when you have the chance to pitch your wares, put in the necessary time and effort to amaze.
- **Be prepared to give more than you get.** In a world of deposits and withdrawals, be the person who asks what you can do for others before you ask what they can do for you.
- **Know the big three.** Before referring a fellow member to someone in your network, be sure you can answer the three questions we discussed in the referral piece topic: Who is their ideal client? Why are they a

good fit for that client? Why is their firm a good fit? And be absolutely sure you can answer these questions about yourself when others ask.

- **Follow up.** The referral has only just begun when you offer a name. Make sure you follow up to confirm a successful connection was made between your two contacts. Your reputation is on the line and you want to be sure the person is reliable if you're going to refer them again.

Key takeaways

Business-to-business groups are a great resource because they:

- Create a recurring commitment to business development for busy accountants.
- Expand your network of professional contacts. You'll meet more people whom you can refer to your clients, thus adding value to the client relationship.
- Generate referrals. The more relevant contacts you develop, the more people who can send business to you.

INDUSTRY AND TRADE ASSOCIATIONS

A professional association is a group of individuals who work in a common field or who share business interests. An aeronautical engineer might join the Aerospace Industries Association, while an accountant might prefer the American Institute of CPAs. In targeted industries or niches, professional associations become a particularly valuable tool for business development. They're a means to expand your professional network, build your name recognition, keep abreast of the latest research in your field, increase awareness of your company and discover what your competitors are doing.

It's all who you know

The more niche focused you are, the more industry and trade associations become an important part of your overarching business development effort. Joining an association offers the following benefits:

- **Grow your network.** Associations help you grow your referral network and make connections that can help your clients. They offer an opportunity to interact with your peers, prospective clients and industry experts in a friendly environment. You have the chance to meet people whom you wouldn't otherwise meet, which is essential for growing your business. You're looking to connect with the best prospective clients or the most promising referral sources — these are the people who can really help you. The chance to network is one of the most important benefits of associations from a business development perspective.

- **Gain exposure.** The other significant business development benefit of joining associations is the chance to establish yourself as a thought leader in your field. You can use these organizations as a means toward building your own reputation and promoting your firm. If you write for a newsletter, speak at a meeting or present at a conference, people will start to recognize your name. You'll emerge as a leader in your field and you can use your membership in one association to provide you with access to other organizations.

- **Access research and resources.** Most associations provide access to resources such as journals, magazines, newsletters, case studies, white papers and books written by experts in your field. Many associations also provide certain items to their members at a reduced cost.

- **Continue your education:** Most associations host national or local conferences, which offer the opportunity to learn about best practices, hear from key achievers in your field and meet and brainstorm with others. Many also offer industry-specific certification programs.

Do your due-diligence

Don't sign up willy-nilly for just any association. First ask yourself two questions: "What benefits does this organization provide to me?" and "What can I contribute to the organization that will subsequently help me?" There are many types of professional associations you might join, from entre-preneur groups to industry associations to civic organizations like Rotary International. There are many resources online to help you find the right group, including the National Trade & Professional Associations of the United States directory published by Columbia Books, the Encyclopedia of Associations and the Associations Yellow Book published by Leadership Directories.

Maximize your investment

Many of these associations charge a fee, so you'll want to maximize your investment once you join.

- **Show up.** Make a point of attending meetings regularly. Membership requires a degree of dedication, so don't overextend yourself by joining too many associations. Focus on the ones that are most likely to yield results.
- **Practice makes perfect.** If networking doesn't come easily to you, practice your elevator pitch and points of conversation beforehand (see later in this chapter for more networking tips). Always have your business cards ready.
- **Hone in.** Network with as many members as possible before determin-ing your "A" list. Then focus your time and energy on getting to know your most promising prospects. Remember, you're on the lookout for both prospective clients and referral sources.
- **Raise your profile.** Consider taking a committee or board position, which will help you build personal connections, or raise your profile by writing, speaking or presenting. You want people to start to recognize your name. This will bring exposure to both you and your firm.
- **Follow up.** Always follow up with the people you meet and convert the time you spent meeting people into tangible business opportunities. Take advantage of opportunities to connect with other members outside of scheduled meetings. Getting to know someone is an important part of building a fruitful relationship.
- **One begets another.** Use your membership in one organization to provide you with access to other organizations. Leverage your knowl-edge and experience to speak at other meetings. Accountants are sought after as guest speakers.

Key takeaways

Joining an industry or trade association will:

- Expand your professional network.
- Provide you with valuable connections to new clients and referral sources.
- Give you a chance to raise your profile in your field by speaking, writing or presenting.

BOARDS

Board membership offers accountants a chance to serve the common good, an outlet for professional development and the opportunity to meet potential "A"-level clients. It's an ultimate win-win-win when working with the right organization and is especially important for senior accountants, who are expected to bring in top-level clients.

A win-win situation

When accountants join a networking group or a trade association, the motivation is clear — they're looking for business development gain, whether that means new clients, new referral sources or increased exposure. But the reasons for joining a non-profit board are often more altruistic. Joining a board is a way to help others and to give back. But that doesn't mean that joining a board can't also be a valuable business development strategy.

Serving on a board helps others and it helps you. The more senior you are in your firm, the more important board memberships become. Joining a board offers the following benefits:

- **Contribute to your community.** For many professionals, joining a board is a way to give back to their community. Accountants possess a unique skill set, which they can use to help a worthy cause.
- **Develop your skills.** In your role as a board member, you can develop leadership skills, hone your public speaking and sharpen your networking abilities. All of these skills will serve you well as you advance in your firm.
- **Build your network.** You'll also likely cross paths with other business leaders, who might become clients or referral sources. The people you meet through board memberships often have the potential to turn into "A"-level clients and referral sources. Many people serve on multiple boards, so membership on one board might beget contacts in another organization, exponentially growing your professional network.

In addition, boards are a valuable business development resource even if you aren't a member. If you are performing an audit for a non-profit organization, you can offer to give the board a presentation on how to interpret financial statements. You'll add value to the client relationship, bring more visibility to your firm and receive introductions to board members. You should also research whether your clients belong to any boards. They might be able to offer a valuable introduction to an organization that would be a good fit for you as a client.

Choose and commit

Accountants are a perennially popular choice when non-profit organizations are looking to fill a spot on their board. Keep these ideas in mind to get the most out of your board memberships:

- **Do your homework.** Before committing, do your research about the board and organization. Ask questions about how the leadership operates and how decisions are made and ask to sit in on a meeting. Inquire about your role and about whether you'll be expected to contribute a specific skill (for example, are they expecting free accounting advice). Talk to other board members about their opinions and experiences. Ask what they like and dislike about serving on the board. Try to answer the following questions: Does the board serve in an advisory role or does it make policy? What's the orientation process for new members? What's the relationship between the board and the staff? How are conflicts resolved? In sum, do your due-diligence to ensure you're making a good choice. Remember, you're joining a board because you want to give back so make sure you choose a board whose mission and structure aligns with what you want.
- **Rationalize the time and resource commitment.** Know what kind of time commitment is required before you commit. Some boards hold infrequent meetings while others convene monthly. Once you know what's expected, check your schedule and make sure you have time for the commitment. You may also be required to make an annual financial commitment to the organization. Make sure you have the time and money to make the commitment worth it.
- **Establish your responsibilities.** Once you've joined, take an active role. Join appropriate committees and share your expertise (for example, train the board on how to read, interpret and make decisions from the organization's financial statements). You can also help grow the board by sharing your network of contacts.

Key takeaways

Joining a board is a means to:

- Contribute to a good cause. Join something you're passionate about, and commit to helping. This shouldn't just be a line on your resume.
- Develop your skills. Like trade associations, boards offer a chance to improve skills like public speaking and writing.
- Grow your professional network. Demonstrate your skills in a new environment and you'll make valuable connections to prospective clients, referral sources and other professionals.

NETWORKING TOOLS AND TECHNIQUES

Ask a group of people whether they would rather go to a networking event or the dentist, and at least a few people would opt for the dentist's drill. But you're unlikely to meet prospective clients while flipping through magazines in the dentist's reception area.

Networking events exist to provide business professionals with the chance to meet others who serve a similar clientele. When you attend a networking event, you should keep two main goals in mind: First, you want to meet other professionals who can help your clients; and second, you want to meet other professionals who might refer new business to you. The tactics for how to succeed at a networking event remain the same whether the mixer is business-to-business or business-to-client. Here's a step-by-step approach to mastering the mixer.

Prep, prep, prep

Don't walk into a networking event without preparing. Know what you want to get out of the event and have a plan for how to achieve your goals.

- **Dress for success.** Dress appropriately for the event. Additionally, bring an ample supply of business cards and pens. They're the two most crucial tools for successful networking.
- **Practice your pitch.** Rehearse your 10-15 second elevator pitch before arriving. You want to be specific but brief. The most important thing to convey is not what you do but what value you provide to your clients.
- **Set goals.** Decide on a target for the number of contacts you want to make or the number of business cards you want to collect. Don't leave the event until you've met your goal. But networking is about more than shaking the most hands; you want to meet the right people. Identify people whom you'd like to meet and make sure to seek them out — these people could be prospective clients for your firm, thought leaders in your industry, valuable referral sources or professionals who could help your clients.

In the moment

Now you've arrived. Smile, be positive and get to work.

- **Be approachable.** This is all about positioning and demeanor. Smile, try to enjoy yourself and don't cross your arms — if you look happy and relaxed, others will be more likely to seek out your company. Acknowledge others with a smile and a nod. If your smile is reciprocated, this will be an easy introduction later in the event.
- **Guide the conversation.** Take a genuine interest in the people you meet and ask good questions. People like talking about themselves. You want to establish points of connection. Remember to give your elevator

pitch and keep the conversation going with a few simple questions: "What do you like most about what you do?" or "How did you get started in your field?" When appropriate, ask elaborative follow-up questions, and if relevant, offer a lead or referral.

- **Don't be afraid to exit.** You shouldn't spend more than 10 minutes with each person you meet. It's perfectly acceptable to excuse yourself politely after a few minutes of discussion. You can simply say "excuse me," or if it's been a productive conversation, establish the next steps and exchange contact details. You can also introduce a third party to get another conversation going while you make your exit.
- **Keep track.** Exchange business cards with the people you meet and write comments on the back of the cards you collect. This will help you remember more about the person when you follow up the next day. Ask others for two copies of their card, one to pass on to someone else and one to keep for yourself. Make sure you've brought a pocket-sized business-card file to keep track of the cards you receive.

The morning after

Shoving all those business cards into a drawer won't help. Make sure you follow up with the people you meet.

- **Create a database of contacts.** Enter each card and the social media information into your contacts database. Software programs exist to simplify this process, including some that allow you to take a picture of the card and then add it to your database. Add a picture from a social media page to their contact entry — putting a face to a name will help you remember who they are.
- **Follow through.** Don't rely on catching up with your new friends at the next event. You need to follow up personally and make good on any promises you made. Do not under any circumstances send a "blanket" email to everyone you met. Customize each message based on your conversation and the notes you made on the back of the business cards. Establish next steps that will help develop the relationship.
- **Repeat.** The more events you attend, the more familiar faces you'll see and the more you'll enjoy seeing them. That familiarity will give you the confidence to keep meeting new people.

Key takeaways

To get the most out of your networking events:

- Prepare for the event by bringing business cards and identifying the people you most want to meet.
- Be your best self. Be approachable, be personable, ask interested questions and engage with the people you meet.
- Go after your goals. Know how to initiate and exit conversations and keep track of whom you talk to. Follow up later to solidify the connection.

CHAPTER 8
PROSPECTIVE CLIENTS

Although clients are most likely the single biggest source of new business for your firm, there comes a time when there's no more juice to squeeze from the orange. You need new clients and prospects are aplenty. The key is to target your prospective clients wisely. Gather the necessary intelligence to win their trust and ultimately their work and continuously learn from your prospecting experiences. And ultimately, don't give up on prospects who don't want your services right now; you don't know what the future holds.

In this chapter, we discuss how to find good prospective clients, how to win them and how to learn from your experiences. Individual topics include:

*   **Ideal client profile:** Identify the type of prospective client you want to target. Once you know who you're after, you can seek them out and figure out how to connect with them.
*   **Prospect intelligence:** Learn everything you can about your prospective client before asking for their business. Research their current situation, understand their needs and build a relationship.
*   **Prospect post-mortem interview:** Whether or not you've won a prospective client's business, you should still ask them what you did well and what you did poorly. You'll learn how to improve your pitch.
*   **Lost prospect cultivation:** Don't write off your lost prospects. Reach out to them, keep in touch and continue cultivating your relationship. There might be a valuable opportunity to work together in the future.

IDEAL CLIENT PROFILE

An ideal client profile identifies the types of clients you want to target. Once you know the personality, demographics and needs of your ideal client, you can seek them out and devise strategies and tactics to connect with them, and ultimately win their business.

Don't stumble around in the dark

When you create an ideal client profile, you maximize your chances of landing more ideal clients. You'll win more work with less effort by targeting your marketing and prospecting efforts. You'll win clients with whom you enjoy working and those clients will in turn produce valuable referrals for you. Ignore your ideal client profile at your own peril. If you do, you'll waste a lot of time looking for new clients and you won't achieve the success you seek.

Know your type

One way to define your ideal client profile is to draw on your existing client list. Analyze your "A"-level clients and identify the traits they share. Define quantitative measures, such as size, type, needs, net worth and annual revenue. Also look for qualitative measures, such as issues the client is trying to solve, specific product needs they have and intangibles such as preparation and readiness, willingness to follow advice, a history of paying their bills on time and niche relevance. If you're looking to launch a niche, analyzing your current client list will only get you so far. To more clearly understand your ideal client, you'll need to perform market research and competitive analysis to define who constitutes the market and which part of that population is underserved by your competition.

No matter which strategy you use, you want an ideal client profile that is neither too restrictive nor too broad. If your profile is too narrow, you won't find enough prospective clients who match it. Make it too general, and your profile will be of no use. If you serve multiple constituencies, make an ideal profile for each one; don't try to mash all your clients into one ideal client profile. Once you've researched your ideal client, convert the information into basic tables. The tables below include sample categories, and you should choose the most relevant categories for each profile you create.

Individuals

Type	High net worth individuals, including executives, entrepreneurs and small business owners, all of whom need the assistance of a sophisticated tax advisor
Income	Adjusted gross income of $250,000 or more
Location	Within 50 miles of office
Age	Over 35

Issues	Complicated returns; tax planning needs
Needs	Tax return includes investment income, Schedule C income or Schedule E income; tax compliance, tax projections, and tax planning services
Fees	$2,000 or more
Intangibles	Provides tax information by March 15; likely has an investment advisor or broker

Entities

Type	Growing enterprises; may be adding entities or expanding into other states
Revenue	$10,000,000 or more
Profitability	$1,000,000 or more
Value	$5,000,000 or more
Employees	50 or more
Location	Within 50 miles of office
Issues	Worried about tax situation; struggling to coordinate personal and business tax issues
Needs	Annual audit or review and tax return work
Fees	$50,000 or more
Intangibles	Pays bills promptly and doesn't haggle over fees; enjoyable to work with; frequently asks for and acts on our advice; not overly demanding

Next, convert the information in the table into a paragraph. Integrate it into your messaging, including your competitive advantage and claims. Use it in your referral piece to explain who your ideal client is (see referrals chapter). For example, here is the entity profile from above, in paragraph form:

"At [insert firm here], we're here to help you grow and prosper. We're looking for growing enterprises that may be in the process of expanding to other states or adding entities. Our clients typically have annual revenue of $10 million or more, have profitability of $1 million or more and employ 50 or more people. They are concerned about their tax situation and may be struggling to coordinate their personal and business tax obligations. Often they need annual audit and tax return work, with fees beginning at $50,000. We enjoy working with clients who ask for and value our advice and who honor their financial commitments."

Key takeaways

To create an ideal client profile:

- Draw on your "A"-level clients. What do they have in common? Include both quantitative and qualitative measures.
- Conduct market research and competitive analysis to define your ideal client in a particular niche.
- Create a profile for each constituency or industry you serve. Convert the table into paragraph form and integrate that copy in general messaging and in your referral piece.

PROSPECT INTELLIGENCE

Prospect intelligence is about doing your homework on a prospective client, getting to know them and engaging in conversation about their needs and wants. At the end of the prospect intelligence phase, you should know enough about the individual and their business, their likes, priorities, motives, preferences and personality to position yourself to win the work. Succeed in prospect intelligence and you'll win more business in less time, earn more per client and generate more referrals.

Set yourself up for success

Prospect intelligence encompasses the first three steps in our sales process: research, relationships and needs (see sales process chapter later in this book).

- **Research:** Before sitting down in person with the prospective client, conduct research to understand their financial situation, business priorities and organizational needs. Armed with knowledge about your potential client, you'll be able to ask insightful questions and get to the root of their needs.
- **Relationships:** To build a relationship with a prospective client, they have to see you as likeable, credible and trustworthy. You should come away knowing your prospect's likes, priorities, motives, preferences and personality traits.
- **Needs:** To conduct a needs assessment, sit down with the prospective client and ask questions to understand their issues, wants and goals. By the end of the meeting, you should be well informed about the prospective client and their current situation, your competition and their decision-making process.

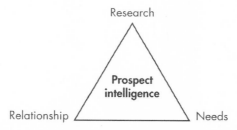

Business development success is as much a function of your ability to do these three things well as it is to position your solutions, negotiate an agreement and ultimately gain commitment.

Play to your strengths

Many people shy away from selling because they feel they don't have the gregarious personality they need to succeed as a salesperson. Yet, contrary to the conventional wisdom, people succeed in sales because they're good listeners and questioners. If you genuinely want to help people, you take the time to understand them.

Consider the following types of accountants, outlined in broad strokes. Both have skills they can leverage during the prospect intelligence process.

- **The introvert:** Many accountants are naturally quiet, reflective and thoughtful. They're likely to invest in prospect research because they like to be prepared. They struggle with relationship-building because they don't easily build rapport with people they don't know. When they prepare questions in advance, they're fantastic at listening and gathering information about the client's needs. Thus, their strengths are research and needs assessment. Fast-tracking like, trust and credibility is their challenge. As a result, the sales cycle is often longer in their case.
- **The extrovert:** The talkative, confident and persuasive accountants are a different challenge. They're less likely to do research and more skilled at building relationships. They have a tendency to sell and tell more than to ask and listen, which makes them their own worst enemy during the needs phase. The sales cycle may be quicker but they have a tendency to lose as many as they win.

The important thing is to follow the prospect intelligence process while being true to yourself. Focus on accentuating your strengths but don't lose sight of your weaknesses. Training can help you overcome your challenges, as you can learn to replicate the skills of the opposite personality type. You can also work in teams, so staff members with complementary skills go out to prospective client appointments together.

For more about how to succeed at prospect intelligence, we go into great detail in the first three topics of the sales process chapter.

Key takeaways

To win more new business:

- Conduct prospect intelligence before you start pitching your services.
- Get to know the prospective client, come prepared with research and ask good questions.
- Don't psych yourself out. Lots of different personality types can succeed at sales.

PROSPECT POST-MORTEM INTERVIEW

A post-mortem interview should be conducted with all prospective clients, regardless of whether you win their business or not. It is a tool for learning how to better pitch your firm to new prospective clients, with the goal of ultimately helping you win more business.

Know your audience

Talking to won and lost prospects is an invaluable source of information about your clients' issues, needs and wants. Once you understand why you won one client and lost another, you can present more relevant, targeted information about your firm to future prospective clients.

Conducting the debrief

The advice provided for lost client post-mortem interviews in the clients chapter can also be applied to interviews with prospective clients. Here's a short review:

- Perform the interview within four weeks after a decision is reached, but not immediately after.
- Interview the client in person or over the phone, not with a paper or online survey.
- Stay objective and don't take the feedback personally.
- Listen attentively during the interview, taking in all the information you can.
- Apply what you learn to your next proposal, presentation or interaction with a prospective client.

Keep in mind that no sales pitch goes perfectly. When interviewing prospects you've won, you should still focus on gathering both positive and negative feedback to learn how to be better next time. And even lost prospects aren't lost forever — ask about other services you can provide now or in the future. These questions are a crucial business development tool.

A list of questions you might ask to help guide the conversation:

Won prospects:

- What led you to choose our firm over others?
- What were the most important criteria you used to make your decision?
- What was the most persuasive aspect of our proposal?
- How much of a role did our written proposal and/or oral presentation play in the selection process? Were they similar in style and content to the others you received?
- What did another firm do better than us?
- What did we do that you thought was good or helpful?
- How well did we interact with your team?
- Were our fees competitive?
- What should we take away from this experience to help us do better next time?

Lost prospects:

- What led you to choose the winning firm?
- What were the most important criteria you used to make your decision?
- What was the winning firm's fee?
- What could we do to improve our proposal and/or oral presentation next time?
- How well did we interact with your team?
- What should we take away from this experience to help us do better next time?
- Would you consider our firm for special work or consulting projects in the future? Do you have anything in mind now?
- Would you recommend our firm to others? Why or why not?

Target acquired

Post-mortem interviews help you understand your clients' needs and to present your products and services more effectively to future prospects. Many of the outcomes found in the lost client post-mortem topic in the clients chapter are applicable here as well. Specific outcomes from prospect interviews include:

- Your sales presentations will become more targeted and more relevant as you incorporate client feedback. This will position you to win more work in the future.
- Your team will improve how they interact during the client courting process, expertly connecting your firm with the right clients and avoiding relationships that aren't a good fit.

Key takeaways

Post-mortem interviews with won and lost prospects help you:

- Learn how prospective clients view your firm.
- Improve the way you introduce your firm to new prospective clients.
- Win more work as you target the right clients and pitch your firm more effectively.

LOST PROSPECT CULTIVATION

You invest a lot of time and effort into cultivating a prospective client and then they choose another firm. Most of us would consider the prospective client to be lost, when in fact the more appropriate classification would be "lost for now." Don't write off your lost prospects. Reach out to them, keep in touch and continue cultivating your relationship. There might be a valuable opportunity to work together in the future.

This isn't goodbye

One of my first sales mentors, back in the days before CRM databases, used to keep an accordion folder that he called his "tickler file." The tickler file was nothing more than a date reminder to call prospective clients, both current and lost. When I asked him why he called people who had already said no, he replied simply: "They didn't say no. They said: no, not now." I took one very important sales lesson from this: Situations can change, dramatically. A client's needs a year ago could be entirely different from their needs today. When it comes to lost prospects, you've already done much of the groundwork. You've established a rapport and demonstrated your point of difference. For whatever reason, you didn't win the work — it could have been a politically motivated decision or one simply based on cost. But the prospect may be unhappy with the firm they chose, or they might decide they need a particular service after all. In either case, if you do your job during the dormant phase — by staying in touch, helping out when they ask — you'll be the go-to person when they're back on the market.

Stay top-of-mind

Follow these tips to cultivate lost prospects:

- **Conduct a post-mortem interview.** Gain intelligence about why the prospect went in another direction. This tells you which of the two types of lost prospects they are: the ones who chose someone else or the ones who decided not to act. During the course of the interview, you'll get a sense for whether it's appropriate to stay in touch (see previous topic for more on prospect post-mortem interviews).
- **Update your database.** Mark them as a lost prospect. In the same way that you report "sales stages," track and report lost prospect activity. Know who's contacting whom, how frequently and with what results.
- **Communicate.** Continue to send appropriate firm communications to lost prospects. That may include the firm's newsletter, niche-specific communications and invitations to informational and hospitality events. If their current firm is less communicative, this will give a sense of what it feels like to warm their hands around the fire.
- **Stay in touch.** For the first year, check in with the prospect quarterly to see if they've had a good experience with the winning firm. You can either call or email, whichever method they prefer. In most cases, if

the experience has not been a productive one, they'll decide to re-bid the work within the first year. Thus it's relevant to be in touch more frequently during that period. After a year, continue to contact them semi-annually, paying attention to specific renewal dates. For example, for an audit client, you might call just prior to the scheduled RFP date.

- **Extend a helping hand.** The point of these calls is not to dig for dirt on your competition but rather to demonstrate a willingness to help. The prospect may be too reticent to ask their CPA certain questions for fear of running the bill or their CPA may be unable to refer them to a specific professional. Think of this as an opportunity to add value through expertise and connections. It doesn't cost you anything and the value-add is significant.

- **Respect their wishes.** If they unsubscribe from your communications, ask them if it's no longer appropriate to stay in touch. It's good to be persistent but don't become a nuisance.

- **As one door closes...** You aren't the right fit for them, but that doesn't mean you aren't the right fit for someone they know. During the lost prospect phase, they've learned that you're reliable, persistent, helpful and a valuable resource. They may know someone looking for an accountant just like you. As my friend Bill Burke would ask, "Is there anyone else I should be talking to?" You won't know if you don't ask.

- **Share successes.** When a lost prospect becomes a client or refers you to a new prospective client, share this internally as an illustration of a best practice. Most people will write off lost prospects. Highlighting when you ultimately convert a lost prospect into a client helps to build the case.

Key takeaways

To turn lost prospects into new clients:

- Remember that people's needs and wants change. Lost prospects don't need what you have to offer now, but they might in the future. You want to remain top-of-mind.
- Think of the lost-prospect phase as a time to demonstrate your value. Make connections, contribute to their success and offer insight and expertise.
- Put a process in place. Schedule quarterly calls and ensure lost prospects are included on appropriate communications mailing lists.

CHAPTER 9
SALES PROCESS

A sales process is a step-by-step process for winning new work. Following a documented, consistent process ensures that everyone is on the same page and generates more reliable results. It also makes it easy to measure your efforts, identify areas for improvement and offer targeted training and assistance.

Follow these steps sequentially and you'll win more work more of the time:

1. **Research:** Before meeting a new prospective client, conduct preliminary research to understand their financial situation, business priorities and organizational needs.
2. **Relationships:** Buyers don't decide on facts alone. Build like, trust and credibility with a prospective client if you want to win their business.
3. **Needs:** Sit down with the prospective client and ask questions to understand their needs, issues, wants and goals. You want to establish the target you need to hit when promoting your services.
4. **Solutions:** Tell the prospective client how you can help them. Connect your capabilities with your prospective client's needs.
5. **Demonstration:** Offer a demonstration event to back up your claims. Make a valuable introduction, review a prior year tax return — anything to demonstrate your value.
6. **Reservations:** Uncover any remaining questions or reservations the prospective client might have. Try to understand the root of the issue.
7. **Assurances:** Respond to the prospective client's concerns. Offer examples of how you've helped other clients and offer guarantees to overcome any roadblocks.
8. **Commitment:** This pivotal step is often the one most feared by accountants. Learn how to ask for a prospective client's business and you'll convert more opportunities into won work.

9. **Next steps:** Once a prospective client agrees to become a client, immediately schedule a next step to maintain momentum in the relationship. The next step could be a phone call, introduction or firm event, among others.

10. **Review:** Review your performance to analyze what worked and what didn't and how you can improve next time.

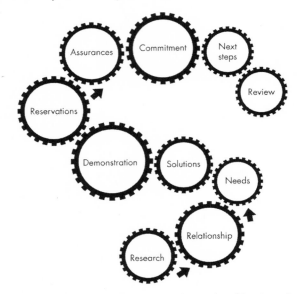

For a step-by-step process like this one to be truly effective, there has to be a connection that links each step. In our model, it's called "goal statements." Before each interaction with the prospective client, establish the goals you need to achieve to keep the sales process moving forward. A goal statement might be to schedule a follow-up call or to decide on a submission deadline for a proposal. It's easy to go into meetings with lots of objectives in mind — understand the prospective client's needs, learn about the competition, find out what they're willing to pay — but without specifically stated goals, your informative conversation may not lead to a tangible next step. You don't need to establish a goal statement for every single stage in your sales process, as many stages will occur within the same meeting. Instead, in advance of each interaction, decide on the goal statements you want to achieve. For example:

Interaction	Goal statement(s)
First call	Schedule a pre-meeting call.
First-round call	Schedule a first-round meeting to build the relationship and complete a more comprehensive needs assessment.

Interaction	Goal statement(s)
First-round meeting	Schedule a second-round meeting if necessary to meet all relevant parties or address specific reservations.
Second-round meeting	Commit to a proposal submission format and date.
Proposal meeting	If necessary, schedule a follow-up meeting to discuss agreement particulars (fee, start date, etc).
Negotiation meeting	Win the business.
Won business	Schedule a next step to overcome doubts and focus energies on moving the relationship forward.
Lost business	Schedule a post-mortem interview.

RESEARCH

Advance research involves creating a profile of prospective clients to understand their financial situation, business priorities and organizational needs. Having this research to draw on during an in-person meeting can prove invaluable in converting a prospect into a client.

Always be prepared

Meaningful prospect research has become a lost art in the digital age. Yet knowledge is power, and in most cases, even a quick look at a prospective client's online presence can better prepare you for the meeting ahead. And for the most promising prospective clients (your big hairy audacious goal clients, the ones you really want to land), advance research is key to making the best first impression possible. Landing these clients could change your business so it's worth taking the time to know everything you can about them. If you walk into the meeting armed with knowledge about your potential client, you'll be able to ask insightful questions and get to the root of the client's needs more quickly. As Mark Cuban, Dallas Mavericks owner and Shark Tank celebrity, said, "Information is power, particularly when the competition ignores the opportunity to do the same."

Compile a profile

The work of compiling a profile about a prospective client can be tasked to an intern, administrative assistant or business development coordinator. The best research involves combing through several sources to assemble the most complete profile possible. Even if you don't have the time or staff resources to do this for every client, try to at least perform some quick research, using Google, LinkedIn or the prospect's website; a little information goes a long way.

The most relevant information differs depending on whether your prospective client is an individual, for-profit entity or non-profit. Here are the most salient points for each type of client (www[29] for research profile templates):

- **Individuals:** You want to gather a brief personal history that includes family background, employment history and education. Evaluate their current business situation, net worth and any current assets, including stock holdings, company ownership, real estate and inheritance. You can also try to find out who their other advisors are (attorneys, wealth managers, etc). Finally, focus on the person, including their civic and community affiliations, philanthropic contributions and any awards and honors they've won.
- **For-profit entities:** Try to uncover general background about their business, including number of employees, annual revenue, customers and competitive advantage. Determine who their key executives are and try to understand their organizational priorities. It also helps to know about their community involvement and any awards they've received.

- **Non-profits:** Summarize their mission and key priorities and look up who is on their board of directors. As with a for-profit business, try to determine business information including number of employees and annual revenue. Look up any available financial information, including 990 forms. Find out who their current auditor is. Try to understand their constituents and develop a sense of event marketing and communications opportunities.

It's always helpful to know who is in a prospective client's network, as you might be able to convert one opportunity into another. Not all this information will be accessible through public records — find out what you can and fill in the rest from what you learn during the face-to-face meeting.

Information is power

Performing advance research on potential clients achieves four main benefits. First, it tells you what you don't know and what you need to learn during the face-to-face meeting. Second, it helps you ask smart questions that uncover the client's true needs. Third, it demonstrates to the client your level of commitment, as other firms will not have gone to the same lengths. Finally, it helps clarify whether the prospective client is a good fit for your firm, and can help you decide how much time you should put into pursuing them.

Key takeaways

Doing research before a meeting with a prospective client will help you:

- Get a leg up on your competitors. Most firms won't do any advance research at all.
- Make the most of the meeting. Even if all you have time to do is skim a few social media sites, it's better than going in blind.
- Win the clients who will change your business. For those clients you dream about, find out everything you can beforehand to give yourself the best shot.

RELATIONSHIPS

As any salesperson knows, a buyer facing a big financial decision doesn't decide based on facts and figures alone. They want to buy from someone they connect with. Therefore, as an accountant trying to woo a new client, you aren't just selling your firm; you're selling yourself. You need to know how to rapidly build rapport with prospective clients, which comes down to three things — you need to be likeable, credible and trustworthy.

How to build a relationship

Keep these tips in mind for establishing that perfect trifecta of talents (likeable, credible and trustworthy).

How to get people to like you

To get people to like you, think of the 3C's: commonality, caring and connection.

- **Ask smart questions.** Your goal is to promote insight and understanding. We'll talk more about how to uncover relevant information in the next topic in this chapter.
- **Listen actively.** Listening doesn't mean waiting to talk; it involves actively paying attention to the prospective client. Instead of thinking about what you're going to say next, focus on what you're going to ask next.
- **Relate to their situation.** Most people find it difficult to admit what they don't know. When someone says they don't know if they have a college savings plan, don't scold them. Instead, empathize with their situation. You can also try to relate the conversation to things you don't know in their areas of expertise.
- **Draw on common interests.** Personally, my main interests are exercise, golf, travel and family. I've found that 99% of the time, I can connect those passions with something that the other person is passionate about. Document what your interests are and try to connect to them in your conversations with prospective clients.
- **Speak their language.** As a client of an accountant, my biggest critique is that accountants struggle to explain their craft in a way that the average person can understand. Instead, they offer a mumbo-jumbo of three letter acronyms, tax codes and big words that are certainly lost on me, if not the majority of us. When asked, "do you understand," we often just nod and say yes because we don't want to appear unintelligent.

How to get people to see you as credible

There are two parts to gaining credibility: first, having the resume to back up your claims; and second, having other people willing to testify to your talents.

- **Establish your credentials.** Your work experience, education, associations and credentials (the letters after your name) all serve to establish your credibility with clients. When you're in a meeting with a prospective client, try to focus on the parts of your background that are most relevant to that person and don't spend too much time talking about your resume. Talents trump credentials in my book, especially when credentials are universally shared.
- **Be a thought leader.** By writing, speaking and presenting, you'll establish yourself as an expert in your field. If others see you as credible, your prospective clients will too.
- **Get others to vouch for you.** More important than your resume is what others say about you through testimonials, references and referrals. When others vouch for your credibility, they're putting their reputation on the line for you. Instead of summarizing your bio, try this approach: "I'm sure you didn't come here to listen to me spout off about where I went to school and where else I've worked so instead of the usual 'let me tell you about myself' speech, I'd prefer to share some of the things that my clients have said about their experience working with me."

How to get people to trust you

Trust is a whole other matter. While likeability and credibility can be established quickly, trust takes time. Trust is built when you come through in the clutch, when you go above and beyond to finish a task and demonstrate that you really care about what's best for the client. There's no secret handshake for getting people to trust you right off the bat, but there are a few things you can do to generate sufficient trust to persuade a prospective client to hire you.

- **Offer third-party references.** It always helps to have other people testify to how you've helped them and how you've exceeded expectations.
- **Demonstrate your abilities.** Often the best way to overcome a prospect's uncertainty is to demonstrate that you can deliver on your claims. One way to do this is to review their prior year's tax return or financial statements for free. Your goal is to find a potential opportunity or possible savings. You might point out that they missed R&D credits or that new legislation will change their tax position moving forward. The goal isn't to undermine their prior CPA, but to demonstrate that you have a unique perspective that may prove a better fit.
- **Put your best foot forward from day 1.** You've already made a good impression, now prove yourself by following through. Send a summary immediately following the prospect meeting that outlines the tasks and timelines that you discussed. By sending this email and following up accordingly, you'll demonstrate commitment, organization, diligence and reliability. It's an easy thing to do and it establishes from day 1 that you say what you mean and mean what you say.

Getting you through the tough times

To move from commodity provider to trusted advisor, you have to build strong relationships with your clients. Those relationships are pivotal to the success of your business relationship. When things hit a rough patch, as they inevitably will at some point, relationships help you overcome the client's automatic reflex to jump ship and go elsewhere. Your client will come to value you, not just the service you provide, and they'll stick with you for the long haul. Think about how many clients leave a firm when a senior contributor leaves — they see the relationship with the individual as far more pivotal than the relationship with the firm. Building relationships with prospective clients early on, and then cementing those relationships over time, is the lifeblood of any business development process.

Key takeaways

To build relationships with prospects and clients, you should be:

- Likeable. Connect to the client, discuss your common interests and listen to their concerns.
- Credible. The fastest way to establish your credibility is through third-party testimonials. It's much more effective than droning on about where you went to school.
- Trustworthy. Trust is harder to build, but it will develop over time if you consistently deliver on your promises.

NEEDS

To conduct a needs assessment, you sit down with a prospective client and ask questions to understand their issues, wants and goals. By the end of the meeting, you should be well informed about the prospective client and their current situation, your competition and the prospective client's decision-making process. Needs assessment is perhaps the most pivotal step in the sales process because it establishes the target you need to hit when promoting your services. If you fail to adequately understand the prospective client's needs, you'll be doing nothing more throwing stuff against the wall to see what sticks.

Aim for a bullseye

The primary goal of a needs assessment is to understand the totality of your prospective client's needs. If you can identify their most pressing needs and offer solutions to address those needs, you'll be in a great position to win the work. Additionally, you want to figure out which of their needs connect with the things you do best. You will be well positioned to win their business if you can demonstrate that your competitive advantage aligns with their needs. Conduct a needs assessment with each and every prospective client. You may win a client without one, but you'll likely leave a lot of opportunity on the table if you don't fully understand their circumstances.

Seek understanding

As Stephen Covey said, "Seek to understand before being understood." This is a mantra to live by with needs assessment. The less you say and the more they talk the better. By the end of the needs assessment process, you should know all of the following:

- **Situation and goals:** You should know the prospective client's current situation, their goals and the role you will play in achieving those goals. This is the meat of the needs assessment process; spend most of your time on these questions.
- **Competition:** You should know who your competitors are, what capabilities the prospective client wants from their new provider and their concerns about their current or prior provider.
- **Decision-making process:** You should know who makes the decision about what firm to hire, how and when the decision will be made and what criteria will be used to select the winning firm.

Prepare your questions

To gather all the relevant information, you need to be an effective questioner. Below we outline three strategies to help you get to the root of the prospective client's needs: the three E's of questioning, a questions roadmap and your issue-solution-benefit narrative.

Three E's of questioning

The "three E's of questioning" is a process for uncovering prospect needs. Questions are asked in the following sequence:

- **Entry** questions: These are broad, open-ended, easy-to-answer questions that get the subject talking. Stay away from yes or no questions.
- **Elaborative** questions: These questions encourage the subject to expand on specific topics of interest.
- **Evaluative** questions: These questions establish how important or urgent the topic is. Often evaluative questions rely on key words such as impact and consequence to provide context (for example, "what's the impact if you do X?" and "what's the consequence if you don't do Y?").

Here's an example in conversational flow:

- Seller asks an **entry** question: "How's business?"
- Prospect replies: "It's been an up-and-down year. Revenue is up but profitability has slipped considerably, particularly in the last two quarters."
- Seller asks an **elaborative** question: "Why do you think that's the case?"
- Prospect replies: "We made several investments in sales support. We added a sales support person and invested in sophisticated CRM software to help us track and monetize our sales efforts. That adversely impacted profitability in the short-run."
- Seller asks **evaluative** question: "How do you think those investments will impact your business a year from now? What would have resulted had you not made those investments?"

Questions roadmap

A questions roadmap is a list of prepared questions by category. Having a prepared sequence of questions ensures that you hit all the important points. Here are some examples:

Current situation questions

- What is the primary mission of your business?
- What are the top three operational or business challenges that you face on a daily basis?

Vision questions

- What are the 3-4 key strategic initiatives for your business this year?
- What is the time frame for accomplishing these initiatives?

Competition questions

- What alternatives is your organization considering?
- Who is your current vendor? Why are you considering leaving them?

Decision-making questions

- What is the time frame for making a decision?
- Who approves the investment and ultimately signs the engagement letter?

For a complete questions roadmap, see our website (www[30]).

Issue-solution-benefit narrative

During the needs assessment, you want not only to understand the prospective client's needs but also to identify the needs that highlight your core competencies. The key to this is your issue-solution-benefit narrative (we talked about how to develop your issue-solution-benefit narrative in the messaging chapter). If you know what you do best, you can ask questions to identify whether the prospective client needs the solutions that you can offer. This allows you to drive the sales conversation in a direction that highlights your strengths and capabilities. Here's an example of an issue-solution-benefit narrative around retirement planning:

Issue	I don't know my number.
Solution	We'll work with you to develop a "Wealth Plan," which includes a cash flow analysis and financial snapshot (includes assets, risks, taxes, etc). We'll also meet with you on an ongoing basis to recalibrate the plan when things change (personal situation, the market, etc).
Benefit	You'll have a roadmap for saving, spending and investing your money for maximum return, and remove doubts about whether you'll have the capital you need to live the lifestyle you envision for yourself and your family.

Here's an example of the questions you might ask to identify if a prospective client faces that issue:

Entry	What are your long-term goals, dreams and concerns?
Elaborate	What information/guidance do you need to make intelligent, informed financial decisions moving forward?
Evaluate	Do you have enough money to retire on? If not, how much do you need?

For a template to create your own issue-solution-benefit narrative questions, see our website (www[31]).

Ask away

Now that you know how to ask effective questions, follow these steps once you sit down with the prospective client:

1. **Understand where they are.** Get a snapshot of their current situation. Ask: Where are they? How did they get there? What keeps them up at night?
2. **Uncover their envisioned future.** Get a sense for where they're going or where they would like to be. Ask: What's your vision for the future? Where would you like to be in X years?
3. **Identify the barriers.** Often prospects are so clear about where they want to go that you only have to ask one additional question to get to the root of their needs: What's preventing you from getting there?
4. **Check all your boxes.** In addition to uncovering their needs, ask about anything else you need to know, including competition, decision-making process, price and delivery timeline. Make sure you understand how factors such as price will affect their decision.

At the end of the needs assessment process, you should have a thorough understanding of the prospective client's needs, who they're talking to, when and how they plan to make a decision and what essential capabilities the winning firm must have.

Key takeaways

To conduct an effective needs assessment:

- Know your target. You need to come away understanding the prospective client's current situation, the competition and their decision-making process.
- Hone your questions. Prepare a questions roadmap beforehand and utilize the "three E's of questioning."
- Focus on what you do best. Ask questions that connect to your issue-solution-benefit narrative.

SOLUTIONS

This is the part of the sales process where the spotlight turns from the prospective client to you. It's your time to shine. You've learned all about the prospective client, and now it's time to talk about what you can offer. The key here is to connect your capabilities with the prospective client's needs. If you drone on about yourself and lose sight of their needs, you're doomed to fail. Draw on your issue-solution-benefit narrative, provide clear examples and metrics and be as succinct as possible. You want to highlight the critical info, not get lost in the weeds.

Make your pitch

Follow these steps when pitching to a prospective client:

1. **Rephrase the issues.** To ensure that you understand the key issues, rephrase them in your own words. If you've interpreted incorrectly and start talking off-topic, you're going to lose the client's business. You might say: "If I understand you correctly, you're looking for a CPA with substantial industry expertise who is committed to providing an outstanding client service experience for an affordable fee. Is that accurate?" Allow the prospective client to restate their needs if your summary is inaccurate. Don't proceed until they have confirmed that your summary is accurate.

2. **Keep it brief.** It's tempting to throw the kitchen sink at a prospective client, especially one who has listed a variety of needs. Instead, prioritize their needs and focus on the top three. By addressing any more than three at this stage, you're just complicating the message. You can address additional points once you've nailed their most pressing concerns.

3. **Provide issue-solution-benefit narratives.** When you prioritize the top three issues, focus on needs that connect to the things your firm does best. Use your issue-solution-benefit narratives to frame your solutions. Begin by describing the issue, then articulate the best features of your solution and finish by summarizing the benefits. For example:

   - *Describe issue:* "During the course of our conversation, you talked about the staff turnover frustrations you've had with your current firm."
   - *Articulate solution:* "Our annual turnover rate for staff, seniors, supervisors, managers and senior managers is 6%, half that of our competitors."
   - *Summarize benefits:* "At our firm, you'll see the same people year after year. Our people will know your business inside and out and you won't have to continuously educate new staff about your operations. The time savings to you are considerable!"

4. **State measures.** The prospective client won't remember everything you say, but they likely will recall compelling statistics. In the example above, including the 6% metric signals to the client that this is an important number, one worth measuring and quantifying. When telling the prospective client about the benefits of your solutions, don't just tell them how they'll benefit, tell them how much. Be precise with your numbers — say "6%," not "about 6%."

5. **Provide examples.** Substantiate issue-solution-benefit narratives with examples of how you've helped similar clients. For example: "A client came to us with similar staff turnover concerns. We invited that client to review team member resumes, interview each prospective team member personally and ultimately provide input in the selection of their audit team. The team has remained intact for the last four years and the client couldn't be happier. They went so far as to say that their 'audit has gone from a painful experience to a pleasurable one.'"

6. **Ask feedback questions.** At the end of each issue-solution-benefit narrative, ask a feedback question to gauge the prospective client's satisfaction with the solution. For example: "Does that address your concern?"

7. **Keep a few in reserve.** You may not cover every issue in your initial presentation. Other concerns may arise at later stages when you ask if the prospective client has any questions or is ready to move forward. Keeping a few of your issue-solution-benefit narratives in reserve will help you address any remaining reservations the prospective client might have.

Dive right in

There's a common belief in sales that you sell yourself, then sell your firm and finally sell your product. As a result, after completing the needs assessment phase, many accountants will start talking about themselves. To me, that's a missed opportunity. I suggest you go straight from understanding the prospective client's needs to suggesting solutions. You'll end up selling your firm and your product in the course of presenting your issue-solution-benefit narratives. And ideally, you will have already convinced the prospective client of your expertise and value during the relationship-building phase. By segueing directly to solutions, you're making a clear argument for your value right off the bat.

Key takeaways

When presenting your solutions to a prospective client:

- Rephrase what they just told you. Make sure you understand the target.
- Share issue-solution-benefit narratives that directly address their three most important needs.
- Use examples and metrics to further substantiate your claims. Be specific.

DEMONSTRATION

The most appealing part of a sales pitch is the product demonstration, where the salesperson shows how the item works. Demonstration events can be difficult to create in accounting, but that doesn't mean you should skip past this step in the sales process. If you think creatively, you can employ a variety of techniques for offering "proof of claims," including providing a legislative update or offering a valuable introduction. These demonstration events will help seal the deal.

De-clutter your pitch

It's easy for prospective clients to discount your competitive claims — "bigger, better, faster, stronger" is just noise to most people until they see proof. In a perfect world, everyone would be able to trial their accountant before hiring them. That's not going to happen, but the next best tactic is to provide a demonstration event to prove that what you say is true. As you'll see below, a demonstration event can take many forms. It doesn't require that you review a prior year tax return or financial statements. It simply requires that you provide real illustrations of your value.

Emulate the infomercial

Think about late-night infomercials; they're littered with demonstrations. My personal favorite is the miracle glue commercial where the salesperson cuts a hole in the bottom of a boat, glues a door in place over the hole and floats the boat down the river to prove that the glue really works. You want to do the same thing in your sales process; before you ask a prospective client to make a commitment, provide a demonstration to eliminate any doubts they might have that your claims are true.

While you can't easily float a boat down the river, you can provide any number of demonstrations to validate your claims. Demonstration events are designed to showcase one or all of the following:

- **Knowledge:** Demonstrate your expertise in a specific service or industry. Example: Ask to review their prior year tax return in search of missed opportunities such as credits and incentives; ask to review their financial statements in search of inconsistencies.
- **Currency:** Demonstrate your understanding of current legislative policy. Example: Provide a legislative update to showcase your knowledge of recent code reform and apply that knowledge to their situation.
- **Efficiency:** Demonstrate your ability to do the work in less time or at a lower cost. Example: Showcase technologies to illustrate proposed time and cost savings, such as how your online submission portal works, how your paperless format reduces client expense, etc.
- **Bench strength:** Demonstrate your team's expertise and experience. Example: Invite team members to participate in needs assessment

and proposal meetings and have them speak about their experience, knowledge and industry expertise.

- **Attention to detail:** Demonstrate how your processes and protocols minimize mistakes.
- **Connections:** Demonstrate the value of your network. Example: Introduce them to experts who can help them ("In the course of our conversation, you mentioned that you could benefit from a no-cost insurance review. Let me introduce you to person X at firm Y").

In short, you don't have to cut a hole in a boat to give a demonstration event. Video testimonials, case studies, awards, referrals, testimonials — these are all demonstration events. Anything you can do to bring your claims to life is a suitable demonstration event.

Key takeaways

Demonstrations are a key part of your sales process:

- In reviewing how they made a decision, clients often point to a demonstration event as the most memorable part of the sales process.
- Demonstrations allow you to walk the talk. They're proof that what you say is true.
- Demonstrations cement your claims and turn them into gains. They show clients how they'll benefit as a result of the things you do best.

RESERVATIONS

After presenting your solutions, you need to uncover any remaining questions or reservations the prospective client might have. Before you jump in with your response, take the time to understand the basis of their reservations. Look beyond superficial answers and get at the real reason they're undecided.

Probe for problems

It's what you ask more than what you say that determines your success in business development. You've had an opportunity to talk in solutions; now it's time to listen again. Ideally, you've done such a masterful job of understanding the prospective client's needs and connecting those needs with solutions that they have no serious reservations about choosing you. In reality, you'll likely encounter several roadblocks. Ask questions to get to the root of the issues so that you can target your response to overcome their uncertainty or hesitation.

Understanding reservations

Not all prospective clients hesitate for the same reasons. Some are just cautious about making a big decision; others have serious concerns about your service. The key to the reservations stage is understanding the real basis behind their hesitation. Reservations generally fall into two categories:

- **Stalls:** There is no specific reason for the prospective client not to move forward, they simply need a little more convincing. Here's an example of how you might better understand why a prospective client is stalling: Prospect: "I really need to talk to X about this."

  Accountant: "If you don't mind me asking, what specific issues do you feel the need to discuss? What insight are you looking to gain from that conversation?"

- **Objections:** There is a specific reason why the prospective client is unwilling to buy from you, such as price or insufficient expertise. Here's an example of how you might discuss an objection with a prospect: Prospect: "Your fee is more than we had budgeted."

  Accountant: "If you don't mind me asking, what did you budget for this work? What outcomes did you hope to achieve at that fee?"

Get to the root of the issue

Follow these steps to understand a prospective client's reservations:

1. **Start with entry questions.** Ask an entry-level question to get the prospective client talking again. For example: "Do you have any questions?" Listen intently to what they say.

2. **Elaborate and evaluate.** Ask elaborative and evaluative questions to better understand the root of the question, the underlying issues and its overall priority.

3. **Ask, don't tell.** Resist the temptation to jump in and answer each question right away. Ask if they have any other questions. Keep going until you've uncovered all their unanswered questions or concerns. Responding to all their questions at once allows you time to organize and prioritize your response and buys you extra time to consider what to say. Questions also tend to intersect, so offering a single response avoids repetition.

4. **Organize and prioritize.** As you listen, mentally organize questions into two broad categories: informational questions that seek elaboration or clarification and reservation questions that highlight concerns. This organization will help when you formulate your response.

5. **Keep a poker face.** This is a particularly difficult thing to do, particularly in the face of mistruth or inaccuracy. Regardless, non-verbal cues can be as powerful as verbal responses. Stay neutral, maintain eye contact and nod in understanding and empathy.

6. **Dig deeper into reservations.** Understand whether the prospective client is just stalling or whether they have a specific objection. Think of a reservation like a dartboard. Before you throw a dart, you know what number you need to hit to win the game; just hitting the board is rarely sufficient. Similarly, overcoming an objection requires a clear understanding and targeted response.

7. **Repeat and rephrase.** Now that all their questions and concerns are out in the open, repeat and rephrase them to ensure that you understood correctly. Give the prospective client the opportunity to correct or add to your understanding.

Key takeaways

To understand a prospective client's reservations:

- Probe why they're stalling. They simply may need a little more convincing.
- Dig deeper into objections. Know what issues you have to address to overcome their hesitation.
- Get everything out in the open. You need a clear understanding of the underlying issues.

ASSURANCES

Now it's your turn to answer questions and address concerns. Create an environment of understanding and empathy; this shouldn't be a combative process. You're trying to create accord, establish consensus and ultimately earn a commitment. The best way to do this is with examples of how you've helped other clients through similar situations. Offer solutions and guarantees to overcome any roadblocks.

Make your case

Once you've identified the prospective client's questions and concerns, follow these steps to address them:

1. **Answer informational questions first.** Many informational questions are closing questions, in which the prospective client asks for clarification to confirm the decision they've already begun to make. Answering these first will help build momentum and move you one step closer to the sale. Closing questions might include: "You mentioned X during your presentation. Can you expand on that?" or "You quoted a variable fee of between X and Y. What accounts for the variability?"

2. **Empathize.** Before you move on to reservations, show empathy for their position. Build understanding with phrases such as, "I can see where you're coming from" or "Another client felt exactly the same way."

3. **Move on to stalls.** As we discussed in the reservations topic, a stall represents hesitancy on the prospective client's part. They still need to be convinced. Speak to a specific solution or benefit of your service that addresses their concern. Layer new information and insight onto existing ISBNs or, better still, add a new ISBN. Don't talk around the topic in the hope that something you say marginally connects with their concern. You have to address the issue specifically if you want to move the process forward. Oftentimes, the prospective client is able to come to a conclusion just by talking about their concerns out loud. Your role is to ask smart questions to help them in the process.

4. **Tackle objections.** An objection is a specific reason that prevents the prospective client from buying, such as price or insufficient expertise. Objections are typically more difficult to counter than stalls. Don't back the prospective client into a corner when responding to an objection. Instead, empathize and acknowledge the issue. Then address the objection head on. In my experience, there are four ways to do this:

   - **Draw on an ISBN.** Go back to the issue-solution-benefit narratives you already delivered. Now that you understand the concern, connect one of these ISBN threads to your response.
   - **Dig deeper.** In an effort to focus on the prospective client's specific issues, you've probably kept an ISBN or two in reserve. Now's the

time to go to the well. Connect those solutions and benefits to the prospective client's concern.

- **Offer examples.** Tell them how you've addressed that same concern with other clients. Remember the power of a demonstration event. Present a case study in a succinct manner.
- **Retreat and regroup.** Sometimes you don't have the ammunition to counter an objection. Maybe you need to consult another party or the prospective client needs to reflect on your offering. It's better to retreat and regroup than to push the issue right then.

5. **Move the process forward.** Once you've addressed their reservations, ask if they're ready to move forward. If they still hesitate, ask, "What's preventing you from moving forward?"

6. **Offer guarantees.** If the prospective client repeats a previously stated reservation, you have one last tool in your arsenal: a guarantee. Think back to the conversation we had about late-night infomercials. Before telling you how to order, they offer a guarantee — return it in 30 days, no questions asked, for your money back. The purpose of a guarantee is to counter apprehension by limiting possible negative consequences. Guarantees are more challenging in the accounting industry, but there are options: "If we don't deliver on our promises within 60 days, we'll discount your fee by X" or "If we don't deliver on our promises within 60 days, we'll provide you with (insert additional service here)." Most importantly, the guarantee has to be meaningful to the prospective client.

7. **Be succinct.** One of the biggest challenges in responding to questions is answering in a structural and concise manner. Go back to the rule of three — provide no more than three key points to address a specific question. Elaborate when necessary but try to keep your responses short. My personal rule of thumb is not more than 30 seconds on each key point, for a maximum of 90 seconds.

8. **Don't lose sight of your goal.** The goal is to get the prospective client to commit to a next step. Sometimes that's a verbal or written commitment to move forward; other times it's another call or meeting. Either way, a next step that brings you closer to commitment is a productive and worthwhile one. Some salespeople feel they've failed if they let a prospective client walk out of the room without making a sale. I don't subscribe to that belief. If you are thoughtful and appreciative in your responses, you're serving the client well.

Key takeaways

To address a prospective client's reservations:

- Answer informational questions first. Tackling these helps build positive momentum toward commitment.

- Address stalls next. Oftentimes, stalls can be overcome by encouraging the prospective client to talk through the issue. Your role is to facilitate dialogue.
- Tackle objections last. Unearth the real issues behind the objection. Make sure you target your narrative as talking around the issue will only exacerbate the situation.

COMMITMENT

Asking for commitment is a pivotal step in the sales process. You've listened to a prospective client's needs, presented your solutions and addressed their concerns, positioning yourself to win the work. Yet for many accountants, gaining commitment is the most challenging part of the process. By asking for a prospective client's business, many accountants feel like they're crossing a line from accountant to salesperson. A staggering percentage of opportunities are lost because accountants wrongly assume that prospective clients will speak up if they're interested in moving forward. It's important to gain comfort in learning how to ask for a prospective client's business.

Make the ask

In my experience, the best way to gain commitment is through a simple process:

1. **Address remaining questions and concerns.** Ask if you answered their questions and addressed their concerns. If you did, move on to the next step. If not, seek to understand what needs further clarification and address the topic directly. Roadblocks have a tendency to snowball if you fail to hit the mark a second time. Give them one more chance to raise any remaining questions. If they don't have any, you have the green light to ask for their business. If they have additional questions, address logistical questions first and reservations second. Follow the process we described in reservations and assurances. After answering their questions and addressing their concerns, ask again, "Any other questions?"
2. **Ask for their business.** It's time to ask. It's important to craft a simple, conversational question to make the ask. My personal preference is, "Are you ready to move forward?" The important thing is that you craft something that works for you; it has to sound genuine.
3. **Silence is golden.** Resist the temptation to talk after you've asked for commitment. The silence may feel like an eternity, but it's important to give the prospective client a chance to deliberate. Don't ruin the opportunity with nervous conversation.
4. **Commit to writing.** If they want to move ahead, convert the verbal agreement into a signatory acknowledgement in the shortest time possible. We strongly recommend that you prepare the agreement ahead of time and give them an opportunity to review and sign it in the room. If not, turn the document around quickly. The more time you take, the greater the chance that hesitation and doubt will creep in.

If you ask for their business and the prospective client says no, it likely either means they've made up their mind to go elsewhere or that they need to reflect on the decision. If they need more time, don't rush or pressure them into making a decision on the spot. This may contradict many sales books you've read but we believe the added time will ultimately lead to the desired outcome. If they choose to go in another direction, you were likely not a good match in the first place. Make sure, however, that you schedule a next step, either a meeting or a phone call, so the process doesn't stagnate indefinitely.

Timing and tone

Keep these key points in mind when asking for a commitment:

- **Look for opportunities to ask.** Not every prospective client needs to see a demonstration event or has reservations that require specific assurances. Some clients like what they hear in solutions and are ready to move forward. If they start asking closing questions — such as how much does this cost or when can you start — pass go, collect $200 and jump to commitment.
- **Build momentum.** In other cases, there are so many questions and reservations that it's easy for the prospective client to lose sight of what you have to offer. In this case, we recommend you summarize the best solutions and benefits of your service before asking for their business. Focus on the ones that most resonated with the prospective client. This will build positive momentum before asking for a commitment.
- **Don't coerce or pressure.** Think how you like to buy. You don't like to be pressured or coerced into a decision you're not ready to make. Let the prospective client determine the pace of the conversation. If they have more questions, answer them. If they have reservations, address them. If they're not ready to make a decision, encourage them to take the time they need. This is a relationship you're nurturing for a lifetime so don't be in any hurry to gain commitment if they're not ready.
- **Foretell what's to follow.** Your actions during the sales process should foretell what's to follow during your relationship with this client. Think of the sales process as an audition for future interaction. Go above and beyond to meet their needs, be patient in allowing them to reach a decision, be flexible in meeting their conditions. Be the person you intend to be for the balance of your working relationship. Congruency goes a long way in the sales business.

Key takeaways

To gain commitment from a prospective client:

- Don't be in a rush to get to commitment. Confirm that you've answered their questions and addressed their concerns.
- Make the "ask" with a short, simple turn of phrase such as, "Are you ready to move forward?"
- If they're not ready to commit, set a next step to allow the prospective client to consult others or reflect on the information.

NEXT STEPS

At the meeting when a prospective client commits to becoming a client, it's important to schedule a next step to maintain momentum in the relationship. You'll help overcome any lingering doubts and instead focus the client's energies on moving the relationship forward. Possible next steps include a follow-up call or meeting, a submission requirement, an introduction to another partner in the firm or an invitation to a firm-sponsored informational or hospitality event. Creating a next step establishes the expectation from the get-go that this will be a relationship of action and achievement. It also gives you the opportunity to discover the client's other needs.

Avoid second-guessing

Think about buying a new car — you've signed all the paperwork and now you're sweating whether you've made the right choice. Aware that many customers suffer from buyer's remorse, the car salesperson tells you to come back in a few days to program the deluxe package options in your new vehicle. This free value-added service is designed to help you push past the natural self-doubt that accompanies a big purchase. The salesperson gets you to focus on how to customize your hands-free navigation, instead of second-guessing the major investment you just made. The salesperson also has the chance to try to pitch their service center for oil changes, tune-ups and other maintenance needs. They've assuaged your doubts while also selling you more services.

Similarly, scheduling a next step with an accounting client helps the client overcome doubts and focus on the task at hand. It's especially important in accounting because there's often a significant time delay between the client's commitment to move forward and the actual work being done — that's plenty of time to reconsider a decision, which is exactly what you don't want. And by learning more about them and their needs and deepening your relationship, you're identifying ways to better serve them. Every next step is a chance to learn more about how you can help them.

Create a focal point

Once a prospective client has committed to join your firm, schedule a next step within a week. The next step may require something of them, like submitting documentation, completing your intake form or filling out a won client post-mortem survey; it may also require something of you, like introducing them to other members of your team, sending them a client welcome package or scheduling a discovery planning meeting. Either way, the next step should be something tangible, it should add value to the partnership and it should occur immediately. Verbalize the next step during the meeting in which the prospect agrees to become a client, and follow up immediately after the meeting with an email summarizing specifics.

Once you've completed the next step, establish another next step, and preferably a timeline of next steps so the client knows when, how and how often they should expect to interact with you, your team and your firm. The more scheduled and frequent the interactions, the less fear the client will have that they've misplaced their trust. It's key to remember that creating a next step isn't something you do once; it should happen every time you interact with a client.

Key takeaways

To prevent clients from second-guessing their decision:

- Schedule a next step, such as a submission requirement or a meeting.
- Make sure the next step takes place within a week of the client deciding to move forward with you.
- Follow one next step with another. You'll make the client feel like a priority and uncover new ways to serve them.

REVIEW

Following each interaction with a prospective client, you should review your performance to analyze what worked and what didn't and how you can improve next time. You may have wowed a prospective client with a presentation or things may not have gone as well as you might have liked; either way, debriefing that meeting gives you an opportunity for continuous improvement. It helps you learn to accentuate your strengths, minimize your weaknesses and improve from your experiences, both good and bad.

Aim higher

Continuous learning serves two goals. First, it helps you get better which means you'll win more work. Second, it conveys something important to the prospect or client — that you're committed to getting better, that you don't have all the answers all the time and that you're open to recommendations and feedback. When you realize you could have done better and you revisit your mistakes with a client, you demonstrate that you're willing to work on your shortcomings. Rarely have I seen this adversely impact a relationship with a client or prospective client.

While the iron is hot

Follow these steps to get in the habit of continual self-analysis:

1. **Capture your thoughts.** Once you've left a meeting, capture your thoughts immediately. You can fill out a form (www[32]), speak into an audio recording device (like your phone) or use an app designed for this purpose. Record both quantitative data and qualitative analysis.

   For example, after a needs assessment meeting, fill out the following form by scoring each outcome on a scale of 1 to 5.

Prospective client	Score
Client has clearly defined their current situation	
Client has shared their goals	
Client has defined success factors to achieve goals	
Client has clarified the role the firm is expected to play in achieving goals	
Competition	
Client has shared the concerns they have with their current/ prior service provider	
Client has clearly defined the capabilities the winning service provider must have	
Client has provided a list of competitors	

Decision-making	
Client has clarified who makes the decision, how it will be made, and when it will be made by	
Client has provided the criteria that will be used to select the winning firm	
Client has defined next steps, including process and timeline	

For the qualitative analysis, structure your comments as follows:

- **Positives:** three things you did well; the things you would repeat
- **Concerns:** three things you didn't do well
- **Recommendations:** three things you would do differently to improve your performance next time

The qualitative feedback is by far the most important. The more specific and substantial your feedback, the easier it will be to improve.

2. **Share feedback with a mentor or coach.** Your business development mentor or coach will hopefully provide additional insights and ideas to augment your own recommendations. For this to work best, your coach or mentor should have immediate access to your feedback. The principle at play here is "better is best" — there's always room for improvement.

3. **Go back to the well.** Keep a running tally of your feedback. Look for commonalities, including things you repeatedly did well and mistakes you made over and over. Remember not to focus only on the negatives; it's just as important to learn how to play to your strengths. If you are using an app to track your feedback, the app may be able to generate comparative reports for you.

4. **Identify training topics.** Know your "best practices" and teach them to others so they can replicate your winning formula. Know your weaknesses and address them in future training or coaching sessions. When possible, supplement theoretical training exercises with live role-play. For example, if you're struggling with the needs stage in the sales process, practice your interview techniques with your mentor or coach.

5. **Add another dimension.** Outside of self-analysis, draw on other opportunities to review your performance, including post-mortem interviews. Ignore client feedback at your peril. There's no one-size-fits-all approach to business development, but if a client says you didn't ask enough questions, keep that in mind during future interactions with that client and other prospective clients.

Key takeaways

To learn what you do well and where you need to improve:

- Take the time to debrief every interaction with a prospective client during the sales process.
- Use a tool to record your thoughts immediately after the interaction while your thoughts are fresh.
- Provide both quantitative and qualitative feedback and share feedback with a mentor or coach.

CHAPTER 10
NICHES

Look at any high-performing accounting firm and you'll find one uniform commonality: They've seen their greatest growth in service and industry niches. One of the core tenets of this book is that firms that want to continue to succeed need to develop specialized areas of service. As sports agent Leigh Steinberg once said, "Very narrow areas of expertise can be very productive. Develop your own profile. Develop your own niche." Remember, society needs people who are well rounded, but rewards people who are well-pointed. We live in a niche world; it's time to make the commitment.

In this chapter, we address the critical considerations in developing a new niche. Individual topics include:

- **Why niche:** Too many firms try to do everything for everyone. Develop a specialized niche expertise and you'll close more new business and command higher prices.
- **Which niche:** Consider your own expertise and experience, the size of the market and the competition when choosing a niche. Complete our exercise to find the best niche for you.
- **Niche levels:** Create niche levels to serve as a blueprint for growing a niche. Understand the investment required to advance in establishing your niche.
- **How to niche:** Follow these specific strategies to succeed in your niche. Strategies include anointing a champion, building your team, conducting research, creating a plan, identifying prospective clients, providing training opportunities and maximizing visibility.
- **Niche plan:** Draft a business development plan that lists your services, goals, strategies and any relevant analysis.

WHY NICHE

Positioning your firm in a niche is about catering to a specific set of clients interested in a particular suite of products or services. A niche can be a service, in which case your firm would focus on a single service that appeals to multiple industries (for example, business valuation). A niche can also be an industry, in which case your firm would offer a broad array of services to clients in a specific industry (for example, technology).

Reel in more fish

Many accounting firms position their business to meet everyone's needs in an effort to capture more work. They figure that the broader their service offerings, the more business they'll develop. In fact, the reality is just the opposite. By offering services to everyone, the firm ends up competing against every firm in the area that claims to provide the same services. When this happens, clients make their decision based on price because they can't differentiate among the competitors. Rather than adopting a generalist approach, take a page out of Henry Ford's book and become better at servicing a segment of the market. As Ford said, "Any customer can have a car painted any color he wants so long as it is black."

Niche marketing has gained significant traction in the accounting industry over the past decade. Niche marketing is about defining narrow categories of people to whom your business can appeal. The accounting firms that have seen the greatest success in recent years are those that have committed to a niche practice development strategy. The AICPA recently released a report on the future of the accounting industry. That report discusses the opportunities that specialization presents for accountants. In part, the report reads: "Emerging opportunities for specialization will allow CPAs to strengthen their expertise and provide additional value to clients, employers and business."

With specialized niche expertise, you'll close more new business and command higher prices. You shouldn't give up on your generalist clientele — they help pay the bills — but your focus should be on becoming superior in a niche. It takes a lot of time to build and ultimately conquer a niche but it's well worth your while to do it right.

There are many benefits to building a niche, including in the following areas:

- **Marketing:** Your marketing efforts become more focused. If you have a niche, you have a clearly defined target audience and you can focus on reaching that narrow segment of the market.
- **Services:** You learn how to best meet the needs of your niche. Because you've chosen to specialize, you aren't bouncing around between issues, but instead are developing a deep expertise in your chosen area.

- **Clients:** You convert more prospects into clients. You're experienced at identifying client needs in your niche and can present a convincing case for your solutions. You win more work in less time and face fewer geographic boundaries in recruiting new clients.
- **Referrals:** You generate more referral traffic. Your niche clients refer you to other clients in your niche and you know where to look to develop high-quality referral sources.
- **Pricing:** You command higher pricing and compete on price less often. You don't have to lower your price to compete; instead, your expertise is your value proposition.

In the following topics, we'll explore how to pick the right niche and how to develop your business in that niche.

Key takeaways

Building a niche helps you:

- Reduce the competition. Now you won't be competing in the same generalist space as everyone else.
- Close more business and command higher pricing.
- Focus your efforts. You'll be catering to a more select group of clients.

WHICH NICHE

It's not uncommon for firms to pick a niche based on the number of clients they have in a particular service or industry. While there's some logic to that strategy, there are many more variables that you should consider in deciding where to invest your talent and resources, including profit and growth potential, the competitive landscape and whether you have personnel with the relevant skills and contacts.

Understand the investment

It takes significant investment in the following areas to be successful in a niche:

- **Messaging:** Your firm will need a mission statement that illustrates what differentiates it from other firms in the niche. The statement should align with the firm's overall marketing message.
- **Marketing:** You'll need a niche-specific marketing effort that should involve generating niche-specific collateral and utilizing social media to position your firm as an industry leader. It also helps to serve as a media source and to join niche-specific associations.
- **Expertise:** Do whatever it takes to become an expert in your niche. Take niche-specific training courses and perfect your niche-specific service specialties. Offer benchmarking to your clients to help them see how they stack up against others in their industry.
- **Commitment:** Establish measurable goals to assess your progress. Ensure that everyone on the team is excited and contributing. Remember, you need total buy-in to succeed in establishing a niche.

Pick wisely

Ask yourself the following questions when considering starting a new niche:

- Do you have a unique expertise? Is your expertise superior to that of your competitors?
- How deep is the well of opportunity? Does the market want what you have to offer?
- Looking at your client base as a whole, with whom did you like working and are they in an industry in which you can sell additional services?

The X factor

The following "Factor Exercise" helps you answer those questions. For each proposed niche service or industry, score your firm on a scale of 1 to 10 in each of the following categories. A 10 means you more than meet the criteria, a 1 means you don't meet any of the criteria. You'll need to perform some preliminary research to accurately complete the exercise.

Factor	Explanation	Score
Personnel	Do we have a passionate champion with relevant skills and contacts?	
Seasonality	Can the work be done during the non-busy season?	
Profitability	Does the type of work or absence of competition support higher margins?	
Clients	Do we already have clients in this niche? Can we sell more services to them?	
Referral sources	Do we have referral sources in this area? Have they been a recurring source of new business year after year?	
Strategic alliances	Can we draw on existing partnerships to deliver technical competence? Do our partners have the relevant expertise?	
Few competitors	Is there an absence of relevant competition in this space?	
Maturity	How established is the industry? Is it growing or in decline?	
Industry definition	How defined is the industry (real estate, construction, etc)?	
Other	Insert other criteria here.	
Tax	Can we sell a full suite of tax services?	
Audit	Can we sell a full suite of audit and accounting services?	
Wealth management	Can we sell wealth management services? If so, which ones?	
Advisory	Can we sell advisory services? If so, which ones?	
Total score		

Armed with this information, you have a strong foundation for determining the services or industries in which you should invest your resources and talent.

Key takeaways

To choose the right niche:

- Consider the investment you'll need to put in to succeed.
- Do your homework to better understand the opportunities.
- Complete the factor exercise to determine where to invest your efforts.

NICHE LEVELS

Niche levels serve as a blueprint for launching and growing a niche. Try to simplify the process as much as possible; having fewer levels makes the process easier to understand and track.

Know the road ahead

Possessing industry expertise is not the same as developing a niche practice. By virtue of serving multiple technology clients, you can certainly claim expertise in the technology sector; however, that is not the same as developing a niche practice in technology. Creating niche levels helps ensure your firm is clear about the necessary investments to build a successful niche.

Track your growth

The following is an example of a three-level niche development model. The required investments are broken into three categories: administration and management, business development and services. As you grow your niche, you progress from level 1 (starter niche) to level 2 (maturing niche) to level 3 (established niche). In the how to niche topic that follows, we'll talk about the specifics contained in the niche model, such as appointing a champion, building your team, creating a plan, identifying prospective clients, providing training and certification opportunities, and maximizing visibility.

Administration and management		
Level 1 (Starter niche)	**Level 2 (Maturing niche)**	**Level 3 (Established niche)**
Appoint a designated champion	Appoint a designated service provider	Add dedicated service providers
Appropriate personnel to teams	Measure niche profitability	Develop a recruiting plan
Draft a business plan	Conduct an internal inspection	Conduct a peer review
Establish quality control standards		
Create a dedicated website	Update web content on a regular basis	
Business development		
Level 1 (Starter niche)	**Level 2 (Maturing niche)**	**Level 3 (Established niche)**
Perform market research	Publish articles in an industry or professional journal	Generate unique industry media (for example, talk radio)

Business development		
Level 1 (Starter niche)	**Level 2 (Maturing niche)**	**Level 3 (Established niche)**
Develop a client screening process	Establish an industry business group	Speak at industry conference/trade shows
Develop a referral source plan	Establish strategic partnerships	Host educational events (for example, seminars or speaker series)
Develop marketing materials	Attend and exhibit at industry conference/ trade shows	Serve as an industry news media spokesperson

Services		
Level 1 (Starter niche)	**Level 2 (Maturing niche)**	**Level 3 (Established niche)**
Compile a skills inventory	Compile a list of niche experts by skill set/ service	Integrate niche experts into service model
Develop a niche services menu	Expand and refine niche services menu	Share service model with pertinent alliance partners
Develop a staff training plan	Provide specialized staff training	Encourage staff to gain industry certifications

Once you have created a niche model, you can establish performance metrics by level (all numbers are hypothetical):

Category/Level	Level 1	Level 2	Level 3
Timeline	1 year	3 years	5 years
Number of clients	20	50	100
Gross revenue – tax	$100,000	$250,000	$500,000
Gross revenue – audit and accounting	$75,000	$175,000	$350,000
Gross revenue – financial services	$50,000	$100,000	$200,000
Gross revenue - advisory	$50,000	$100,000	$200,000
Total revenue	$275,000	$625,000	$1,250,000

Category/Level	Level 1	Level 2	Level 3
Designated champion(s)	1	1	1
Designated staff	2	4	8
Designated strategic alliance partner(s)	0	1	2
Other (insert additional criteria here)			

Each firm should customize its niche levels depending on the marketplace and its available resources and talent. Though there aren't uniform metrics for niche development, we would suggest the following rules of thumb: First, don't start a new niche until you've moved your prior niche from level 1 to level 2; and second, expect to invest 3-5 years to successfully move a niche from level 1 to level 3.

Key takeaways

Niche levels help you:

- Set benchmarks for the development of a niche.
- Establish expectations for the performance of a niche.
- Develop a roadmap for becoming the pre-eminent firm in your niche.

HOW TO NICHE

In the previous topic, we laid out a plan for growing and tracking a niche. Now we'll talk about some of the specific items discussed in the niche-level model. Specifically, this will include appointing a champion, building your team, conducting research, creating a plan, identifying prospective clients, providing training opportunities and maximizing visibility.

Appoint a champion

Without a champion, your team is rudderless. The niche champion corrals the group effort, sets targets and makes sure everyone stays on topic. The champion is the voice, face and spokesperson for the group both internally within the firm and externally with clients, prospective clients, associations, boards and media. There are two schools of thought for whom to choose as your champion. Many who have successfully launched niches in large local and regional firms suggest selecting a firm partner as your niche champion. We believe niche practice development provides an unparalleled opportunity for firms to develop senior managers en route to making partner. A successful niche champion will possess three skill sets that all "partners of tomorrow" will need: technical competence, the ability to lead and manage others and business development acumen. Consider assigning a business development-savvy partner to mentor the niche champion if they don't possess the necessary business development acumen.

Build your team

Niche staff members should bring a cross-section of experience to the team. The team should include a mix of staff accountants, senior accountants, supervisors, managers, senior managers, directors and partners. All individuals should have demonstrated an interest in the chosen service or industry. The champion should host a lunch n' learn session with niche team candidates to explain the opportunity, skill requirements and commitments. Once the team is chosen, everyone should meet regularly and the niche champion should delegate specific tasks with stated timelines, spread the workload and recognize outstanding effort and contribution.

Conduct research

Beyond the factor exercise described in the "which niche" topic, there's significant additional research to be done by the team before a plan takes shape. This research includes a more comprehensive analysis of the opportunity, including understanding the market, the competition and the required service capabilities of a winning competitor. This information will be essential when you craft your competitive advantage and claims.

Create a Plan

A niche plan is similar in form to a general business plan. As a general guide, consider covering the following:

- **Know the market and how you fit in.** Write a succinct statement explaining what services you provide, develop an ideal client profile and research any industry trends that would affect your business development strategy. List your current clients in the niche and categorize them as "A"-level, "B"-level or "C"-level clients or referral prospects.
- **Decide on your goals.** Figure out what you want to accomplish with your business development efforts. Make your goals specific and measureable and state up to three total goals. Develop a general strategy for reaching your goals and state up to three total strategies.
- **Create a budget.** Include a business development expense estimate, so you know what you have to work with when planning your business development tactics.
- **Develop a marketing strategy.** Tackle the four P's of marketing: product, price, placement and promotion. You need to know what you're selling and how you'll price your services. Will you market yourself as the low-cost provider to garner broad appeal or will you set a high price to target a luxury market? You also need to decide how you'll promote your services to make them visible to your target market.
- **Know the competition.** Research your top three competitors. Keep things as realistic as possible. Figure out your strengths and weaknesses and what you do better than the rest. Connect your competitive advantages to the most common client issues. For each issue, articulate your solution and the benefit the client will enjoy as a result of that solution.

In the following topic, we provide a specific template to follow when creating a niche plan.

Identify prospective clients

Armed with your ideal client profile, identify a list of suspects. There are a number of online tools where you can generate a list of prospective clients based on specific search queries. These lists tend to be inexpensive to purchase, but they're not necessarily accurate or up to date. If you're willing to spend more to get a current list, we recommend you hire a researcher to clean up the initial suspect list and convert it into a prospect list (remove duplicates, validate current information, correct contact information, etc). It will be the best $1,000-$2,000 you'll spend. Invest the time and resources to get this right.

Provide training and certification opportunities

One of the defining characteristics of niche expertise is currency, or being up-to-date about changing legislation, policy and procedure. Make sure to provide all team members with the necessary training opportunities to stay on the cutting edge. And keep in mind this wisdom from classical guitarist Andres Segovia: "To teach is to learn twice." Encourage those who go through training to internalize what they learn by teaching it to others.

Maximize visibility

To raise your visibility, generate intellectual capital by speaking and publishing as much as possible; join industry-specific associations and work to the front of the room by taking on positions of responsibility; become the go-to expert for local media; and do more than the traditional marketing platform requires by supporting multiple social media channels, blogging and sponsoring events.

Key takeaways

Developing a niche requires that you make the following significant commitments:

- Appoint a niche champion. This is an important and essential first step. The champion must be technically proficient, a willing leader and manager of others and skilled at business development.
- Build a team. Even with an outstanding niche champion, it takes a village. The niche team is that village.
- Go after your goals. You can't do niches halfway. You have to commit to developing a plan and putting yourself out there.

NICHE PLAN

Before you get started on building your niche, it's important to create a short business development plan to guide your activities. Your business development plan should list your services, goals, strategies and any relevant analysis.

Know where you're going

Your niche business development plan should cover the following:

- **Services:** Succinctly state what services you provide.
- **Target market:** Define your target market, including important demographics such as size or geographic location.
- **Industry trends:** Include analysis of any relevant industry trends, such as major growth or decline within certain segments of your market.
- **Current clients:** List your current clients in that niche. Categorize them as "A"-level, "B"-level or "C"-level clients. Do the same for your referral sources and prospective clients.
- **Goals:** Define your business development goals. Make them specific and measurable. Include up to three goals.
- **Strategies:** Lay out the strategies you'll employ to reach your goals. These should not be specific actions, such as weekly newsletters, but rather should be broad in nature. Include up to three strategies.
- **Budget:** Know how much money you have to work with when planning out your business development expenses.
- **Marketing:** Develop a marketing strategy that addresses your product, price, placement and promotion. Decide how you'll market yourself.
- **Competitive analysis:** List your top three competitors and their strengths and weaknesses.
- **Strengths and weaknesses:** Detail your strengths and weaknesses in your new niche.
- **Value proposition:** State your competitive advantage and claims.
- **Monthly topics:** Outline specific actionable business development tasks by month.

Your final plan should be about three to five pages long. You can access a blank template on our website (www[33]). The following example is excerpted from a niche plan that was developed for a firm's consulting practice:

Goal 1: Create an umbrella approach to marketing the firm's consulting services.

- *Strategy 1:* Leverage data mining software and partner knowledge to identify prospective clients.
- *Strategy 2:* Create podcasts that can be streamed live to clients and archived for future reference.
- *Strategy 3:* Include a note with every customer submission document detailing the firm's expanded consulting service offerings.

Goal 2: Identify the firm's core consulting services and create a targeted marketing approach for each to reach non-client prospects.

- **Strategy 1:** Write articles for trade publications.
- **Strategy 2:** Develop a list of center of influence referral sources for each service type.
- **Strategy 3:** Track results to better understand which marketing activities offer the best return.

Goal 3: Provide training to give partners and staff an opportunity to learn more about the firm's consulting offerings and how they benefit clients.

- **Strategy 1:** Host a monthly "consulting spotlight topic" training.
- **Strategy 2:** Host a monthly cross-selling meeting to discuss best practices and success stories.
- **Strategy 3:** Present a consulting case study at every other business development pipeline meeting.

Key takeaways

A niche plan should:

- Provide a roadmap. Follow your plan as you develop your niche.
- Lay out your goals and your strategies for achieving those goals.
- Provide analysis of your target market, competition and strengths and weaknesses.

CHAPTER 11
MANAGEMENT

Sales management is the wonderful meeting point of process and motivation. To succeed in business development, you need to have the right people and the right processes. After all, business development isn't something that everyone likes to do. Reliable and repeatable business development success depends on putting processes in place to manage and track effort and performance, and on tasking people with coaching, mentoring and motivating others. As you go about building your business development management structure, keep in mind these words from Oscar™ winning actor, Tom Hanks: "If it wasn't hard, everyone would do it. It's the hard that makes it great."

This chapter is stuffed with business development management best practices. Individual topics include:

- **Compelling saga:** A compelling saga states your firm's business development goals. It unifies employees around a common purpose.
- **Sales stages:** Sales stages are the key milestones that exist between identifying a new prospect and winning or losing that prospect's business.
- **Know your strengths:** Every individual in a firm needs to understand their own talents and how to leverage them for business development.
- **Staffing:** To sustain a commitment to business development, we recommend appointing or hiring a business development champion, a business development coach and a business development coordinator.
- **Firm business development plan:** A firm business development plan forecasts new business revenue and outlines business development strategies. When followed, it represents your roadmap to success.
- **Targets and KPIs:** Targets represent the goals you need to achieve to succeed each year. KPIs, or key performance indicators, are the steps

required to reach the target. Set these wisely to guide your business development efforts.

- **Individual business development plan:** An individual business development plan outlines what each contributor is expected to do to realize their business development goals.
- **Business development meetings:** Schedule regular meetings to discuss business development performance. Recognize key contributors, acknowledge best practices and offer assistance in dealing with issues and challenges.
- **Database management:** Use a sales database to aggregate information on clients, prospective clients and referral sources. Mine this data to identify best practices and areas for improvement.
- **Reports:** Generate reports regularly to track how you're doing and, more importantly, to tell you what you need to do moving forward. Go beyond the data and provide analysis.
- **Coaching:** Task your business development coach with driving your business development efforts. The coach should outline goals, monitor performance and offer suggestions.
- **Mentoring:** In addition to coaching, create an informal mentoring program so colleagues can learn from each other.
- **Accountability:** Hold employees responsible when they fail to meet their business development goals.
- **Compensation:** Adopt a hybrid compensation model in which employees earn year-end bonuses for hitting certain goals while also earning commissions for their business development successes throughout the year.
- **Recognition and reward:** Recognize and reward good work by your employees to reinforce positive behaviors. Don't overlook the importance of verbal praise — a sincere thanks is often the most valuable reward you can offer.

COMPELLING SAGA

This topic draws on the work of Chris Warner and Don Schmincke, who wrote the book "High Altitude Leadership: What the World's Most Forbidding Peaks Teach Us About Success." It's a fantastic book and we highly recommend you read it.

A compelling saga is a statement that sets a goal for a firm's business development efforts. That goal usually involves defeating an enemy, pursuing an ideal or fulfilling a purpose. The compelling saga statement sets the context for how success or failure will be defined.

Rally the troops

Oftentimes, a firm's mission or value statement doesn't suitably rally the troops from a business development standpoint. They need something more specific and more motivational to drive their efforts. A good compelling saga achieves this by unifying employees around a common goal. It makes a clear case for why growth is important and for what success looks like.

Forward, march

There are three types of compelling saga statements: ones that target an enemy, ones that seek to achieve an ideal and ones that aspire to fulfill a purpose. For example:

Type	Company	Statement
Enemy	Lexus	Beat Benz.
Ideal	Citicorp	Become the most powerful, the most service-able, the most far-reaching world financial institution that has ever been.
Purpose	Harley Davidson	Fulfill dreams through the experience of motorcycling.

I prefer compelling sagas that are driven by an ideal or purpose. Focusing on an enemy combatant can seem overly confrontational, plus the industry landscape changes so rapidly that the fiercest competitor today may not be a relevant competitor tomorrow. And remember that much like a slogan, your compelling saga can change with time.

Consider this compelling saga from Bay Area accounting firm DZH Phillips: "Win by creating opportunities." It's a great compelling saga because it ties together the firm's many constituencies. Everyone wins by creating opportunities — opportunities for clients, for colleagues, for partners, for their families.

Follow these steps to craft your own compelling saga:

- **Conduct a SWOT analysis.** Prioritize the results to create a top 5 list of strengths, weaknesses, opportunities and threats.
- **Craft individual statements.** Ask everyone on your business development team to write down one or more compelling saga statements for the firm's business development effort. Individuals can draw on the SWOT analysis, as well as on their own perspective and personal experience. Ask everyone to articulate and defend their statement.
- **Write a single statement.** Debate the merits of each statement and combine them as needed to craft a single compelling saga that everyone can support.
- **Create a graphic that captures the statement.** The graphic for the example referenced above was a checkered flag and finish line with the words, "win by creating opportunities." I like the visual because the flag and finish line are universal symbols of success, and because "win by creating opportunities" is an inclusive concept that applies to all of a firm's constituencies.
- **Use the statement.** Include the statement and graphic in internal business development communications, including firm business development reports (see culture chapter for more on business development reports).
- **Bring the saga to life.** I've seen firms create employee and customer awards and recognition programs around their compelling saga, integrate the compelling saga into building décor and promote the saga through "treasure and trinket" giveaway items. The point is that crafting a compelling saga is not just an exercise. It has to permeate all your business development activities.

Key takeaways

Crafting a compelling saga helps you:

- Set a target, goal or destination for your business development efforts.
- Unite all contributors in pursuit of that common goal.
- Drive performance and set the standard for how success will be defined.

SALES STAGES

Sales stages are the key milestones that exist between identifying a new prospective client and winning or losing that prospect's business.

Structure your sales process

There are many steps between researching a prospect and winning their business — you have to build a relationship with the prospective client, uncover their needs, sell your firm and close the deal. The point of creating sales stages is to formalize this process, ensuring consistency and discipline from everyone involved. You'll also learn where in the process you need to improve your efforts and you'll significantly enhance the quality and accuracy of your sales forecasts.

Track your progress

Follow these four steps to set up a sales stage process at your firm:

1. **Choose your stages.** Different firms use different names for the stages of their sales process. You should choose between six and ten stages that best resonate with you. My own rule of thumb is the fewer the better; the simpler your sales stages are, the easier they'll be to understand and quantify. Here are three ideas of how you might break up your sales process. In the process that follows, we'll use the **third option**.

Lead stage	Unqualified leads stage	**Research stage**
Opportunity stage	Market and prospect intelligence stage	**Needs assessment stage**
Proposal stage	Qualification of prospects stage	**Proposal stage**
Negotiation stage	Needs assessment stage	**Decision stage**
Closed – won	Proposal stage	**Closed – won**
Lost – incumbent	Conversion stage	**Lost – incumbent**
Lost – competitor	Closed – won	**Lost – competitor**
Lost – no decision	Lost – incumbent	**Lost – no decision**
	Lost – competitor	
	Lost – no decision	

2. **Create a checklist for each stage.** This will provide a basis for determining whether a prospective client is ready to move from one stage to the next.

Research stage	• You have completed the client research profile and confirmed the client fits the firm's ideal client profile.
Needs assessment stage	• You know all of the following about the client: their current situation, their goals, the role you will play in achieving those goals. • You know all of the following about your competition: who your competitors are, what capabilities the client wants from their new provider, the client's concerns about their current/prior provider. • You know all of the following about the client's decision-making process: who makes the decision about what firm to hire, how and when the decision will be made, the criteria that will be used to select the winning firm.
Proposal stage	• The client understands the strengths of the firm and the individual team member. • The client has confirmed the firm's understanding of their needs, agrees with the firm's solutions and understands the benefits.
Decision stage	• The client confirms that any remaining objections have been addressed. • The client has agreed with the work schedule and fee agreement. • The client has signed a document committing to move forward.
Closed – won	• The client has signed an engagement letter or agreement and has completed a won client post-mortem survey.
Lost – incumbent	• The client has decided to stay with their current provider and has completed a lost client post-mortem survey.
Lost – competitor	• The client has decided to go with another provider and has completed a lost client post-mortem survey.
Lost – no decision	• The client has decided not to act at the present time.

To ensure your sales stage reporting is accurate, don't allow individuals to change a sales stage unless each item on the "sales checklist" has been checked. You can use software programs to help you manage your sales stages. For example, there are mobile applications that allow you to create your own checklists and update them with ease from your phone.

3. **Track the value of your sales pipeline.** Using your best guess, assign a conversion probability percentage to each stage (in the example below, the firm assumes that 15% of the prospective clients in the "needs assessment" phase will ultimately come on as new clients). Use real data to refine your percentages over time.

Stage	Conversion probability
Research stage	5%
Needs assessment stage	15%
Proposal stage	35%
Decision stage	65%
Closed – won	100%
Lost – incumbent	0%
Lost – competitor	0%
Lost – no decision	0%

Multiply the opportunity value of each prospective client by the conversion probability to arrive at a pipeline value.

Client name	Opportunity value ($s)	Conversion probability (%)	Pipeline value ($s)
Client X	$25,000	Needs Assessment Stage – 15%	$3,750
Client Y	$2,500	Decision Stage – 65%	$1,625
Client Z	$7,500	Research Stage – 5%	$375

4. **Use the data.** Use the information you've collected to improve your sales forecasting. By carefully tracking your sales stages, you'll be able to project sales numbers by person and time period. You can also use this data to train your staff in stages where you are losing the most opportunities. You should also glean best practices from individuals who are consistently successful in specific stages.

Key takeaways

Sales stages enable you to:

- Better forecast future sales on an individual and firm-wide level.
- Ensure everyone has a clear idea of how to successfully pursue a sales opportunity.
- Train individuals in aspects of the sales cycle where they're falling short.

KNOW YOUR STRENGTHS

This topic draws on the work of Benson Smith and Tony Rutigliano, who wrote the book "Discover Your Sales Strengths: How the World's Greatest Salespeople Develop Winning Careers." It's a fantastic book and we highly recommend you read it.

Understanding your personal strengths is crucial to your business development success. As a business development coach, I ask all my clients to read the bestselling book "Discover Your Sales Strengths" and to take the Gallup StrengthsFinder assessment, which identifies their top five talents. The book, grounded in extensive Gallup research conducted over 40 years and based on hundreds of thousands of interviews with sales managers, salespeople and clients, teaches individuals to focus on their personal talents and strengths, and then guides them in transforming those assets into business development success.

Put your best foot forward

To make the most of your sales opportunities you need to recognize your own talents and understand your client's preferences.

As an example, here are my five signature themes, as determined by the StrengthsFinder assessment, along with illustrations of how I've used my strengths in the sales arena.

Achiever	My achiever theme gives me the energy to work long hours without burning out. It's what pushes me to make one more "inconvenience call" at the end of the day.
Maximizer	My maximizer theme leads me to focus on doing more for my best prospects and clients. That's where I direct my energy.
Strategic	My strategic theme helps me to see patterns where others see complexity. This helps me to be a problem-solver and solution-finder.
Ideation	My ideation theme helps me to improve upon existing ideas, innovate and find connections between seemingly disparate concepts. This creativity is my competitive advantage.
Futuristic	My futuristic theme helps me to focus on vision and what could be. Better is best is my personal mantra.

The "Discover Your Sales Strengths" book is particularly useful for relating your talents directly to business development. It dispels several longstanding sales myths and focuses on connecting your strengths profile to techniques, skills and strategies that will help you to sell more effectively.

Your top talents

To put your best skills to work, follow these steps:

1. **Buy the book.** Purchase "Discover Your Sales Strengths" by Benson Smith and Tony Rutigliano.
2. **Take the test.** Go to strengthsfinder.com. Enter the code in the jacket sleeve of your book and take the StrengthsFinder assessment. As an alternative, you can access your top five signature themes report or your entire 34 signature themes report at gallupstrengthscenter.com.
3. **Study the results.** Print your top five signatures themes report. Read the "sounds like" examples for each of your themes in the appendix section of the book. This section includes concrete examples of each theme in the real world (for example, it might help you to recognize how to channel your "maximizer" theme in identifying "A"-level clients and referral sources).
4. **Share with others.** Share your top five signature themes with colleagues. Discuss ways to leverage your talents in the business development arena.
5. **Find additional resources.** Visit Gallup's Strengths Center at gallupstrengthscenter.com for questions and to access additional coaching resources, including Tony Rutigliano and Brian Brim's follow-up book, "Strengths Based Selling."

Use your knowledge

Arm yourself with this knowledge and you'll be able to escape outdated ideas about selling. You'll connect your own talents with the three most important facets of business development: building relationships, solving client needs and persuading others to commit. You'll also learn to understand your clients' strengths and the most effective way to sell to them. Knowing how to tailor your sales pitch to each client is much more valuable than a one-size-fits-all approach to business development.

Key takeaways

To make the most of your own strengths:

- Read "Discover Your Sales Strengths." This book connects your talents to business development.
- Take the Gallup StrengthsFinder assessment. Based on decades of research, it will give you insights into your strengths and talents.
- Convert that knowledge. You need to understand yourself and your clients to sell effectively.

STAFFING

To sustain a commitment to business development, we recommend that firms fill three critical roles: business development champion, business development coach and business development coordinator.

It's their job

Without a dedicated staff in place to support a firm's business development effort, business development becomes an afterthought. When business development slips to this precarious position, bad things happen, particularly in a poor economy when you don't have a steady stream of unsolicited new clients. The business development team — champion, coach and coordinator — are charged with making business development a constant priority for the whole firm.

Build your team

To build an effective business development team, craft clear job descriptions to avoid overlap. Once the team is in place, everyone should meet regularly, identify strengths and weaknesses and stay on top of business development trends.

Consider filling the following three business development roles at your firm:

1. **Business development champion:** The business development champion is a high-ranking member of the firm, typically a partner, who has been a prolific source of new business for the firm for many years. The champion can't be someone who lives by the motto, "do as I say, not as I do"; this person leads from the front by example. The champion can probably draw on a strong professional network and will ideally have helped launch a niche. The champion should be an engaging communicator, likeable, personable, approachable and friendly. The champion may provide some or all of the following:

   • Partner liaison. They serve as the partners' eyes and ears in business development.
   • Budgeting and allocation of resources.
   • Communication. As the face of the business development effort, they often speak at staff, partner and business development meetings.
   • Mentoring. They mentor staff and train other mentors.
   • Managing. They supervise the business development coach and coordinator.
   • They also perform any of the tasks assigned to the coach, if the firm doesn't have the means to hire for this role.

2. **Business development coach:** Because business development is such a foreign skill-set for many accountants, it can be helpful to bring in a business development professional to provide direction and guidance.

The business development coach can draw on experience working with other types of professional service firms and may be able to bring a different perspective on how the non-accounting world drives business through relationships. This person is typically paid hourly or put on retainer; the cost isn't necessarily significant but the benefit should be exponential. This person may also be able to act as an outside sales rep. In any case, their contributions help drive revenue that offsets their fees. The coach may provide some or all of the following:

- Individual coaching.
- Group training.
- Devising business development plans for the firm and for individuals.
- Forecasting.
- Compensation consulting.
- Coordinating the business development meeting. They set the agenda and lead the meeting.
- Reporting and analyzing business development progress. This may include benchmarking against other firms.
- Performance evaluation.

If your firm can't afford to have someone consult for you, draw on the resources within your firm and on industry resources, including webinars, convention workshops and media articles.

3. **Business development coordinator:** Hiring a business development coordinator is often the first significant step for firms making a long-term commitment to business development. This person is pivotal for managing all the "behind the curtain" work that is necessary for maintaining a business development culture. As the firm's business development commitment increases, this person will eventually become overrun with work. At that point, consider adding temporary help in the form of a business development intern or paid part-time assistant to perform some of the administrative tasks. The coordinator may provide some or all of the following:

- Managing and maintaining the firm's sales database and generating applicable reports.
- Procuring lists, mining data and coordinating mailings supporting campaign initiatives.
- Generating customized proposals.
- Generating client/prospect/competitor intelligence.
- Distributing and maintaining sales and marketing collateral.
- Organizing business development special events, such as B2B mixers and client informational and hospitality events.
- Orchestrating the firm's bi-weekly business development meeting.
- Conducting post-mortem research by following up with lost prospects, won prospects and lost clients.

- Organizing the firm's business development marketing calendar.
- Scheduling meetings, generating and sending correspondence and conducting miscellaneous "follow-up" for the firm's partners, business development champion and business development coach.
- Performing unsolicited lead generation functions.

In addition to the three roles listed above, you might consider hiring an outside sales rep. This person would be paid to bring in new business by drawing on their professional network or conducting unsolicited lead generation campaigns.

Key takeaways

To help create a business development-centric culture:

- Build a dedicated business development team.
- Appoint a business development champion, and hire a business development coach and a business development coordinator.
- Ensure clear roles, constant communication and a commitment to continuous improvement.

FIRM BUSINESS DEVELOPMENT PLAN

A firm-wide business development plan is your firm's blueprint for business development success. It forecasts new business revenue by type and lays out strategies to make the forecast a reality. The simpler and more stream-lined it is, the more achievable it will ultimately be. As the great Winston Churchill once said, "Let our advance worrying become advance thinking and planning." Drafting a business development plan creates a sense of purpose and a belief that the vision is attainable.

Strategize

To keep your plan simple, we suggest you choose three key objectives. Objectives typically fall into three general categories:

1. **Sales-focused:** Establish strategies to promote significant revenue growth, both overall and in niche practices.
2. **Marketing-focused:** Clarify the firm's competitive advantage and claims. Increase marketing promotion through print and electronic media, social media and events.
3. **Team-focused:** Develop a firm-wide business development culture that values the contributions of all and strives to foster an environment of collegiality, mutual support, trust and accountability.

For each objective, we recommend you choose not more than three strate-gies, and break each of those strategies into not more than three sub-strat-egies. Thus in a business development plan, there are not more than 27 strategies (3 x 9) contributing to the overarching business development goal. It may sound like a lot but several of them will intersect. A plan might look like this:

Objective 1: Increase new business by $1M by end of year			
Strategy A: Improve business development processes	Measure	Person responsible	Timeline
i. Better utilize sales database to track sales stages			
ii. Classify clients as "A"-level, "B"-level and "C"-level to better allocate resources			
iii. Involve partners in setting business development targets and KPIs			
Strategy B: Develop niche practices	Measure	Person responsible	Timeline

Objective 1: Increase new business by $1M by end of year			
i. Perform market research on future niche areas			
ii. For each niche, appoint a niche champion who is responsible for developing niche service options			
iii. Promote niche practices through blog posts, company website and conferences			
Strategy C: Generate more referrals	*Measure*	*Person responsible*	*Timeline*
i. Create a one-page ideal client profile for each partner			
ii. Institute a referral compensation program			
iii. Emphasize importance of asking existing clients for referrals			

Repeat for two other objectives

Plan ahead

To create a firm-wide business development plan:

- **Establish targets.** See topic later in this chapter for how to establish targets and KPIs. Break down targets into subsets of the overall new business target (for example, by service, niche, industry, individual contributor, etc).
- **Set priorities.** You may have already set priorities in a strategic plan. If not, connect your firm's vision with business development strategy. For example, if you want to make a greater investment in niches, highlight specific niche objectives and strategies in your plan, such as joining associations and demonstrating thought leadership.
- **Simplify.** Keep it simple. Adhere to the planning format we outlined above.
- **Aye aye captain.** Assign a leader to each objective and assign lieutenants to each strategy within each objective. Clear leadership creates focus, responsibility and accountability.
- **Set realistic timelines.** Don't be in a rush to achieve everything out of the gate. Stretch your commitments over the year. Nothing is more deflating than failing to hit objectives on schedule. Give yourself some breathing room to ensure you achieve what you set out to do.

- **It takes a village.** Use all the resources at your disposal. If you're fortunate enough to have a business development team, explore ways for them to complement what others are doing (for example, by conducting prospect research, planning events, initiating warm-calling campaigns, etc).
- **Get outside of the box.** Just doing what other accounting firms are doing will only get you so far. Look outside of the accounting profession for ideas and suggestions and consider inventive strategies that change the face of your business development effort. If you have sales or marketing clients, ask them for insight and advice. Seek counsel from your younger staff who aren't as encumbered by the existing paradigm.
- **Measure and manage.** Make sure that your strategies are measurable. Establish graduated measurement terms (weekly, biweekly, monthly, quarterly). The smaller the goal and the shorter the time period, the more likely it is that you'll achieve it.
- **Debrief.** A plan is a living, breathing organism, subject to change. Review positives and concerns to identify points for improvement. It's okay to tack if the water is choppy!
- **Report.** Keep relevant parties updated about where you are to target. Communicate relentlessly about the plan.

Key takeaways

To create a firm-wide business development plan:

- Craft objectives in three broad areas: sales, marketing and team.
- Adhere to the rule of three in drafting your plan. Identify three key objectives, and up to nine strategies per objective.
- Assign responsibilities and set realistic timelines. Measure and manage performance and don't be afraid to re-think the plan if something's not working.

TARGETS AND KPIs

Targets are your benchmark for success. They represent what you need to achieve to succeed each year. Miss your targets and you'll notice the hit to your bottom line. To hit your targets, you need to have clear expectations about the amount of effort required. That's where key performance indicators (KPIs) come in — KPIs establish the steps you need to take to reach your target. Without KPIs, you have no rationale for how to allocate your business development efforts and no way of knowing if you're doing enough of the right things to ultimately realize your targets.

Choose targets wisely

While many accounting targets are set according to a rigorous methodology, business development targets are more often than not chosen randomly. Sometimes the target is set according to the individual's prior performance; other times it's chosen by asking the individual how much business they think they can generate. Often once the target is established, the individual is left on their own to figure out how to reach the end in mind. As a result, they are unable to break down the task into specific actions and behaviors needed to execute the commitment they've just accepted.

Know the effort required

The goal in establishing KPIs is to make targets seem less intimidating by focusing on behavior instead of results. Think of it like losing weight — losing 50 pounds sounds unattainable but losing one pound per week sounds doable. Take it one week at a time and 50 weeks later, you will have hit your goal. For accounting, we recommend an approach that focuses on two types of KPIs:

- **Communications:** The number of personalized communications aimed at generating new business. This includes phone calls and individual emails, but excludes generic communications like newsletters.
- **Meetings:** The number of face-to-face business development meetings.

I find that limiting the number of KPIs is helpful because it makes it easy for accountants to understand what's expected of them. Additionally, I never set goals with a timeline of longer than 90 days. Thus, each accountant knows how much effort they need to put toward business development in the next quarter if they hope to hit their target.

Connecting targets and KPIs

To understand the connection between targets and KPIs, consider the example below for an accountant with a target of generating $50,000 in new business. Using conversion probabilities, the accountant is able to figure out that they need to find 100 unqualified leads if they hope to hit their target (to simplify the example below, we've assumed the accountant is generating all their new business from unsolicited lead generation efforts).

Target

New business target	$50,000
Average new client ($'s)	$10,000
Number of new clients to hit target	5

KPIs

Number of unqualified leads required	100	50% conversion probability
Number of qualified leads required	50	100% conversion probability
Number of first-round communications required	50	50% conversion probability
Number of needs assessment meetings required	25	40% conversion probability
Number of proposals required	10	50% conversion probability
Number of new clients won	5	

The conversion probabilities vary from person to person. Those new to the target and KPI process will have to make assumptions about their conversion probabilities. Those with historical year-over-year data will have real numbers on which to base those probabilities.

Devise a roadmap

Follow these steps to set your business development targets and KPIs:

1. **Choose your targets.** I typically try to set three business development targets per contributor: total business development goal in dollars, percentage of business development goal from recurring versus non-recurring work and quarterly business development goal in dollars. For contributors with previous business development experience, use historical data as a basis for your projections. Remember to account for their other responsibilities (for example, a target would drop if a contributor takes on another responsibility that's not focused on business development). In the absence of historical data, use other quantitative measures to set targets, such as industry norms, historical performance by similar candidates, time availability, extent of network and business development talent.

2. **Reach higher.** Build in some wiggle room by skewing conversion ratios so minimal underperformance doesn't spell disaster. For example, rather than estimating that 50% of proposals will result in new clients, estimate that 40% will.

3. **Set objectives and goals.** Identify specific initiatives and strategies to get to the target. Your KPIs should ultimately connect to these initiatives and strategies. For more on this, see the chapters on individual and firm business development plans.

4. **Establish KPIs.** KPIs are your roadmap to the target. Use conversion probabilities to estimate the number of leads, communications, meetings and proposals needed to generate the number of clients and dollar value of new business desired. While $50,000 may seem like an insurmountable target to a staff accountant who bills 1,600 charge hours per year, establishing specific expectations makes the goal seem a lot more attainable. Account for busy seasons when establishing timelines. Remember, the fewer KPIs you measure, the easier they are to understand and track. (www[34] — see our website for an interactive spreadsheet that lets you calculate what you need to do to reach your targets.)

5. **Modify KPIs.** As a coach or mentor, be prepared to adjust an individual's KPIs from month to month. If an individual fails to meet their KPIs one month, the KPIs increase the next month to ensure they appropriate the necessary effort to get back on target.

6. **Reward effort, coach performance.** Don't allow individuals to get frustrated if their effort doesn't bear fruit immediately. Results take time and once the effort is there, you can coach them to help improve their performance. If the effort isn't there though, you're unlikely to be able to manufacture success. Conduct regular debriefs to build on what's working and identify areas for improvement. Look at where you lose opportunities by sales stage to identify opportunities to train and coach.

Key takeaways

To meet your business development goals:

- Establish targets to provide clear performance expectations.
- Establish KPIs to make business development effort both measurable and manageable.
- Simplify by minimizing the number of KPIs and shortening the timeline.

INDIVIDUAL BUSINESS DEVELOPMENT PLAN

An individual business development plan outlines what each contributor is expected to do to realize their business development goals. Laying out a clear plan helps everyone focus their efforts, sidestep distractions and build momentum toward the goal. The plan is purposefully simple and focuses on encouraging individuals to put in the required amount of effort. The idea is that if everyone does enough of the right things, results will follow.

Connect the vertebrae

When deciding how to direct your business development efforts, think about where your personal and professional interests intersect. We call this concept the "backbone." Your professional commitments are the vertebrae and your personal interests are the backbone. The points of intersection between the backbone and vertebrae represent an opportunity to do more things you're passionate about in your work. For example, if you're a wine connoisseur and you're looking for a new place to network, consider joining a high-end wine club, instead of the local chamber of commerce. You'll meet high net worth individuals at a club like this, and because you like wine, you'll enjoy the experience a lot more and get more out of it.

Professional		Personal
Wine club		Food and wine
School PTA/board of ed		Kids
Conservation group		Environment
Private golf club membership		Golf
Board of directors		Symphony/ballet/theater

It's all about effort

Follow these steps to create individual business development plans:

1. **Choose your targets.** The firm-wide business development plan identifies initiatives for the firm to pursue. Convert those initiatives into specific commitments. For example, if you're launching a niche practice, you'll need to dedicate more time to becoming a thought leader and establishing a presence at industry groups.
2. **Establish KPIs.** Establish KPIs for each source of new business (clients, colleagues, wheels of influence, centers of influence, strategic alliances, unsolicited lead generation, etc). If you plan on generating

new business primarily from certain sources, adjust your effort goals accordingly. For example, if you're attempting to grow a niche, you'll want to expand your efforts to include centers of influence, strategic alliances and unsolicited lead generation.

3. **Outline commitments.** As we talked about in KPIs, we like to simplify effort goals into two categories: communications and meetings. List the number of each you need to make on an annual basis, and break those down into smaller quarterly, monthly and weekly targets. Be sure to discount busy periods as it's unlikely your effort will be linear over the course of a year. (To automate the process of figuring out your KPIs, see www[34] on our website.)

4. **Identify contacts.** Identify the individuals and organizations you'll prioritize for each source of business. Include "A"-level clients, wheels of influence who have been a reliable source of new business year after year, strategic alliances you intend to cultivate and associations you plan to network. It's important to put names to your commitments, otherwise it's easy to avoid following through. This will also help your coach or mentor when they're discussing progress and performance.

5. **Focus on your grades.** "A"-level, "B"-level and "C"-level contacts are not created equally. Allocate your resources disproportionately to your "A"-level contacts. Go after prospective clients who align with your ideal client profile.

6. **Track your actuals.** Now that your plan is complete, it's important to report your actuals on an ongoing basis. Reporting actuals to target underscores variance, which leads to a continuous improvement discussion about positives, challenges and areas for improvement. It also allows you to reset KPIs to get to target. Underperform in one period and your KPIs will logically increase in the next.

7. **Change for good.** During the course of executing your plan, you may find that certain strategies work better than others. Don't be afraid to shift the focus of your plan accordingly. A plan is nothing more than a proposed list of commitments to get to the finish line. If one commitment is working better than another, switch lanes.

Your final business development plan (www[35]) should be a very simple 1-4 page document that lists the number of communications and meetings by type of new business. It should also include the names of contacts and organizations you plan to cultivate to meet your goals.

Key takeaways

To develop an individual business development plan:

- Convert firm-wide initiatives into specific commitments.
- Focus on two primary effort goals: communications and meetings. Do enough of the right things repeatedly and results will follow.
- Add names to metrics. Create a list of people to contact and focus on the most promising leads.

BUSINESS DEVELOPMENT MEETINGS

Business development meetings are regularly scheduled meetings where the firm's business development pipeline and production take center stage. The goal of these meetings is to recognize key contributors, acknowledge best practices and offer assistance in dealing with issues and challenges. These meetings are an important feature in firms that have successfully established a company-wide business development culture (see culture chapter).

Short, sweet and to the point

You want to encourage good attendance, active participation and brevity at your business development meetings. Contributors at all levels should be invited to attend, as well as strategic alliance partners and other third-party service providers. Physical attendance, however, should not be required. A "dial-in" option should be available for those working off-site. It's up to each firm to decide on meeting frequency; what's most important is that you stick to a regular schedule and communicate the agenda ahead of time. We recommend that firms schedule at least two business development meetings per month of not more than 45 minutes each. We also suggest that the agenda differ between these two meetings to keep the meetings feeling fresh. To get the most out of these short meetings, the meeting facilitator must work hard to keep contributions brief and on topic.

Diversify your approach

The following approach involves two meetings per month. The first 45-minute meeting focuses on the business development pipeline; the second 45-minute meeting looks at broader business development topics.

Prior to the meeting

The first step is to make sure that everyone is aware of and prepared for the upcoming meeting. Communicate with presenters about the format and what's expected of them. Enlist the support of an administrative assistant or business development coordinator to prepare and polish any presentation materials (case studies, presentation slides, etc). At least 24 hours before the meeting, send out an agenda that highlights specific contributors and that includes a sales database snapshot. Here's a sample snapshot that uses the sales stages described earlier in the chapter.

Sales database snapshot

Stage	# of accounts	Recurring ($'s)	Nonrecurring ($'s)	Total ($)
Research	31	$312,000	$291,000	$603,000
Needs assessment	22	$110,000	$55,000	**$165,000**

Stage	# of accounts	Recurring ($'s)	Nonrecurring ($'s)	Total ($)
Proposal	12	$22,000	$97,000	**$119,000**
Decision	7	$34,000	$71,500	**$105,500**
Closed – won	32	$227,000	$98,400	$325,400
Change orders	12		$46,000	$46,000
Total new business		$227,000	$144,400	$371,400

Performance since last meeting

New business generated as of (enter last meeting date)	$301,000
New business generated since (enter last meeting date)	$70,400

Performance to target

Target	$590,000
Variance to target	($218,600)
% of target met	62.9%
% of pipeline value to convert to meet target	**56.1%**

To calculate the "pipeline value," sum the quantified opportunities that are being actively pursued (the numbers that are bolded above). Divide the "variance to target" by "pipeline value" to arrive at your "percent of pipeline value to convert to meet target." This number should be at or below 50% if you expect to hit your target with accounts that are already in the pipeline. If that number exceeds 50%, it suggests you need to either convert more early stage leads into real opportunities or generate more opportunities than the ones currently listed in your database.

Break out targets by quarter and measure performance to quarter-end target. If you're in February, measure performance to the end of March Q1 target; if you're in May, measure performance to the end of June Q1 + Q2 cumulative target. If you have access to prior year data, make year-over-year comparisons and use those comparisons to forecast year-end performance (for example, if we did X at this time last year and ended up at Y by year end, we can realistically expect to do Z by year end this year). In addition to projecting content onto a screen during the meeting, email appropriate documents to attendees ahead of time or produce relevant handouts for in-room distribution.

During the meeting (first meeting of the month)

The first meeting of the month lasts 45 minutes and breaks down into four sections.

- **Snapshot report (5 minutes):** The meeting facilitator summarizes key data points in the snapshot report, highlights individuals who have contributed "wins" since the last meeting and asks them to talk about any best practices that contributed to the win.
- **Updates (20 minutes):** The facilitator goes line by line through the sales database report and asks individual contributors what they're actively doing to move the sales process forward. If they make excuses such as, "I haven't heard back from them", the facilitator should reiterate the importance of verbalizing goal statements to move the sales process forward. Record any commitments made (if a staff member says they're going to call a client this week, write that down to hold them accountable).
- **Referrals (15 minutes):** All individuals are asked to summarize what referrals they've given and received in the prior two weeks. Record the description and monetary value of each opportunity listed.
- **Any other business (5 minutes):** Open the floor to any attendee to discuss any other business development topic.

During the meeting (second meeting of the month)

The second meeting of the month lasts 45 minutes and breaks down into six sections.

- **Snapshot report (10 minutes):** The meeting facilitator summarizes key data points in the snapshot report, highlights individuals who have contributed "wins" since the last meeting and asks them to talk about any best practices that contributed to the win.
- **Presentation (15 minutes):** This can take numerous forms — it might be a case study describing a recent client win or a summary of a presentation that a firm member recently gave at a B2B group or niche meeting. The goal is to inform, educate and promote a specific initiative that is helping to drive the firm's overarching business development effort.
- **Challenges (5 minutes):** This section is a chance for anyone to seek advice and counsel from others if they're having trouble with a particular prospective client. Oftentimes, the conversation focuses on connections ("Does anyone know anyone who knows or is affiliated with X?").
- **Best practices (5 minutes):** This is a chance for a senior business development figure to teach and coach others. They might highlight topics like referral best practices, client service best practices and networking best practices.
- **Testimonials (5 minutes):** Attendees recognize other people in the room who have helped them in their business development efforts. This often results in attendees thanking their colleagues for referring them to an existing firm client, referring them to potential referral sources or assisting them in closing a particular opportunity. The goal is to support a team approach to business development. It's also a great time to recognize the contributions of more junior staff members.

- **Any other business (5 minutes):** Open the floor to any attendee to discuss any other business development topic.

For both meetings, it's crucial to keep the conversation moving and on topic. The meeting facilitator should remain upbeat and lighthearted so attendees enjoy the meeting, but shouldn't be afraid to cut off or redirect individuals who drift off-topic or talk for too long. Start and end on time and remember that everyone in the room is busy; your business development meetings should be an effective use of their time.

After the meeting

Send copies of documents generated during the meeting to all attendees, including update and referral reports. Encourage the managing partner, partners and other relevant staff to acknowledge contributors who weren't present at the meeting (for example, they might send a company-wide email praising a junior staff member who referred a potential opportunity).

Key takeaways

Good business development meetings:

- Involve all business development contributors. That includes staff members of all levels and outside contributors like strategic alliance partners.
- Are short, fast-paced and fun. Avoid repetition and keep the agenda moving.
- Acknowledge contributions and encourage practical discussion. The things that are shared in the room should ultimately improve your business development efforts.

DATABASE MANAGEMENT

A sales database aggregates all your information about clients, prospective clients and referral sources in one location, allowing you to keep track of important information, including contact details, meeting notes, mailing dates, interactions and so on. This centralization of information helps you automate the sales process and target your communications. Additionally, sales databases are an important business development tool because they make it easy to aggregate and mine your data to identify best practices and areas for improvement. Without a sales database, you'll waste a lot of time parsing client data.

Selecting a database

A sales database can be expensive, so make sure you know how you're going to use it. If you only need basic functionality, you can choose a relatively inexpensive system. More expensive options will offer additional features; it's up to you to decide whether they're worth paying for. When making your selection, keep these factors in mind:

- **Customization.** Every firm has its own measures and metrics so you're going to want to create custom fields. Choose a database that allows you to easily create as many custom fields as you want or you'll have a difficult time tracking the information you care about.
- **Reporting functionality.** Select a system that allows you to create reports within the database software. All your reports will be housed in one place and they'll update automatically when you add new information. This is much easier than exporting content to another program and creating reports there.
- **Additional features.** Some databases offer features such as direct mail and email so you don't need a separate database for email or direct mail campaigns.
- **Ease of use.** Even if a database does all of the above, if you can't figure out how to use it, it's not worth very much. Make sure the database company offers high-quality customer service and easily accessible video tutorials.
- **Cloud-based or on-premise.** Cloud-based sales databases are accessed online through a web browser. These services are typically billed on a subscription basis. It's also possible, though less common, to choose an on-premise option that usually requires a larger upfront cost.

Salesforce is the current industry leader among sales databases though there are plenty of other options that you might consider, depending on what you need in terms of features and price.

Maximizing your sales database

Keep these tips in mind to get the most out of your sales database:

- **Align with your accounting software system.** Make sure you use the same fields in your sales database as you do in your accounting data management system. This helps eliminate confusion when entering new information into either system. Preferably you would merge your sales and accounting databases into one to minimize duplication and human error.
- **Learn how to use it.** Task everyone with entering their own leads. It's easy to do and doesn't take much time. Some databases offer a mobile app so users can enter information from their phone immediately after a meeting. In addition, designate someone as the gatekeeper to monitor entries, answer questions and create reports. This will ensure that everyone is using the system correctly.
- **Take advantage of reporting functionality.** One of the biggest advantages of sales databases is the ability to generate snapshots of how the firm is doing, who's bringing in business, where it's coming from and when it's coming in. For more on how to use reports, see reports topic later in this chapter.
- **Use the customization functionality.** If you're only using your sales database to enter contact information, you're not taking full advantage of the system. You should be able to customize fields so you can track everything from the first point of contact to the needs assessment meeting to the reason you ultimately won or lost their business.
- **Track the sales process.** Create fields in the system for each of your sales stages. This will help you understand where in the process you're losing the most prospects. You can use that information to develop individual training plans that develop strengths and address weaknesses.

Key takeaways

Use your sales database to:

- Track prospects, clients and referral sources. Include contact information and notes on all interactions.
- Generate reports. Use the information you gather to see how you're doing and how you can improve.
- Track the sales process. Diligently record where you are in the sales process with each prospective client and use that information to improve your efforts.

REPORTS

Reports are an important facet of business development communication. They tell you where you are, and how you got there. More importantly, they tell you what you need to do to get where you want to be. The key in getting the most out of your reports is to go beyond the data to provide analysis on how to improve. Highlight best practices and suggest actionable next steps. Keep it simple and focus on key points.

Types of reports

Business development reports should be sent to all relevant business development contributors, but not to the whole firm (that's the purpose of the firm-wide business development report — see culture chapter). These reports are more frequent and more detailed than the firm-wide report, which is just a snapshot to keep everyone on the same page. There are several types of business development reports you can create:

- **Comparative team report** (www[36]): Compares team performance year-over-year for recurring, nonrecurring and total new business year-to-date. Allows the group to gauge their contributions and output over a comparable time period. Highlights and explains positive and negative variances.
- **Individual performance report** (www[37]): Tracks each individual's business development contributions and measures their progress in meeting quarterly and year-end targets. Presents variance in both dollar and percentage terms, and ranks contributors according to percentage to target. Highlights and explains positive and negative variances.
- **Niche report:** Documents how much revenue is being generated from each industry or service niche. Also records individual contributions to niche revenue.
- **Referral source report** (www[3]): Tracks who is directing the most business to the firm. Offers suggestions for how to leverage that information.
- **Benchmarking report:** Uses comparative data to benchmark your firm against other firms to provide insight into the success of others. If you're part of an accounting member organization like CPAmerica, Crowe Horwath International or CPAConnect, you have access to an abundance of comparative data you can use to generate this report.

Give me the numbers

Follow these tips when generating your reports:

- **Do it often.** Resist the temptation to wait until there's enough movement to justify producing performance reports. Produce them weekly, biweekly or at the very least monthly. The more frequently they arrive, the more importance they carry and the more effective they are at changing behavior.

- **Make it immediate.** It often takes too long to collate the data and communicate results. Performance results need to be up-to-date to have any bearing on behavior. If you use a sophisticated sales database, you can generate reports instantaneously and send them by email to all contributors.
- **Simplify.** Most reports include too much information. Cut the "nice to know" information and focus on the "need to know." You should be able to snapshot the key takeaways from a report in 30 seconds or less. Any longer and you'll lose the reader.
- **Inaccuracy kills.** Make sure your data is accurate. Put the onus on individual contributors to update the database. If they fail to do so, it reflects poorly on them. Don't send "asterisk" emails after the fact (for example, the recent report excluded A, B and C from contributor Z).
- **First we, then me.** Most people scan a report looking for their own name, seeing how they stack up against the competition. Buck that trend by emphasizing the collective we first. Focus on the team's performance, highlighting individual contributions in the process. Then praise individual contributors who have exceeded expectations. Don't focus on the negative. The underperformers will fret enough without you adding to their misery.
- **Harness the power of comparison.** Listing performers from first to worst eliminates the need to highlight individual underperformance. Underperformers should recommit to the process for fear of appearing at the bottom of the list again.

Key takeaways

To generate business development reports:

- Go beyond the data. Provide analysis and highlight best practices.
- Produce comparative team and individual performance reports on a regular and frequent basis.
- Benchmark your performance against other firms. Keep an eye on the industry leaders.

COACHING

It's important to have a business development coach to drive your firm's business development efforts. To paraphrase a recent Harvard Business Review article: If a world-class athlete uses a coach to improve, why should business developers go it alone? The coach can be an outside consultant or a member of your firm with a track record of business development success. The business development coach has three principle responsibilities: establish KPIs and targets, help individuals draft a business development plan and coach individuals to make sure they stay on track.

Prioritize business development

Appointing a business development coach is a key step in ensuring that you stay on track with your business development goals. Requiring all business development contributors to report on a regular basis to a business development coach can be a necessary evil in making sure that business development doesn't become a forgotten pursuit, particularly during the seasons when other work takes precedence (for example, filing deadlines in tax or year-end windows in audit).

Appoint your taskmaster

My suggestion is that firms commit this responsibility to an outsider who isn't politically handcuffed; sometimes the role of business development coach requires "tough love" that colleagues struggle to provide to one another.

Coaching sessions usually fall into two categories: group coaching sessions that cover a particular topic and 1-on-1 coaching sessions personalized around an individual's plan and activities.

Group sessions: In these sessions, the coach discusses educational and informational topics like sales process in a group setting. It's common to organize these sessions by title (all seniors and supervisors) or by expertise (all tax accountants). The content should be question-oriented and conversational. Instead of reading a prepared presentation about "best practices," the coach should present a case study followed by a "how would you" conversation. These sessions shouldn't last more than an hour. For firms that follow the training recommendations outlined in the culture chapter, we recommend substituting group coaching sessions with one-hour training workshops.

1-on-1 sessions: In these sessions, the coach discusses specific goals within an individual's business development plan. These sessions should last between 30 minutes and one hour. Break the session down into four parts:

- **Review prior commitments.** Did they complete their commitments and what were the results? Ask questions to help the individual understand why things worked or didn't work. The goal is to help instill good habits. If the individual didn't do what they committed to, see the accountability topic later in this chapter.

- **Build on group classes.** Connect content from an earlier group session to the individual's business development effort. For example, if the most recent group session covered the importance of relationships, ask the individual to describe how they build credibility, get prospective clients to like them and ultimately establish trust.
- **Make a plan.** Establish business development tasks between now and the next meeting. Apply a measure or metric to each commitment to ensure it can be quantified (for example, introduce client X to partner Y by date Z). Try not to overcomplicate the to-do agenda; cap the number of commitments at three.
- **Summarize commitments.** Restate commitments verbally at the end of the meeting and send an email detailing those same commitments by end of day.

The function of a coach is two-fold. First, you want to ask questions to help others arrive at the right answer. Second, you want to provide expertise, insight and ideas to supplement what they already know. Resist the temptation to scold individuals if they fail to honor their commitments. Instead, try to understand the reasons, try to get them to commit to the process going forward and help them understand the consequences of their choices. Additionally, resist the kneejerk reaction to change the plan if an individual isn't honoring their commitments. Shifting the focus won't necessarily change their results. Finally, ask what you can do to help their business development effort. Sometimes there are practical things that you can do to "kick-start" their progress like introducing them to a B2B group or helping them better articulate their elevator pitch.

To make sessions less intimidating for more junior staff, you might consider offering 1-on-2 sessions so you get the benefit of the small group without making participants feel like they're on the hot seat.

Recommended meeting frequency

The following table serves as a guide for how often group and 1-on-1 meetings should occur:

Category	Tier 1	Tier 2	Tier 3
Group session frequency	Monthly	Monthly	Bimonthly
Group session duration	1 hour	1 hour	1 hour
1-on-1 session frequency	Biweekly	Monthly	Bimonthly
1-on-1 session duration	1 hour	30 minutes	30 minutes
Total monthly time commitment	3 hours	1.5 hours	0.75 hours
Total annual time commitment	36 hours	18 hours	9 hours

You can organize tiers in two ways, either by title or by the dollar value of business development target, as titles are not always indicative of business development contribution.

- **Tier 1:** The firm's largest business development contributors (each individually carries more than 5% of the firm's total business development target).
- **Tier 2:** The firm's other significant business development contributors (each individually carries between 1% and 5% of the firm's total business development target).
- **Tier 3:** The firm's newest business development contributors (each individually carries less than 1% of the firm's total business development target).

Key takeaways

To benefit from business development coaching at a firm:

- Assign an outside consultant or an experienced business developer within the firm to take on the role of business development coach.
- Deliver group content in an engaging and conversational format. Make it an opportunity to share, discuss and learn from each other.
- Focus 1-on-1 sessions on specific commitments that help individuals execute their business development plan.

MENTORING

Good mentors think creatively, are interested in helping others, communicate and listen well and are talented at motivating others. Their mentoring ability comes from their own expertise, experience and knowledge and from their understanding of the firm's culture. Mentoring is a mutually beneficial arrangement — the mentor gains proficiency in teaching and the mentee receives advice from a trusted source.

Building bonds

Mentoring is a great way to build like, trust and credibility internally among colleagues. Business development benefits aside, forging bonds among colleagues helps boost morale, promote engagement and improve workplace productivity. From a business development point of view, one of the biggest benefits of mentoring is what I affectionately refer to as the "ride along." When junior staffers accompany their mentors to client meetings or B2B groups, they get to witness business development in action. These staffers don't usually directly interact with clients and prospective clients. Mentoring gives them the chance to do so.

Follow the leader

Here's a process for creating a business development mentoring program:

1. **Assign individuals to teams within the firm.** We recommend assigning mentors vertically through a firm so that each team resembles a pyramid, with more junior people at the base and a single business development-focused partner at the top (for example, eight staff accountants connected to four seniors to two supervisors to a manager, senior manager and partner). This forges connections among individuals in the firm and builds a sense of responsibility and belonging. It also creates a little internal competition, which can be a helpful motivator.

2. **Assign individuals within each team to a mentor.** This may be someone immediately above them in the org chart, or someone more senior. Provide mentor training that outlines mentor traits and methodology, including how to ask questions, how to listen and how to use creative thinking to craft solutions. Mentoring doesn't come naturally to everyone and basic training equips mentors with the necessary skills. Not everyone in your firm needs to mentor someone — if someone is a poor communicator and listener, they'll probably make a poor mentor, and a poor business developer for that matter.

3. **Design your mentoring program.** There's no one-size-fits all approach; mentoring sessions can be formally scheduled or can occur on an as-needed basis. Most important is that mentees feel comfortable talking with their mentors. Group meetings typically follow a debrief format with the mentor discussing successes, challenges and recommendations. The mentor ensures that everyone has a chance

to contribute and prioritizes the most important points. The agenda for individual meetings should be driven by the mentee. The mentor might start the session with an open-ended question: "Tell me what business development topics you'd like to discuss today?" For each topic identified, the mentor should use the three E's of questioning (entry, elaborate and evaluate) to gain broader perspective and a clearer sense of priority. Summarize any commitments verbally at the end of the meeting and send a summary of those commitments in writing at the earliest opportunity.

Remember that mentoring requires confidentiality. What's said between the mentor and mentee should remain private unless the mentee gives the mentor permission to share the issue with a third party. Additionally, mentors should not hesitate to consult the firm's business development coach if they don't know how to address a particular problem. In most cases, mentors will be able to draw on their own experiences to help their mentees; but in cases where they don't know the answer, they can do more harm than good by tackling a problem they're ill-equipped to solve.

Key takeaways

Remember these tips to get your mentoring program off the ground:

- Mentoring requires specific skills, traits and experience, as well as a basic level of training.
- Mentoring is a great way to build business development teams within a firm. Being part of a team creates a sense of belonging and responsibility.
- Mentoring provides the mentor with coaching experience and the mentee with a confidential outlet to share issues and challenges.

ACCOUNTABILITY

Firms often struggle to instill a consistent commitment to business development among employees. Employees often let it slide and try to skate by with excuses. To counter this habit, you need to hold employees accountable when they fail to meet their business development goals. Demonstrate the natural consequences of their actions so contributors understand how their decisions impact the greater good. Focusing on these consequences will hopefully cause them to double down on business development tasks and will help develop a firm-wide business development culture.

Focus on the future

The idea here is to help your employees understand the results of their actions so that they'll make better decisions in the future. You have to be willing to let them fail. For example, if an employee neglects to follow up with clients and his manager learns about this and does it for him, the employee isn't going to change his behavior. Instead, the manager needs to demonstrate the adverse effects of the employee's decision.

There are a number of ways to highlight the natural consequences of not following through on business development commitments. Don't begin the conversation until a contributor has demonstrated a repeated pattern of underperformance. Your approach should vary depending on the individual's personality (for example, some individuals will care more about money, while others are primarily concerned with career advancement). Here are a number of ways to approach the conversation:

- **How it impacts their performance:** As a first step, I like to use statistics with contributors who didn't meet their goals. I can easily show them how neglecting part of the sales process will impact the amount of new business they'll ultimately generate. I demonstrate that the fewer KPIs they hit, the less likely they are to realize their target. It sounds simple, but you would be amazed how many people don't make this connection. Once you've made this point, give them the chance to turn it around; if they don't improve, elaborate on the consequences listed below.
- **How it impacts their career advancement prospects:** Firms need people who are technically competent, able to lead and manage others and skilled at bringing in new business. Employees who aren't making an effort to meet their business development goals don't meet those criteria. Thus it can be effective to point out to contributors how their business development failings will hamper their opportunities for advancement in the firm.
- **How it impacts their compensation:** If employee compensation is tied to a goal system as well as commission (as suggested in the compensation topic later in this chapter), it's easy to convert projected

revenue into compensation. For some, money isn't a particularly big driver, but for others, a hit to compensation is the single fastest way to get their attention. Understanding an employee's personal goals and aspirations will help you to determine if this is a pain point to press.

- **How it impacts their clients:** I've had a lot more success motivating accountants with this tactic. Many accountants are driven by a desire to serve their clients. It can be a powerful motivator to point out that they're under-serving their clients by failing to meet client up-selling, cross-selling and referral commitments.
- **How it impacts others in the firm:** For those who aren't motivated by money or career advancement, you might have the best luck by highlighting how their choices impact friends and colleagues in the workplace. Meeting business development targets means the following for others: advancement opportunity, job security, increased compensation and better benefits, among other opportunities.
- **How it impacts the firm:** If you have established a strong commitment to growth, articulate the consequences as they relate to the firm's ability to meet its goals. Underperformance directly impacts a firm's ability to achieve what it has set out to accomplish.

Key takeaways

To successfully establish natural consequences you should:

- Understand each individual's drivers so you highlight the most relevant consequences.
- Connect key performance indicators to performance so they see the tangible connection between effort and results.
- Connect their choices with consequences that impact them and others.

COMPENSATION

In most firms, employees receive a base salary plus a bonus tied to individual or overall firm performance. The bonus is intended to incentivize the individual to invest in desired behaviors, such as increasing their charge time or realization rate. For business development contributors, we're suggesting firms adopt a hybrid compensation model: employees earn the standard bonus package at the end of the year, but they also receive commissions for their business development successes throughout the year.

A shot in the arm

This hybrid model for compensation aligns the firm's goals with an individual's best interests — if an individual is tasked with bringing in more new clients and succeeds, the firm gets more revenue and the individual gets a bonus. But in many cases, these rewards follow long after the individual has completed the work. Doling out commissions throughout the year can help drive more sales by immediately linking the action and the reward.

Show me the money

There are two parts to creating a hybrid compensation model:

1. **Establish bonus goals.** Select up to four goals for each individual, with easy-to-measure metrics. These don't have to be exclusively business development goals, but if you want to establish a firm-wide business development culture, every employee should have some kind of business development goal, even if it's attending business development classes or joining a B2B group. Prioritize the most important goals and assign corresponding percentages. Evaluate individuals on a recurring basis and score each goal at the end of the fiscal year. If 20% of their bonus depends on completing their business development goal and they meet their goal of generating $30,000 in new business, then they would receive 20% of their total bonus allocation. For example:

    | Increase per annum charge time to 1,600 hours | 50% |
    | Increase realization rate to 87% | 20% |
    | Generate $30,000 in new business | 20% |
    | Mentor a minimum of three staff accountants | 10% |

2. **Supplement bonuses with direct commissions.** We recommend that firms augment bonus pool incentives with immediate payouts as new business is generated, executed, billed and collected. Paying out these commissions quarterly rather than at the end of the year provides a tangible "shot in the arm" that motivates employees to do more of the same. The key to making this system work is to have clear rules and good recordkeeping. Consider the following tips:

- **Assign commissions.** Decide how you'll split the commissions. For the total commission paid on new business, I would allocate 2/3 of that amount to the individual who initiates the lead and 1/3 to the individual who closes the lead. If more than one person initiates or closes a lead, I would split the commission accordingly. Occasionally, a lead will come in that can't easily be assigned to one person (for example, a walk-in). In these cases, I would think of the initiator as the firm (the firm gets the initiator commission) and assign the standard closer percentage to the individual who closes the lead.
- **Establish clear written standards.** Know what constitutes initiating and closing a lead. For example, initiation requires that the individual actively initiate the lead; that could mean identifying the prospective client through research, making initial contact by phone or meeting the prospect at a board meeting. Closing requires that the individual actively contribute toward converting the prospect into a client; that could mean attending a needs assessment meeting, generating a proposal or negotiating the terms of the agreement.
- **Carefully track initiators and closers.** Once a prospect becomes a client, clearly assign and record contributions so individuals can't go back and change the facts. A year later, it's easy for people to misrepresent how much they contributed.
- **Assign an arbiter to officiate any disagreements.** Hopefully these are few and far between if the standards are clear and the firm embraces a spirit of inclusion. Most often this person is the firm's business development champion.
- **Don't pay until you've collected the money.** Only pay on work that has been completed and collected. If the work has been done in one quarter but the funds haven't been physically collected, the commission will be counted in the next quarter's calculations.
- **Supplement compensation with recognition.** It's one thing to receive monetary rewards for your contributions, but many people care more about recognition (see next topic).

Key takeaways

Your compensation scheme should adhere to the following guidelines:

- Reward individuals at year-end for their business development contributions as part of a "goals" system.
- Supplement the goals program with more immediate commissions on new business generated.
- Reward the initiator more than the closer, pay commissions on a quarterly basis and have clear standards in place to make sure everything goes smoothly.

RECOGNITION AND REWARD

Recognition and reward — the two words are often used interchangeably, yet they're different concepts. Recognition typically takes the form of verbal acknowledgement, such as praise, admiration or appreciation. Reward typically takes the form of a tangible non-cash gift. Both are valuable tools for increasing the productivity of your staff. By recognizing and rewarding employees, you reinforce positive behaviors, incentivize employees to contribute to the firm's overarching goals and foster a sense of teamwork.

Recognition: Taking the time to say thank you

Recognizing employee contributions might seem like an obvious idea, yet it's done infrequently and poorly in many workplaces. Managers move on to the next activity without taking the time to acknowledge effort and contributions. This is especially true in industries like accounting where there's a succession of seemingly never-ending milestones. To many employees, receiving sincere thanks is more important than receiving a tangible reward. Start thanking your employees for doing a good job and you'll find that they become more loyal, more team-oriented and more invested in their work. You will have powerfully reinforced the desired behavior and set an example for others to follow.

When recognizing employee contributions, do it in a timely, specific and sincere manner. Follow these steps:

- Thank the person by name.
- Specifically state what they did that is being recognized. Specificity is key because it identifies and reinforces the desired behavior.
- Point out the value added to the team or firm by the behavior.
- When possible, offer praise first privately and then publicly.
- Finish by thanking the person again by name.

Reward: Encourage team successes

A rewards program acknowledges employees for significant accomplishments in a formal way. These programs are important because they show that major achievements are critical to business success. They also drive employee performance by aligning individual and firm interests. In my experience, the best rewards are group-centric (for example, lunch on the company credit card or tickets to an entertainment event). Team awards elevate everyone's performance and help build collaboration, cooperation and teamwork. Rewards should offer a chance for staff to bond; otherwise, when giving gifts like a bottle of wine, all you're doing is substituting cash for cash-in-kind. Additionally, research suggests that non-monetary awards work better to incentivize performance than cash prizes.

There are several companies that offer to create rewards programs based on business development effort and output. While these are a good source of ideas in terms of program design, communication, tracking and fulfillment, it's not necessary to outsource this responsibility. To create an effective in-house rewards program:

- **Establish KPIs.** Identify the behaviors and achievements you want to reinforce and thus reward. Set specific measurable effort and performance targets.
- **Assign a budget.** Figure out how much money you're willing to spend on your rewards program.
- **Ask the group.** Rather than offering unexciting prizes, ask the team to create the rewards program. Have the group give input to an awards committee, which will make recommendations to the partnership group.
- **Focus on team.** Encourage team versus individual rewards. As part of your effort to build a firm-wide business development culture, create team goals where everyone wins or loses together. One for all and all for one.
- **Combine reward and recognition.** Combine individual acknowledgement with group reward. Individual success and collective celebration are not mutually exclusive. Just because one person exceeds expectation doesn't mean the whole team can't enjoy that success.
- **Publicize.** Use your firm-wide business development report to highlight individual and team accomplishments. Make others see what they're missing if they're not giving it their all.
- **Go viral.** Publicize awards celebrations on your Facebook page and other social media sites. Give prospective hires a glimpse of what it will feel like to be part of the team.
- **Stretch.** Continually push the boundaries of KPIs and awards. Make the targets harder to reach and the rewards ever more attractive. Try setting an audacious goal with a lucrative award. You won't know whether it's possible until you try, and if you meet the goal, the return on investment will far exceed even the most lavish reward.

Key takeaways

Recognition and reward play an important role in motivating individuals and teams:

- Think of recognition as an informal way to praise and acknowledge effort and contribution. Look for opportunities to praise in private and public.
- Focus on reward as a way to motivate team contributions. Enlist the help of the group to create a meaningful and attractive rewards program.
- When possible, combine recognition and reward to maximize impact and motivate desired behaviors.

CHAPTER 12
CULTURE

Everyone wins when a firm has a great culture. The firm attracts top talent because they're known as a great place to work, where employees enjoy their jobs. The firm in turn benefits because their employees are empowered, enthusiastic, creative and invested in doing their jobs well. Just like any business, accounting firms need to build a strong internal culture, but it's just as imperative that they build a commitment to business development into that culture. Accounting firms can enjoy periodic success without first establishing a business development culture —the market might improve or a business developer could have an unusually good year. But firms cannot achieve repeated success over the long haul without first establishing the key tenets of a commitment to business development. They must continually underscore the importance of business development, track performance, recognize and reward effort and ensure a commitment to continuous improvement. Ultimately, the firm as a whole needs to see business development as an important priority at all times, not just as an urgent priority at specific times.

This chapter offers suggestions for how to instill a firm-wide commitment to business development. Individual topics include:

- **Partner meetings:** Don't allow business development to be pushed aside at partner meetings. A commitment to business development starts at the top.
- **Staff meetings:** Staff meetings are an unparalleled opportunity to establish business development as a firm-wide priority. Use the time to share successes, establish priorities and rally the troops.
- **Lunch n' learn sessions:** Invite employees to enjoy lunch on the firm while they learn about the rudiments of a particular product or service. Hopefully they'll walk away more comfortable talking about the topic with clients and prospective clients.

- **Firm business development report:** Regularly send out a high-level report on business development performance to the entire firm. Be humorous and make it an easy read. Your goal is to keep everyone up-to-date on the latest business development happenings.
- **Training:** Institute a firm-wide training program to instill in your employees the business development skills they'll need to thrive in leadership positions. Invest in your employees starting on their first day. Don't wait until they move up the ladder to start teaching them business development know-how.
- **Pass the torch:** Put in place strategies to make business development an enduring commitment that survives the test of time.

PARTNER MEETINGS

For a firm to enjoy repeated success, its partners have to care about business development and be engaged in it, or at the very least be aware of it. Yet at partner meetings, business development often takes a backseat to day-to-day issues such as efficiency, process and human resources. Don't let this happen. Partners must appropriate the necessary time and energy to such a critical topic at their meetings.

Don't fall by the wayside

Here are a few suggestions for how to incorporate business development into your partner meetings:

- **Make it part of the standing agenda.** This is step number one. It's easy for business development to get bumped by more pressing issues. Make sure it's a recurring item on the agenda.
- **Invite the business development team.** When appropriate, invite your business development coach and coordinator to the meeting so they feel a sense of ownership over the issues and solutions. Make them feel part of the team.
- **Report and analyze business development progress.** Build on the dashboard you create for regular business development meetings to provide the partners with a progress snapshot. Provide year-over-year comparisons and future forecasts and use visuals to bring your talking points to life. The dashboard needs to be short and high-level; this is not the time to get lost in the weeds. Go beyond just reporting the numbers and provide analysis and recommendations.
- **Look on the bright side.** Make sure to provide optimism that it's possible to get where you want to go. Focus on what you need to do, instead of focusing on what's going wrong. Come prepared to present new ideas, creative strategies and new product and service suggestions to spark the conversation.
- **Talk big picture.** Discuss other aspects of the firm's business development initiative, including its commitment to coaching, mentoring and training. Highlight specific instances where the long-term investment in a firm-wide business development culture is paying off (for example, a lunch n' learn session resulted in the launch of a new service offering that is now generating new business).
- **Invite contributions.** Invite partners to contribute ideas and suggestions. Make sure they feel part of the solution.
- **Build commitments.** Bind partners to the plan through specific commitments. Applaud triumphs. Set goals to meet before the next partner meeting.
- **Celebrate success.** Immediately after the meeting, partners should recognize individual contributors who were praised in the meeting. They could stop by at their desk, drop them a personal email or acknowledge

them in a firm-wide communiqué. People can never be thanked enough. Let them know you appreciate them. Inspire continued performance.

- **Minute the meeting.** Summarize the key takeaways and action items and send a copy to all meeting participants.

Key takeaways

Use the business development portion of your partner meetings to:

- Invite key contributors into the room to provide information, analysis and insight.
- Strategize and plan. Commit partners to specific action steps.
- Recognize contributors. After the meeting, let them know how meaningful and significant their help has been.

STAFF MEETINGS

Staff meetings are a time for your firm to share information, announcements and areas of focus. Much like partner meetings, staff meetings are typically over-subscribed with agenda items. Three pounds of potatoes in a one-pound bag, as my mother would say. Because of that, it's easy to rush past important agenda items, including business development-related topics. Don't let that happen. Staff meetings are an unparalleled opportunity to establish business development as a firm-wide priority. If your typical staff meeting runs for one hour, you should allocate at least five minutes to business development. Use the opportunity to share successes, establish your business development priorities, reaffirm targets and goals and rally the troops around your firm's compelling saga.

Running an effective staff meeting

You need to strive to make your staff meetings, and particularly the business development section, as engaging and productive as possible. Start and end on time; if you're consistently running long, schedule more frequent meetings but don't make each meeting longer. Enter the meeting with a clear agenda that matches your firm's priorities. If you're making a push to sell more services to existing clients, include the campaign as an agenda item. Stay on topic and don't allow the meeting to become a time for griping about company problems. Don't waste your staff's time by talking about topics that are irrelevant to most people in the room. The goal of the meeting is to make sure everyone is on the same page.

Assert your place

Here are a few suggestions for how to structure the business development section of the meeting:

- **Summarize business development performance.** Snapshot year-to-date information about how you're doing. Provide variance-to-target analysis and year-over-year comparison data. Quickly summarize "where we are and where we expect to be."
- **Hand over the floor.** Instead of having your business development champion or coach do the talking, let your business development coordinator deliver most of the content. Give them the stage to showcase their contributions, understanding and acumen.
- **Celebrate successes.** Don't rush right to the bad news. Spend some time highlighting recent wins. Share best practices and lessons. Congratulate individuals who contributed to this period's business development successes. Praise both effort and performance; results don't always tell the full tale of the tape. Give out awards and rewards to further substantiate and motivate.

- **Discuss areas for improvement.** This meeting isn't just about cheer-leading; next summarize areas for improvement. Focus on the benefits the group will realize if they invest in these strategies.
- **Make it a forum.** Invite questions and encourage conversation. Invite attendees to discuss their own experiences. Ask "how would you do X?" instead of saying, "Here's how I would do it."
- **Look ahead.** Summarize the firm's upcoming marketing commitments, including communications, B2B events and B2C mixers. Demonstrate the firm-wide volume of effort to business development.
- **Set priorities and goals.** Highlight specific priorities. Convert those priorities into actions. For example, "I want each of you to identify three clients to talk to about X by the end of the week." Everyone should leave with a clear business development goal.
- **Lead the rally cry.** Remind everyone of your compelling saga, the driving force behind your business development effort. End on a high note. You want people to leave motivated and inspired.
- **Minute the meeting.** As always, summarize key takeaways after the fact. Circulate to all staff and alliance partners, even those who didn't attend. Make sure you have a record of what everyone committed to do.

Key takeaways

Keep these goals in mind when running your staff meetings:

- Meetings should be productive and focus on discussing objectives, setting goals and communicating office activities.
- Business development should have a prominent and recurring place on the agenda.
- During the business development section, you should recognize contributions, establish priorities and goals, invite participation and motivate the group to act.

LUNCH N' LEARN SESSIONS

Lunch n' learn sessions are a great vehicle for introducing new product and service offerings to your entire team. Over the course of an hour, employees are invited to enjoy lunch on the firm while they participate in a presentation describing the rudiments of a particular product or service. The best lunch n' learn sessions are engaging, participative and fun, and provide attendees with the necessary knowledge to promote the product or service to clients.

Know thyself

One of the biggest challenges in launching a firm-wide business development initiative is educating staff on what the firm does. This is particularly true of firms that offer a broad array of services or that work with strategic alliance partners to provide non-accounting services. Accountants are unlikely to promote a business development opportunity if they don't understand the topic and don't feel suitably equipped to discuss it with a prospect or client. Lunch n' learn sessions provide accountants with the necessary information to start a conversation, before ultimately connecting the client with a content expert.

Food for all

The best lunch n' learn sessions focus on how the product or service helps clients, rather than concentrating on the nuts and bolts of how it works. Worst case, the audience leaves with a better understanding of the topic; best case, members of the audience commit to bringing it up with suitable clients. A key point: For lunch n' learn sessions to be effective, you need to provide lunch (the finer the dining experience, the better). Make the event sufficiently inviting if you want people to come.

Here are a few more suggestions for getting the most out of your lunch n' learn sessions:

- **Create a recurring calendar appointment.** Schedule sessions on a recurring basis, with flexibility during busy seasons. Lunch n' learn sessions should be a fixture on your firm calendar, not something that pops up occasionally when someone has an idea. Presentations can be delivered either by people in the firm or by strategic alliance partners.
- **Invite everyone.** Send an open invitation to everyone in the firm. When appropriate, invite strategic alliance partners, clients and other interested parties. Don't exclude — include!
- **Make the content engaging.** Give presenters a format to follow, including total time, how much time to allocate to group exercises and whether they're required to provide handouts or case studies. Don't allow presenters to rattle on for 60 minutes. Require that they build in activities that engage the audience. Make it fun.
- **Allow time for questions.** Build in sufficient time in the agenda for Q&A. Prepare your own questions in advance in case you don't get

many from your audience. These sessions are also a chance for presenters to polish their presentation skills, which includes handling live Q&A.

- **Start and finish on time.** Time is everyone's most precious resource. Respect it. Start on time even if people don't show up on time. Those who are late will get the message.
- **Provide collateral.** Put together a "fact sheet" for participants ahead of the meeting. After the meeting, work with your business development team to put together an informational sheet on the featured product or service.
- **Quiz attendees.** End with a short quiz to test what attendees have learned. See how much of the material they have absorbed.
- **Follow up.** Provide attendees with a brief session evaluation. Use feedback to help the presenters improve and make the sessions better. For those who show interest in the product or service, conduct a 1-on-1 session to discuss client and prospect opportunities. When possible, come to meetings armed with client data analysis (for example, a list of clients who have been identified as suitable candidates for the product or service).

Key takeaways

To generate as much new business as possible from lunch n' learn sessions:

- Make sessions available to everyone in the firm, as well as to strategic alliance partners.
- Make sessions engaging. Dialogue is always better than monologue.
- Follow up with interested attendees to convert information into action.

FIRM BUSINESS DEVELOPMENT REPORT

Firm-wide business development reports play an important role in communicating targets and performance to all staff. The report has to be interesting, compelling and newsworthy. You want people to look forward to receiving it. We recommend breaking the report into three parts:

- **Race report:** A visual graphic and numeric table highlighting individual progress toward a goal.
- **Rear-view mirror:** A look back at individual effort and production, success stories, best practices and recent wins.
- **Crystal ball:** A look forward to the next period's targets; a list of individuals to keep an eye on.

Play to win

Not everyone attends business development meetings. Outside of your staff meeting, the business development report is the primary source of information for many people regarding business development progress and performance. It showcases success and quietly acknowledges underperformance. It doesn't shame those who are falling behind, but there is a subtle subtext to the comparison that inevitably occurs when you position one performer alongside another. Nobody wants to be in last place.

A friendly competition

Here are a few suggestions for creating a firm-wide business development report:

- **Create a backdrop for the "Race Report."** Pick a visual image with a clear start and finish line (for example, Tour de France bike race, lines on a football field, horse racetrack, rock climbing mountain, etc.) Photoshop participant headshots onto caricature bodies — if it's not fun, it's not worth doing. Here's an example using a horse racetrack.

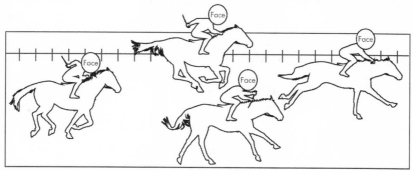

- **Name your report.** The report name will typically take its lead from the visual graphic you select (for example, the Tour de [insert firm name] for a bike race, Mount [insert firm name] for a climbing expedition, etc).

- **Create a graphic template.** While the content has to be interesting and compelling, the visual look of the report is important too. Make sure it's an eye-catcher.
- **Report consistent metrics.** Report percentage of total business development target year-to-date. Include variance to target as a percent, rather than a number, to level the playing field. Thus, irrespective of the dollar value of new business generated, individuals are measured by percentage of target.
- **Establish a timeline.** The ideal reporting timeline is monthly. Enough can change in a month to ensure that a certain amount of "jockeying" takes place on the leader board. Report actuals within five days of the end of the month to ensure the information is current. There shouldn't be a large delay between collecting and distributing the information.
- **Comparison is competition.** Position participants side-by-side on the graphic. Comparison creates a sense of internal competition and a desire to improve one's standing.
- **Include everyone.** Report the progress of all contributors, regardless of their title. Don't shy away from putting someone on the board if they've developed zero new business to date. There's a double goal here: Just as high achievers get to bask in the glow of their success, underperformers are motivated to improve because they have nowhere to hide.
- **Celebrate success.** Aside from the comparison graphic, recognize individual achievement and contributions. Congratulate individuals who have surpassed their cumulative quarterly or year-end target or who have contributed to the success of others.
- **Recognize effort.** Results don't always tell the whole story. Acknowledge individuals who have put in a lot of effort, for example by making the most calls or booking the most meetings. You want to encourage these behaviors, even if they aren't paying off immediately.
- **Share best practices.** Talk about specific wins. Use case studies to illustrate best practices.
- **Talk about the future.** Don't just look backward. Talk about future goals and expectations. Highlight individuals you think are about to "break out" from the pack. Use the opportunity to highlight business development initiatives (for example, this month is midyear tax planning month, or this month's credits and incentives focus is on R&D tax credits).

Key takeaways

To create your firm-wide business development report:

- Make the report a fun and easy read. Be humorous.
- Use a relevant race report graphic that resonates with your firm.
- Report progress by all contributors. Look both backward and forward.

TRAINING

A firm-wide training program helps instill in your employees the business development skills they'll need to thrive in leadership positions. In this topic, we suggest a framework for cultivating those skills throughout your organization.

Invest in your employees

An employee training program accomplishes two things: First, it helps you nurture essential skills in your employees; and second, it helps improve employee retention. Employees are more likely to remain at firms that clearly value them and are invested in helping them grow. You'll cultivate a workforce that is productive, driven and passionate. And by implementing an effective training program, you will have given your employees the skills they need to move up in the firm, providing a significant return on your investment as your staff accountants rise to become seniors, supervisors, managers and partners.

From day one

For business development training to be relevant and meaningful, it should:

- Start soon after an employee joins the firm.
- Focus on reorienting the employee's attitude toward business development, so they think of it as a way to help their clients. Business development is about a lot more than making a sale.
- Develop each individual's business development skills, including dialogue, listening and presentation.
- Encourage a more complete understanding of the services and solutions the firm offers.
- Provide individuals with practical experience in active business development settings. Don't limit your training to classroom theory.
- Facilitate active participation in internal business development meetings and other aspects of the firm's business development culture.

This is the only time we're going to shamelessly plug our own product. To help you institute the ideas proposed in this book, we've created a series of online workshops that offer practical business development training. These online workshops are engaging and participatory and build on the ideas in this book. They offer a level of depth for business development training for accountants that is difficult to find elsewhere. The workshops are organized as follows:

- **Content:** The workshops are designed to help accountants develop the skills they need to succeed in business development. Each workshop focuses on a practical business development tool, technique or strategy, such as conducting needs assessments or handling live Q&A. It explains why the concept is important and outlines specific processes for putting the content into action. Workshop topics include:

- **Sources of new business:** Clients, colleagues, wheels of influence, centers of influence, strategic alliances, unsolicited lead generation
- **Clients:** Client service values, client service principles, tax planning, discovery planning
- **Messaging:** What clients want, competitive analysis, competitive advantage, elevator pitch, issue-solution-benefit narrative
- **Marketing:** Proposals, crafting presentations, delivering presentations, handling live Q&A
- **Sales process:** Relationships, needs, solutions and demonstrations, reservations and assurances, commitments, next steps and review
- **Management:** Compelling saga, staffing, targets and KPIs, individual business development plans, coaching, mentoring

- **Format:** A typical workshop lasts one hour and includes an audio presentation, two in-class activities, a continuing education assignment and a quiz to test what you learned. Each workshop also comes with accompanying resources including a workbook and any relevant forms and spreadsheets.

  - **Activities:** The in-class activities ask you to reflect on your own experiences and performance, brainstorm ideas with your coworkers, prepare mock presentations and more. They are designed to encourage you to actively engage with the material.
  - **Continuing education:** The continuing education assignment helps you develop practical skills. You can't master business development just by sitting in a classroom. Our assignments send you out to practice what you've learned.
  - **Quiz:** Participation and quiz scores are tracked in an easily accessible dashboard, which enables you to tie participation and performance to compensation and advancement in your firm.

- **Frequency:** Our content is available on-demand, which means you can watch the workshops on your own schedule. You can complete each class individually or along with your coworkers. All the workshops are available on our website.
- **Pricing:** Our workshops offer an incredibly affordable way to provide business development training to your entire firm. We offer two licensing options — a "single workshop license" and a "workshop series license." Specific pricing is available at www.ReplacingTheRainmaker.com.

The goal of these workshops is to help you convert the ideas in this book into new business. The workshops don't just help you better understand the content; they help you develop the skills you need to apply the ideas in real-world situations. At the end of the workshops, you should be able to quantify the dollar value of the classes. Please visit our website to watch a two-minute workshop welcome video and learn more about our workshop series. You can also watch an entire workshop for free.

Even if you don't take advantage of our workshops, you should adhere to these principles when creating your own training program:

- **Make it fun.** Training sessions should be participation-driven, interactive and engaging. Build in demonstrations and live role-plays to bring the content to life. Encourage dialogue versus monologue. As with selling, ask more than you tell.
- **Know your audience.** Customize the delivery based on your subject matter and audience. Delivery options include classroom teaching, self-paced learning, mentoring, computer-assisted classes and special projects.
- **Convert theory into practice.** Use case studies to demonstrate real-world examples. Encourage senior staff to take junior staff to client and prospect meetings to give them firsthand experience with business development.
- **Provide networking opportunities.** Give your participants homework. For every one-hour class, participants should be encouraged to spend at least twice that amount of time in active business development situations. You could throw mixers, take out a firm-wide membership to the local chamber of commerce or require that everyone join a BNI group.
- **Lean on your business development coach.** This person is responsible for delivering the bulk of the content. Give opportunities to senior staff to lead trainings when applicable.

Key takeaways

To create an effective training program that develops talent in your organization:

- Begin business development training as soon as an employee joins the firm.
- Put ideas into practice. Provide opportunities for employees to develop their skills, both in and out of the classroom.
- Consider using the online workshops we provide to develop practical business development skills. The workshops are upbeat, engaging and participatory.

PASS THE TORCH

It used to be that business development was seen as the responsibility of the minority, those known as rainmakers. As we've talked about elsewhere in the book, future business development success will require an endemic commitment to business development by the entire firm. Future leaders must be "three tool players" to contribute effectively in the partner room: They need technical competence, leadership and management ability and business development skills and contacts. Training the next generation of business developers is central to a firm's long-term organic success. We've touched on a number of "passing the torch" strategies in several topics to date, including:

- **Compelling saga:** Involve your team in crafting a compelling saga that sets a goal for the firm's business development efforts (see management chapter).
- **Mentoring:** Assign individuals to a team, and choose a mentor for each team. The mentor's job is to listen, ask questions and help devise creative solutions. Mentoring is a great way for junior staff members to witness business development in action (see management chapter).
- **Coaching:** Appoint a business development coach to drive the firm's business development efforts. The business development coach is charged with establishing KPIs and targets, helping draft business development plans and coaching individual staff members (see management chapter).
- **Training:** Begin business development training as soon as an employee joins the firm. Develop each individual's business development skills, including dialogue, listening and presentation (see training topic earlier in this chapter).
- **Compensation:** Institute a hybrid compensation model, in which employees earn year-end bonuses for hitting certain goals, while also earning commissions for their business development successes throughout the year (see management chapter).
- **Rewards program:** Create a rewards program that acknowledges employees for significant accomplishments in a formal way. Ask for group input about what the rewards should be, and consider choosing group-centric awards, rather than individual prizes (see management chapter).
- **Staff meetings:** Don't let business development fall off the agenda at staff meetings. This is your chance to establish business development as a firm-wide priority. Use the opportunity to share successes, reaffirm your priorities and rally the troops (see staff meetings topic earlier in this chapter).
- **Lunch n' learn sessions:** Invite employees to enjoy lunch on the firm while they learn about the rudiments of a particular product or service. Hopefully they'll walk away more comfortable talking about the topic

with clients and prospective clients (see lunch n' learn sessions topic earlier in this chapter).

Remember that business development, like any process, should be mined for continuous improvement. Often, the most valuable ideas will come from more junior personnel who aren't stuck in the old paradigm. Embrace their ideas and encourage business development at all levels. Applaud it, create opportunities for it, reward it. The firms that survive and thrive will be those whose staff both deliver good work and generate new business.

Key takeaways

To pass the torch to the next generation of business developers:

- Instill an endemic commitment to business development by the entire firm.
- Embrace ideas from more junior personnel who aren't stuck in the old paradigm. Encourage business development at all levels.
- Encourage accountants to develop technical competence, leadership ability and business development skills. All three skills are necessary at high-performing firms.

CHAPTER 13
ALLEGIANCES

Accounting firms can form allegiances with other firms or organizations to provide a broader range of services. By partnering up, firms can enhance their reputation for size, depth and strength. They can draw on more resources to meet the totality of their clients' needs. As business strategist Curtis E. Sahakian said, "Partnering is the quickest, most effective way to re-engineer a business."

In this chapter, we make the case for three different types of allegiances. Individual topics include:

- **Accounting member associations:** Join an industry association such as AICPA or CPAmerica to gain access to benchmarking data, marketing support, networking opportunities, joint engagements and referrals.
- **Coalitions with other accounting firms:** Align your firm with a partner firm. Both firms cross-refer work when they can't meet a client's or prospective client's needs.
- **Allegiances with financial services professionals:** To offer a full-suite of services to clients, expand your range of services to include financial services. You'll become a one-stop finance and accounting resource, while also securing a strong recurring revenue stream.

ACCOUNTING MEMBER ASSOCIATIONS

Most accountants and firms are already members of accounting industry associations, such as AICPA or CPAmerica, because they are a valuable resource in areas such as practice management, education, publications and so on. Yet there is another often unintended benefit of joining these associations — they can be incredibly valuable from a business development standpoint by offering benchmarking data, marketing support, networking opportunities, joint engagements and referrals.

Accept a helping hand

There are many business development-focused reasons to join an accounting association, including:

- **Benchmarking:** Firms aggregate data so that members can analyze their own performance. This data can help you understand what niche areas are growing most rapidly, what firms are doing to succeed in a niche and how firms are generating new business.
- **Networking:** Members can learn from the best practices of other group members. Often similar firms in different geographic areas have the opportunity to learn from each other, without fearing that they're collaborating with a competitor.
- **Referrals and joint engagements:** Firms cross-refer clients and collaborate on engagements to expand the level of depth and expertise they can offer to a client. Two local firms might pair up to compete against a larger firm or two firms in different geographic areas might partner up to serve a client who would otherwise seek out a national firm.
- **Marketing support:** Many associations offer pre-written copy that can be used in firm communications, including brochures, newsletters and emails. This provides firms with a steady stream of content at no additional expense.
- **Teaching opportunities:** Most associations conduct educational webinars in a variety of services and industries. You can raise your profile by leading a webinar in your area of expertise.
- **Publicity:** Some associations allow you to highlight your industry-related credentials or experience. You become a go-to resource when others in the association need your expertise, which helps enhance your reputation as a thought leader in your industry.

Consider your options

There are many accounting associations that you can join, from small local options to large national ones. Some of the most notable associations include:

- **AICPA:** This national organization includes hundreds of thousands of individual members in dozens of countries. It hosts large conferences, publishes a journal and other accounting industry news and offers a multitude of resources and networking opportunities. For those building a niche, it can be a source of valuable speaking opportunities.

- **CPAmerica:** This association offers memberships to firms, rather than to individual accountants. Firms must meet certain criteria to join and only one firm is allowed in each geographic area. Benefits include advice, information sharing, CPE training, marketing support and access to consultants. Member firms support each other and sometimes partner up.
- **Crowe Horwath International:** The international extension of CPAmerica, this association includes firms from around the world. Like CPAmerica, firms must meet certain criteria to join and firms often partner to offer joint services to clients.
- **CPAConnect:** This companion to CPAmerica is one of the largest associations of small independent accounting firms. There is no limit to how many firms can join and larger CPAmerica firms coach smaller firms in their geographic area. Member firms gain mentorship, connections with similar firms and access to a large network of resources.
- **2020 Group:** This group offers some of the same benefits as CPAmerica, but at a much lower fee. Member firms across the world gain access to marketing content, benchmarking data and association resources, but there's less of a sense of community than with CPAmerica.

If you can't find an association that adequately serves your needs, consider creating one. Look for nearby firms that might be interested in forming a regional accounting group. This makes particular sense for firms with different specialties and ideal clients, so that work can be cross-referred.

Key takeaways

Consider the following when joining an accounting association:

- Associations provide a variety of business development benefits, including marketing support, benchmarking, networking, joint engagement opportunities, referrals and more.
- While business development is often not the primary driver for joining an industry association, don't skip out on the many benefits such organizations provide.
- From individual CPA associations like AICPA, to small practice groups like 2020 Group and CPAConnect, to mid-size practice associations like CPAmerica and Crowe Horwath International, there's an association to fit everyone's needs.

COALITIONS

Coalitions are a way for accounting firms to align themselves with each other for business development purposes. When one firm can't meet the needs of a prospective or existing client, the "ally firm" joins the fray.

Howdy partner

In short, the idea behind coalitions is that the firms serve as resources for each other and as one another's best source of new business. These coalitions work best in the following three cases:

- **Coalitions with larger or smaller firms:** Different-sized firms team up and refer clients who don't fit their ideal client profile. The smaller firm refers work that is too large or complex; the larger firm refers clients with less complicated needs or seeking a less expensive option.
- **Coalitions with specialized service providers:** Firms refer clients to each other when they lack the expertise or experience to do the work. An obvious example of this would be a firm that specializes in tax partnering with a firm that focuses on audit.
- **Coalitions with similar firms:** When independence rules preclude one firm from doing the work, they refer the client to the ally firm. Often these firms work in the same geographic area and serve similar types of clients. Coalitions are particularly valuable to assurance and advisory departments because a firm that does an audit for a client will be conflicted out of doing a valuation and vice versa.

On rare occasions, these coalitions are formalized, but usually the arrangement is more informal. Both parties have an understanding that they'll work together, cross-refer clients, serve as a resource for each other and not solicit one another's clients.

Everyone play nice

Forming coalitions with other firms helps you better serve your clients. By offering an alternative solution when you can't perform the work, you hopefully eliminate the need for clients and prospective clients to seek out a new firm that offers everything they need under one roof. Coalitions help make friends out of competitors, and protect against poaching by the other firm. They also generate a steady stream of business if your partner firm sends valuable work your way.

Align

There are two ways to cultivate coalitions:

- **Pre-existing relationships:** Individuals in each firm draw on an existing relationship. Often, two individuals will have worked together at a past firm, where they built trust and rapport over time. The two individuals establish a coalition and their new firms support the alliance and agree to cross-refer.

- **B2B industry groups:** Join or start an industry group of practitioners in a particular area, such as a valuation B2B group or an audit B2B group. Referrals will flow among members of the group when one member firm can't perform the work, particularly because of an independence conflict.

Once you've identified prospective partners, the keys are to:

- **Gain clarity.** Have a clear understanding about the scope and purpose of the coalition. It's preferable to have an agreement in writing, but it isn't required.
- **Invest the time.** Like any relationship, you get out what you put in — so invest the time to better understand the other firm's ideal client and competitive advantage. Be able to recognize when a good referral walks in the door. Communicate progress and next steps.
- **Track new business.** As we talk about in the referral tracking topic, keep tabs on business in and out. Try to maintain a balanced ledger (see referrals chapter).
- **Steward referrals.** Even though you trust the other firm, you still want to steward every referral to ensure the client is well served. As with any referral, the quality of the other person's work reflects on you.

Key takeaways

To form coalitions with other firms:

- Build a bridge with another firm. You can create alliances with all types of firms, including ones with similar expertise, specialized services or of a different size.
- The agreement doesn't have to be formal but the general understanding, scope and purpose should be clearly articulated.
- Invest the time to deepen the relationship and understand the other firm's capabilities.

FINANCIAL SERVICES PROFESSIONALS

More and more accounting firms are offering an expanded range of services to their clients, including financial services. Rather than referring out these opportunities, firms can market themselves as a one-stop finance and accounting resource, while securing a strong recurring revenue stream.

Become a trusted advisor

Accountants need to become trusted advisors to their clients so they are seen as the go-to person for all types of financial decisions, not just for specific accounting-related questions. They need to be capable of advising clients on issues across multiple disciplines and when they don't have the required expertise, they need to know where to turn. In short, they need to play quarterback. All of this requires a reliable network of resources and expertise, and financial services professionals are an important part of such a network. Partnerships with financial services professionals are a key part of securing your value to your clients. If clients can't turn to you for all their financial needs, they'll likely find an accountant who offers a broader range of services.

Put a smile on their face

Consider partnering with a financial services professional or firm who can assist with a number of client needs, including health benefits, executive compensation plans, 401k investments, estate planning, defined benefit plans, retirement projections and so on. All of this will help your clients to grow and prosper. Happy clients mean more referrals and more business, and by serving your clients well, you'll defend against poaching by your competition. Your firm will become a "hub" for your clients, who will see you as a go-to resource and appreciate the time you save them by handling all their needs in one place.

A little extra dough

There's also significant money to be made from a partnership with a financial services professional, particularly if your firm is licensed for investments and insurance. Financial services professionals generally bill per project and typically generate high realization fees and commissions that far exceed the firm's hourly rate. This results in a value-added billing system that is often quite lucrative for all parties. Additionally, it frees up accountants from performing most of the strategic and advisory work, leaving them to focus on other core responsibilities.

Making the relationship work

Keep these tips in mind to build a successful relationship with a financial services professional:

- **Build trust.** Accountants across the firm need to build a level of trust with the financial services professional. Make sure the financial services professional is a frequent face around the firm. Invite them to business development meetings and have individual accountants schedule lunches or appointments so everyone can get to know each other.
- **Host lunch n' learn sessions.** Your staff needs to understand the value offered by the financial services professional. Offer lunch n' learn sessions to educate staff on specific products, such as life insurance or defined benefit plans.
- **Visit clients together.** Make it clear that you're part of the same team by having the financial services professional come along on client visits. If a financial question comes up that the accountant isn't qualified to answer, you'll have an expert already there who can pitch in.
- **Be tactical.** Now that you're offering this service, you need to persuade clients of its value. The best way to do that is to offer an idea that will immediately save or make them money. Demonstrate the value right off the bat.

Key takeaways

Partnering with a financial services professional helps you:

- Become a one-stop finance and accounting resource.
- Defend against client poaching because your clients are already well served.
- Generate significant revenue. Fees and commissions can be quite lucrative.

CHAPTER 14
NON-ORGANIC GROWTH

Everyone wants to do it the "organic way" these days. But sometimes, slow and steady doesn't win the race. Sometimes you have to pursue non-organic growth strategies when the opportunity presents itself.

In this chapter, we present two strategies for growing your practice in a non-organic manner. Both are options to consider when contemplating growth beyond your walls:

- **Practice combination:** Formally combine practices with another firm to increase your firm's physical footprint and expand your areas of expertise. Well-executed practice combination results in new staff, more ideal clients, improved process efficiency and enhanced niche expertise.
- **Practice continuation:** A practice continuation agreement offers a succession plan for a firm in the case that the firm's partner dies or is permanently or temporarily incapacitated. By agreeing to take over another firm's business in such an event, you're positioning yourself to gain business down the line.

PRACTICE COMBINATION

Practice combination is an increasingly popular strategy for practice growth, particularly in urban markets where size, breadth of service and niche expertise are necessary to compete. Well-executed practice combination results in new staff, more ideal clients, improved process efficiency and enhanced niche expertise.

Analyze the market

Practice combination provides a faster growth trajectory than organic growth and offers a quick route to niche specialization. Typically practice combination achieves one or more of the following goals:

- **Expertise:** You add qualified, experienced staff, especially senior managers and managers who are particularly hard to come by.
- **Processes:** You improve speed and minimize expenses.
- **Clients:** You gain new clients, and not just any clients, but clients who meet your firm's ideal client profile.
- **Niche notoriety:** You add expertise and experience in a specific service or industry niche.

While many types of firms are practice combination candidates, the most common are young firms looking to merge into bigger firms and older firms whose partners plan to retire soon. Here's the rationale for each:

- **Get 'em while they're young.** A young firm might be interested in practice combination as a means to add services they don't currently provide, eliminate concerns about their ability to staff certain jobs at peak times, sell more to their existing clients and assure an eventual exit strategy for their partners. For the bigger firm, this kind of deal is about the people — they're adding people who will be around for the long haul and who will ultimately become partners.
- **Provide an exit opportunity.** An aging firm might be interested in practice combination as a means to protect and monetize an asset the partners have spent a lifetime building and to ensure that loyal employees are taken care of. Additionally, as partners age, the value of their practice drops and health issues become a greater concern, all of which makes practice combination appealing. For the bigger firm, this kind of deal is about the clients — the other firm's partners aren't going to stick around for years, but hopefully their clients will.

Find the right match

If you're interested in practice combination, follow these steps to find the right partner.

1. **Create your ideal candidate profile.** For example:

Location	In metro/downtown [insert city here]
Revenues	Upwards of $400,000 to $2,500,000 annually
Gross profit	Drops 40%+ to the bottom line
# of partners	1-3 partners
Practice make-up	Has a balance of individual and commercial work; has industry specialization (real estate, professional services, etc); has service specialization (litigation support, forensic accounting, family law, financial planning, asset management, audit, etc)
Scenario 1	A younger group that needs help and support and whose personnel would be looking to stay on for the long haul
Scenario 2	A person or persons in their late fifties or early sixties with 3-4 people in their office who have a great practice but are looking to transition out in the next 1-3 years

2. **Acquire a list of candidate firms.** There are many websites that allow you to apply search criteria to identify firms that meet your profile.

3. **Communicate with candidates.** Write a series of articles that make the case for practice combination. We recommend a tiered communication approach. The first article establishes a basic understanding of practice combination; the second article probes whether there's a reason to move forward; and the third article addresses how to execute the idea:

    •   *Article 1: Why combine practices? Why combine practices now?*

        Include a letter with this article outlining who your firm is and explaining that you're pursuing practice combination opportunities. Detail your ideal candidate profile and provide contact information. Also include an article about practice combination that explores its benefits and challenges. Benefits might include increased revenue, employee security, spreading overhead costs, exit strategy and specialization. Challenges might include the cultural fit, financial terms and business plan. This article isn't pitching your firm specifically; it's advocating generally for practice combination.

- **Article 2: Why combine practices with (insert your firm name here)?**

  This is your opportunity to tout the advantages another firm will enjoy through combining with yours. The list is unique to your firm, but is likely to include some of the following: the quality and size of your staff, your technical expertise, your processes, your service offerings and financial security. You want to make the case for merging with your firm by showing that you have the means and experience to pull it off.

- **Article 3: How would a practice combination agreement work with (insert your firm name here)?**

  Give details of how everything would work. For younger firms, you would establish a path to partnership for the partners of the incoming firm with the standard terms and conditions of partner exit. For older firms, you would outline the financial terms of the deal, including valuation, down payment and timeline. You wouldn't necessarily give specific numbers, but instead would explain how the financial terms would be structured.

These articles can be sent electronically, but using snail mail increases the likelihood that someone will open and read your communiqué. A general rule of thumb is to send one article a month for three months. Send all three articles to each candidate firm, unless you get a definite answer that they're not interested. Make sure all three articles contain relevant and eye-catching graphic elements.

4. **Make warm calls.** Call each of the contacts on your mailing list within seven days of your letter being delivered. Ahead of making the call, craft a simple call script like this:

   > "My name is (insert your name) and I'm calling from (insert your firm name) as a follow-up to a practice combination letter and article we mailed you last week. Do you recall receiving it?"

If no:

   > "Our firm is looking to combine our practice with (insert geographical area)-based firms that are looking to merge with a firm for succession or other purposes."

If yes:

   > "Does practice combination make sense to you? Is it something you'd consider if the right opportunity came along? Do you have any interest in exploring practice combination with (insert your firm name) now or in the near future?"

If no:

> "Thank you for your time."

If yes:

> "Tell me a little about your firm?
> 1. What's your balance of individual and entity work?
> 2. Do you specialize in any industries or niches?
> 3. Do you specialize in a particular service or services?
> 4. Talk about your firm culture.
> 5. What are your annual revenues?"

If you're the business development coordinator or coach charged with identifying candidates prior to a call or meeting with a partner in the firm, close with: "I'm going to have (insert name) contact you to initiate the conversation and explore the opportunities. Thanks for your time today and I look forward to meeting you in the not-too-distant future."

Remember, the script is only a guide; you shouldn't sound like you're reading from a teleprompter. Always leave a message as it creates a record of your efforts and call back within five days of the next mailing if you don't reach anyone initially. Try to anticipate the questions you'll be asked by candidates (how does a practice combination agreement work, can I continue to generate a salary after I sign the practice combination agreement, etc.) and don't make up answers to questions you can't answer.

5. **Go to Plan B.** If you get zero response to your first three efforts, send remaining candidates a letter making the case for practice continuation (see next topic). Practice continuation agreements create a back-up plan for firms in the event of an interruption in leadership due to death or incapacitation. In this case, one firm contracts another firm to serve as a continuing practitioner. Often this is a good option for firms that don't want to be acquired but don't have a succession plan, and sometimes by exploring practice continuation, you might discover the other firm is more open to practice combination than they originally indicated.

6. **Look for a cultural fit.** If you uncover interested parties who don't meet your ideal candidate profile, take a hard look at cultural fit before determining whether to combine practices. When practice combinations go wrong, it's usually because of a culture clash. Be sure you like, trust and respect the other party.

Key takeaways

Consider practice combination as a way to:

- Effectively grow your practice through a non-organic growth strategy.
- Gain talented staff, more ideal clients, improved process efficiency and enhanced niche expertise.

- Keep growing. Practice combination is a lot like having kids. One is easy, two is hard, but three isn't that much harder. Once you have a template to follow, the machinations of practice combination aren't as daunting as they might sound.

PRACTICE CONTINUATION

A practice continuation agreement offers a succession plan for a firm in the case that the firm's partner dies or is permanently or temporarily incapacitated. The firm signs an agreement with another firm that commits to take over the practice in such an eventuality. Your firm might consider entering into practice continuation agreements with aging firms in order to position yourself to take on their business down the line.

Set yourself up for the future

Given the number of baby boomer accountants approaching retirement, there are a plethora of firms out there with aging partners and no exit strategy. If you're a larger firm, entering into a practice continuation agreement with one or more of these firms can be a prudent business development strategy. You're positioning yourself to gain business down the line, and in some cases, you'll end up acquiring the other firm's business sooner than you thought. Circumstances change, and a firm that is interested in a practice continuation agreement now, might be willing to consider combining practices in a few years. Because the other firm has already vetted you and built a relationship with you, they're likely to turn to you first; you're in a prime position to acquire that firm and their clients. And you don't need to sit around and wait for other firms to come to you. Seek out firms that would be a good match and suggest forming a practice continuation agreement. If you're interested in combining with another firm and they rebuff your advances, suggest a practice continuation agreement as a fallback. Think of these agreements as bridges to future transactions; they're long-term investments that will eventually help grow your practice.

Look for a good fit

Consider the following when seeking another firm for a practice continuation agreement:

- **Culture:** If you're going to take over their practice one day, there needs to be a cultural fit. If the other firm has different values or standards, it's going to be difficult for you to retain their staff.
- **Client service:** You're entering into this agreement in hopes of one day gaining the other firm's clients. But if you don't offer a similar client service experience, those clients are unlikely to stick around.
- **Fees:** Similarly, the other firm's clients will need to be comfortable with your billing rates and procedures. If you bill at significantly different rates, it may be difficult for clients to adjust.
- **Niches:** Consider your core competencies and those of the other firm. If they have different areas of specialty, consider whether you're interested in branching out, or whether you would rather partner with a firm that will reinforce your existing areas of expertise.

Key takeaways

When considering a practice continuation agreement, consider the following:

- Think of practice continuation as a long-term non-organic growth strategy. You'll gain new business down the line.
- The combination of your practices might come sooner than you think. The other firm might re-evaluate and decide they're now open to merging.
- Practice continuation is an ideal strategy for smaller, single-partner or aging firms that lack an exit or succession strategy.

CLOSING COMMENTS

Thanks for reading this far. We hope you learned a thing or two and will be able to apply these ideas in your business development endeavors. We encourage you to visit our website at ReplacingTheRainmaker.com to better understand how we can help you convert the ideas discussed in the book into tangible new business. Our website includes:

- **Book:** Purchase additional copies of the book in paperback, hardcover or ebook format.
- **Resources:** Follow the numbered (www) references in the book to access forms, templates and spreadsheets.
- **Workshops:** Many of the topics described in the book are available in workshop format. Each workshop runs for one hour and includes a workbook complete with activities, a continuing education assignment and a quiz.
- **Consulting:** Ian is available on a per diem or retainer basis to consult with firms either in person or remotely.
- **Marketing support:** Access our team of researchers, writers, graphic designers, web developers, social media specialists and videographers.
- **Alliances:** "Replacing the Rainmaker" has built alliances with several trusted service providers, including financial services professionals, software service providers and others.
- **Speaking:** Ian is available to speak on a variety of business development topics.
- **Academy:** A semi-annual three-day boot camp to give program participants an opportunity to interact with other accounting professionals and learn about business development best practices. Offered in San Francisco and other to-be-determined locations.

Thanks again for reading this book and please visit ReplacingTheRainmaker.com to continue your journey.

ABOUT THE AUTHOR

Ian Tonks is a business development consultant. He provides coaching and consulting services to professional service firms, including several Bay Area law, accounting and engineering firms. Previously, he spent seven years as president of an international multi-sport camp and sporting goods provider and three years as associate vice president of advancement and athletics at a Bay Area university. A native of England, Ian holds a bachelor's degree in sports science from the University of Northumbria and an MBA in strategic leadership from Dominican University of California. He lives in Novato, California, with his wife and daughter.